AF478308

This Morning, This Evening, So Soon

This Morning, This Evening, So Soon

James Baldwin and the Voices of Queer Resistance

Hilton Als and Rhea L. Combs

National Portrait Gallery, Smithsonian Institution,
Washington, D.C.
in association with DelMonico Books • D. A. P. New York

Donors

This Morning, This Evening, So Soon: James Baldwin and the Voices of Queer Resistance

has been made possible through the generous support of:

The Ford Foundation

Tommie L. Pegues and **Donald A. Capoccia**

Additional support has been provided by the Portrait of a Nation Gala.

This publication has been supported by Fred M. Levin and Family, The Shenson Foundation, in memory of Nancy Livingston Levin.

Notes on the Contributors

Hilton Als, a staff writer at the *New Yorker*, curated the 2019 exhibition *God Made My Face: A Collective Portrait of James Baldwin*. He won the 2017 Pulitzer Prize for Criticism and recently published *God Made My Face: A Collective Portrait of James Baldwin*.

Rhea L. Combs, the director of curatorial affairs at the National Portrait Gallery, Smithsonian Institution, recently cocurated the award-winning exhibition *Regeneration: Black Cinema, 1898–1971*, organized by the Academy Museum of Motion Pictures in Los Angeles. Her scholarship reexamines American history and culture by focusing on artists from diverse backgrounds, particularly those working in film, photography, and portraiture.

Contents

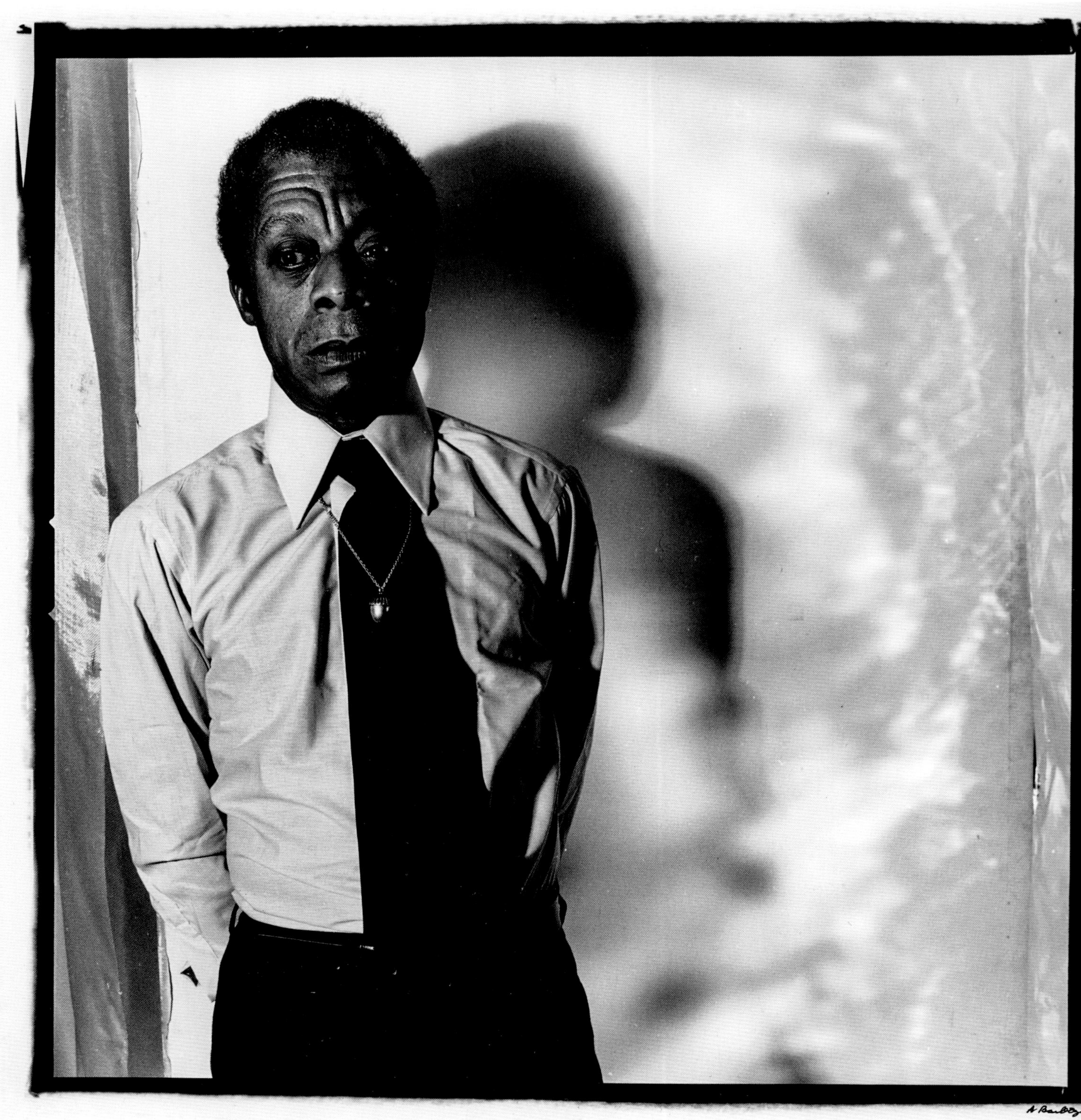

James Baldwin, 1975
Anthony Barboza
gelatin silver print, 33.6 × 33.3 cm (13 ¼ × 13 ⅛ in.)
J. Paul Getty Museum; gift of the Loewentheil Family

Foreword

It's ironical indeed, but it's only black artists in this country—and it's only beginning to change now—who have been called upon to fulfill their responsibilities as artists and, at the same time, insist on their responsibilities as citizens.[1]
—James Baldwin

A century after his birth, the timeless words of James Baldwin (1924–1987) still ring clear. An award-winning author and activist, Baldwin penned essays, novels, short stories, and plays that were not only examining his life and Black life in general, but also interrogating the founding principles of the United States. Unapologetically and fervently, Baldwin explored ideas of civil rights, love, queer identity, and masculinity. *This Morning, This Evening, So Soon: James Baldwin and the Voices of Queer Resistance* provides an opportunity to honor Baldwin's legacy as an American artist while simultaneously recognizing his circle of friends who offered him counsel, comradery, and community.

This exhibition takes part of its title from a short story by Baldwin, originally printed in *The Atlantic* in 1960, when a byproduct of racism in the United States is making people feel like "strangers in their own land." The narrator, like Baldwin, has lived abroad and is returning to the United States after being away for several years. Biographer David Leeming describes the story as being "about the American artist's responsibility—specifically, the African American artist's responsibility—to redeem his nation."[2] So much of Baldwin's work combines personal and public insights. And in many ways, his writings can be viewed as self-portraits. However, instead of a paintbrush or a camera, his pen and typewriter made vivid connections between Black interiority and larger societal ideas. Understanding Baldwin's artistic approach felt important when developing an exhibition dedicated to his life and enduring legacy.

This project would not have been possible without Hilton Als. I want to extend deep gratitude to Hilton for accepting my call in 2022. At that time, we talked and brainstormed about Baldwin's influence. After Als's critically acclaimed exhibition *God Made My Face: A Collective Portrait of James Baldwin* opened at David Zwirner Gallery in New York, in 2019, iterations of that show traveled to galleries throughout the country, and interest in Baldwin reached fever pitch. Taking a conceptual approach, Als challenged the history of portraiture as a representative, singular image of a person. He disrupted and decentered the notion of rugged individualism to posit that identity and personhood is a confluence of many things, notably being in community with others; we are social beings after all.

Fortunately for the National Portrait Gallery, there were still a few ideas that we thought could be pursued when thinking of Baldwin, particularly when considering his life over the arc of a century. Our rich conversations centered on Baldwin's identity, his social circles, and his relationship with the church. We also discussed how homophobia within the Black church and society writ large impeded him in many ways. Although, we acknowledged that his stature afforded him the privilege and platform to confront America's contradictions on race and sexuality more than others in his circle. From our wonderful musings, an exhibition that married Baldwin's commitment to civil rights and his queerness—featuring text by Als—was developed.

For this project, Hilton and I conscientiously embraced different ways of thinking about history. Art and ephemera are interspersed throughout the exhibition to highlight lives from both historical and contemporary perspectives. The featured artists not only remark upon the enduring legacy of James Baldwin but also reflect some thinkers who traditionally have been left out of the discourse.

1. James Baldwin, "Sidney Poitier," *Look*, July 23, 1968, 50–51.
2. David Leeming, *James Baldwin: A Biography* (New York: Knopf, 1994), 170.

It feels particularly apt to present this exhibition on James Baldwin at the National Portrait Gallery. Not only is this a museum dedicated to art, history, and biography, but many of the ideas Baldwin explored in his writings and speeches were headline news when the institution first opened in 1968. That year, the nation experienced tumult, tragedy, and triumph with the assassinations of Baldwin's friend and ally Martin Luther King Jr., as well as Democratic presidential hopeful Senator Robert F. Kennedy. These atrocities were coupled with Olympic medalists Tommie Smith and John Carlos silently protesting racial discrimination by bowing their heads and raising black-gloved fists in Mexico City, as the crew of Apollo 8 became the first humans to orbit the moon.

Since its founding, the Portrait Gallery's mission has been to present individuals who made significant contributions to the United States. For decades, this translated to a preponderance of portraits representing an elite class of primarily landowning gentry and a dearth of portraits from a diverse array of people. When trying to tell a more complete story, one must intentionally find representations of individuals of historical significance who were once excluded from the museum's original vision. More recently, the Portrait Gallery has been reexamining its approach to what subjects it considers for its permanent collection and its special exhibitions.

This special exhibition marks the centenary of an extraordinary American and artist. We better understand Baldwin, his enduring influence, and the significance of his writings, speeches, and teachings by featuring him alongside the friendships he made with other queer artists and activists of color—his chosen family. It is the collection of artist-activists brought together here, along with a few others we did not have the space to include (looking at you Maya Angelou and Nikki Giovanni, to name only a couple), who were intellectual and emotional buttresses for Baldwin to share his ideas and fulfill his creative pursuits. Providing an opportunity for art and politics to join forces allows us to present what Baldwin and his queer contemporaries could fight for in the world—civil rights—even as their sexuality had to remain at least partly hidden. These individuals remind us to live bravely and beautifully; and in the words of James Baldwin, to always "keep the faith."

Huge gratitude to the Ford Foundation for their early and critical support, as well as Tommie L. Pegues and Donald A. Capoccia, whose contributions helped make this project possible. I also am thankful to the institutions and the artists who generously lent works to this important exhibition.

Rhea L. Combs, PhD
Director of Curatorial Affairs
National Portrait Gallery, Smithsonian Institution

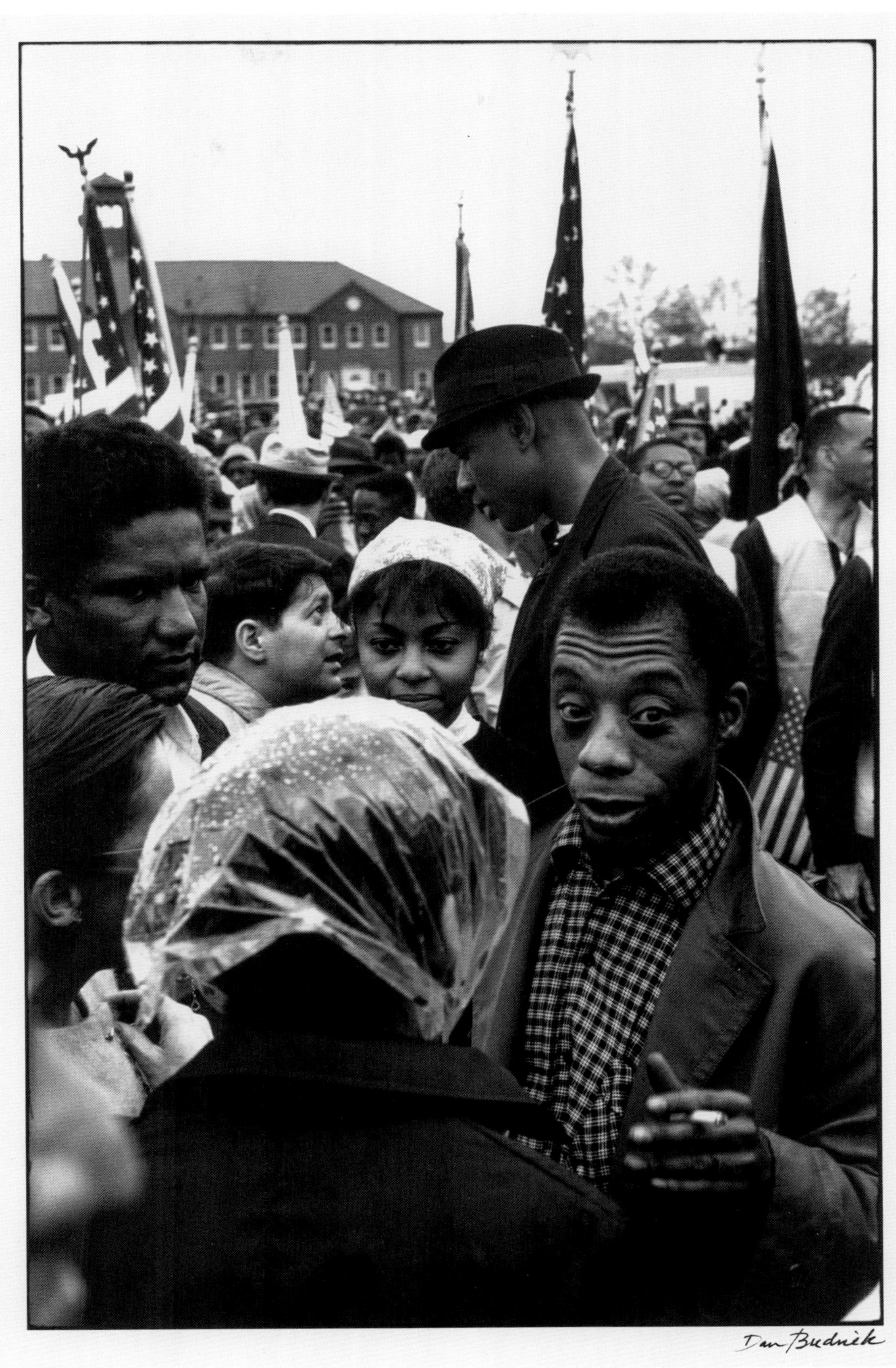

Selma to Montgomery—James Forman and James Baldwin, City of St. Jude staging area, Montgomery, Alabama, March 25, 1965
Daniel Budnik
gelatin silver print (printed 1998), 11 15⁄16 × 8 in. (30.3 × 20.3 cm)
National Portrait Gallery, Smithsonian Institution

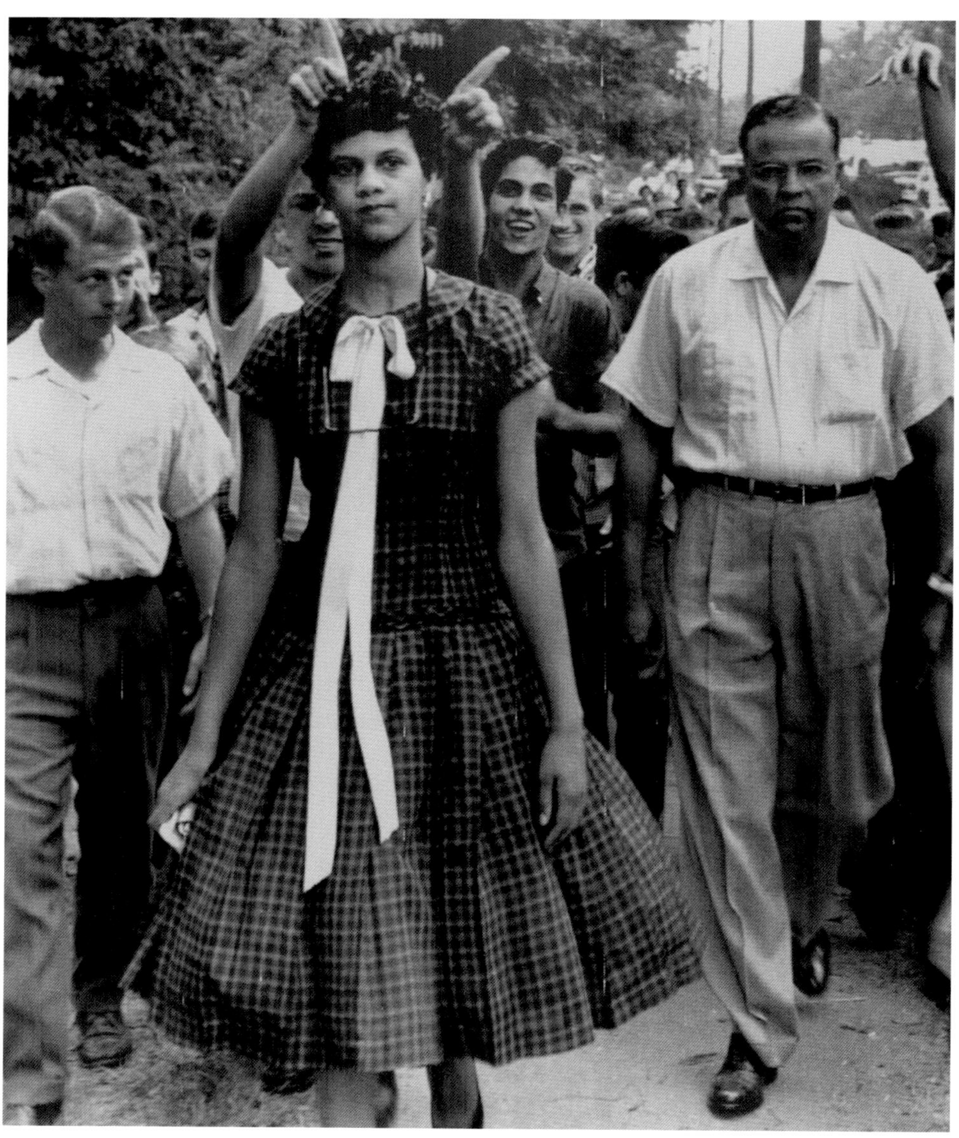

Youths Taunt Dorothy Geraldine Counts in Charlotte, NC, 1957
Douglas Martin
gelatin silver print, 9 x 7 in. (23 x 18 cm)
Prints and Photographs Division, Library of Congress, Washington, D.C.

Introduction

Hilton Als

At some point during the early part of his career, the American author James Baldwin (1924–1987) was asked if he'd be interested in writing the biography of the great Black writer and polemicist W. E. B. Du Bois (1868–1963). The book never happened, but I can imagine why Baldwin was interested in his titanic forefather. Like Baldwin, Du Bois was an author and thinker whose work was not inseparable from his commitment to his race, even as he strived to be himself, which is to say, an artist.

This great schism in Baldwin—between the public figure and the public self—has been remarked upon in the past but without much understanding. Many writers and theorists relegate Baldwin to one spot or the other. He's portrayed either as a polemicist, who produced a work of great rhetoric—as in his non-fiction masterwork, *The Fire Next Time* (1963)—or as a queer artist, whose major novels, notably *Another Country* (1961), were a cry for integration and national acceptance of the Other. In *This Morning, This Evening, So Soon: James Baldwin and the Voices of Queer Resistance*, we encounter these two Baldwins, so to speak, but they are brought together in a gallery space where he and close friends, such as the musician Nina Simone (1933–2003) and the playwright Lorraine Hansberry (1930–1965), author of "A Raisin in the Sun" (1959), are alive with the energy of change and resistance.

Born in Harlem in 1924, Baldwin immigrated to Paris in his early twenties with just forty dollars, and no French. He had left his native land to face what had gotten obscured in Manhattan: himself, and his artistry. A frequent critic for *The New Leader* and other socially conscious publications, Baldwin was often asked to comment on the postwar Black American scene. But by 1948, he had had enough; he could not speak for his people or *a* people without learning how to speak for and about his own experiences. In order to be the writer he wanted to be, he had to face himself. France became a kind of mirror. And it was there that Baldwin published his seminal essays, many of which were collected in his groundbreaking volume, *Notes of a Native Son* (1955). While living largely in Paris, he also wrote his novel about queer desire, *Giovanni's Room* (1956). In that landmark work, Baldwin was able to talk about what he could not openly discuss in a homophobic America: what love looked like and felt like in a gay society. (The Supreme Court did not end sodomy laws nationwide until 2003.)

In short, time and distance gave Baldwin the opportunity for reflection. After nearly a decade in Paris, however, he felt compelled to return to the United States. He caught a glimpse of a picture of Dorothy Counts facing a hostile white crowd as she made her way to integrate a high school in North Carolina. "The photo made me furious," Baldwin recalled. "Everybody else was paying their dues, and it was time I went home and paid mine." By the time he made the journey, in 1957, during the early heady days of the civil rights movement, he knew who he was: a writer whose identity was inseparable from the struggle, an artist who knew that the personal was always political, and a man who recognized that power never rests from the need to declare itself.

In the United States, Baldwin got to work at once. He spoke and wrote incredible essays about the civil rights movement, such as "Fly in the Buttermilk" (1961), while marching with activists ranging from Bayard Rustin (1912–1987) to Joan Baez (b. 1941). A freedom fighter and scholar, Rustin was also a gay activist who worked closely with Martin Luther King Jr. (1929–1968) to organize 1963's historic March on Washington. But he could not be out in that world; homosexuality had no place of honor in the Movement.

Baldwin's sexuality, while known because of his writing, was not a feature folks talked about, either. Meanwhile, Baldwin was becoming friends not only with King but with Medgar Evers (1925–1963) and Malcolm X (1925–1965). With them, Baldwin quested his fellow countrymen by asking, "Why don't we live in a better world—a color blind world where all humanity was honored?" Hansberry was another of Baldwin's queer friends who worked tirelessly for Black people to be heard. And, like Baldwin and Rustin, she could reveal only so much about her personal life within the context of the Movement.

This Morning, This Evening, So Soon: James Baldwin and the Voices of Queer Resistance is a reckoning of sorts, one that not only celebrates these activists for their work on the front lines of the civil rights movement, then and now, but also affirms their queer lives. This gathering of loved ones is in line with what Baldwin knew growing up. He had always been responsible for others. As the eldest of nine, he helped his mother take care of her charges. When his tyrannical father, David, died in 1943, it was nineteen-year-old Baldwin who assumed financial responsibility for his siblings. For a time, he worked in a munitions factory in New Jersey. So, this kinship of the like-minded—supporting Hansberry's success and the accomplishments of their mutual friend Nina Simone, for instance—was part of what Baldwin knew from his experience as a son and elder.

Here, we honor Baldwin's spirit—and legacy—of teaching the children so they, in turn, can teach the children. Because elements of his legacy reside in the lives of the queer artist-activists who came up alongside him and even those who emerged later, such as the legendary Texas Congresswoman Barbara Jordan (1936–1996) and the radical, loving artists Marlon Riggs (1957–1994), Essex Hemphill (1957–1995), and bell hooks (1952–2021). Each, in his or her or their own way, lived what Baldwin preached from his exile and return to his beloved, troubling, and vexed country: that love and insight may not equal a win, but they always add up to a giant step when it comes to progress.

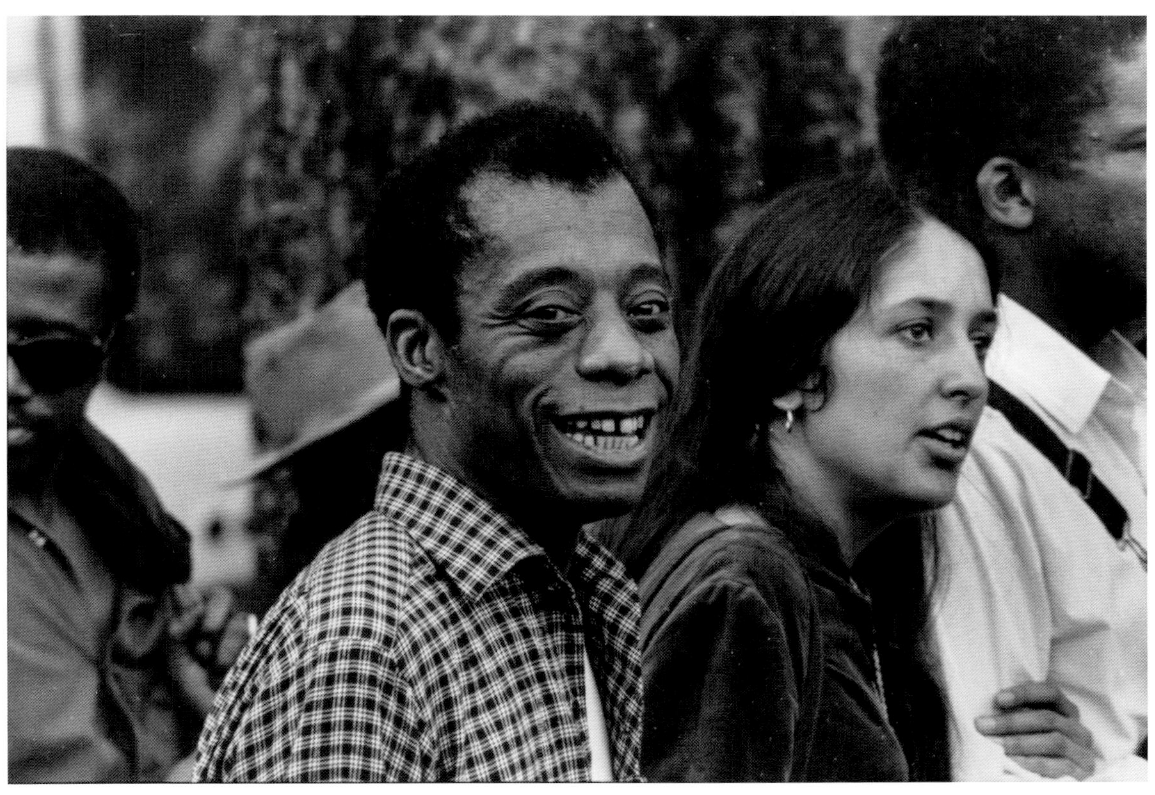

James Baldwin and Joan Baez in Selma, 1965
James Karales
gelatin silver print, 4 11/16 x 6 7/8 in.
(11.9 x 17.5 cm)
National Museum of African American History and Culture, Smithsonian Institution

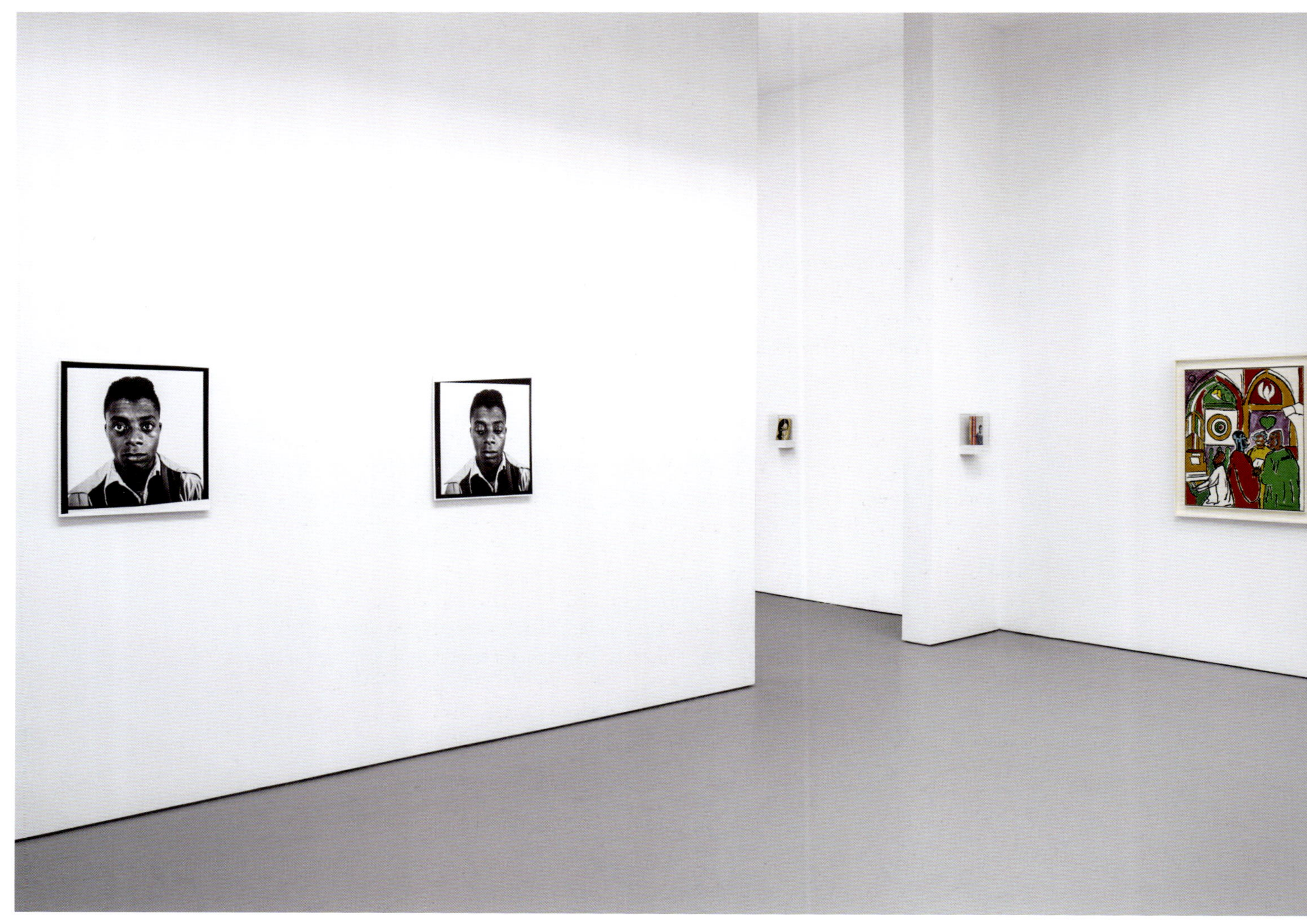

Installation view of **God Made My Face: A Collective Portrait of James Baldwin,** David Zwirner, New York, 2019. Two portraits entitled **James Baldwin, Harlem, New York**, c. 1945, by Richard Avedon, are shown on the left.

In Conversation: Hilton Als and Rhea L. Combs

This conversation between authors Hilton Als (New York) and Rhea L. Combs (Washington, D.C.), which focused on the objectives of This Morning, This Evening, So Soon: James Baldwin and the Voices of Queer Resistance*, was held via Zoom on December 5, 2023. The following transcript has been edited for length and clarity.*

RLC: This project follows a very successful show you pulled together for Zwirner Gallery several years ago. That exhibition examined Baldwin's life in important interior ways; and for a figure who's very popular, it felt as if you were trying to honor his mind and body. That said, I am wondering, what are you hoping will be accomplished with this specific project?

HA: First of all, this show at the National Portrait Gallery is a great opportunity to reconfigure some of those themes. It is a great opportunity to talk about an aspect of Baldwin that only gets passing reference in the literature about him, and that is the queer family that he made by choice as opposed to the family that he inherited by birth. Of course, one of the great things about his essays is his ability to talk about his mother and his siblings and how his family, his mother in particular, was supportive of him becoming a writer and how he had real adult responsibilities very early on because she had so many damn kids, right?

RLC: [Laughter] Yes.

HA: He had big responsibilities very early on, and one of the things that is so moving about his life was that he was able to create another structure for himself. I am also glad a Baldwin-themed show of his work is in Washington, D.C., because that is where *The Amen Corner*, his first play, was produced. Owen Dodson, who was in the drama department at Howard [University] for many years, was the first director to put it on, a queer friend. Baldwin had never been to a university before he went to Howard to see and meet with Dodson.

So, I think the wonderful thing—well, there are many wonderful things about this project, but a significant part of the experience has focused on how Baldwin assembled this queer family. After *The Amen Corner*, Baldwin goes on to work with and live with other gay men of color: Beauford Delaney, he got to come to Paris; Baldwin's brother David, and Bernard Hassell. And then, there were the more luminary names who came through to be with him and to sit at what he called the "welcome table" in Saint-Paul de Vence. That group includes Miles Davis, Caryl Phillips, Josephine Baker, and Toni Morrison. I think one of the things that is essential to our understanding of Baldwin is this ethos, this way in which he made families wherever he lived.

I also think that our show is about the ways in which the political and the personal meet. I don't think people know very well that Baldwin was very close to Lorraine Hansberry or Nina Simone. The people represented in the show not only learned from him as a family member but also became his teachers. It's really a show about how the personal and the political converge and how the chosen family happens.

RLC: And how critical that chosen family was to his understanding and moving through the world.

HA: Yes, well, I think writers, by nature—and by necessity—are lonely. And I think we're showing some of the ways he alleviated that isolation. I think politics really helped him because politics connected him with Bayard Rustin and other people he would not necessarily have gotten to know without his activism.

RLC: It's interesting how you said that activism became a way for him to find his chosen family—one that was political, personal, artistic, and creative as well, wouldn't you say?

HA: I would absolutely say that. I think that he wanted to speak to like-minded people.

RLC: And do you find that through these diverse connections he had with people, as friends, lovers or whatever, that it influenced or even challenged what he was discussing in his writing, specifically with regard to race, sexuality, and sexual orientation in the United States?

HA: I think what you're saying is incredibly important, but also, let's not forget his life and work as an integrationist. One of the super important people in his life during that period, from 1949 on, was Marlon Brando. He and Baldwin were deeply close friends, and there are great photographs of them together at the 1963 March on Washington. Brando had grown up in—I'm not going to say that he was a bohemian—but he was exposed to bohemianism in New York—in that his environment was inclusive. Baldwin was certainly a precursor to people like the painter Bob Thompson and the writer LeRoi Jones (later Amiri Baraka), to name a couple. All of those people who came in the mid-to-late fifties benefited from the bohemianism that Baldwin had lived through and fought for in the 1940s in New York.

RLC: The café society, if you will.

HA: Yes, café society was a little less rough. I'm talking about the bohemianism of people like Marlon Brando, and they were not known people at that time. The point I'm trying to make is that another aspect of the show, which we don't get to cover as much as we would like to, is Baldwin's work as an integrationist personally and professionally.

RLC: Thank you for making that important point.

HA: It's always funny, right, you want to do everything with one show but. . .

RLC: That's the beauty of having the companion book. It allows us to tease out some of the ideas that are either merely touched upon in the exhibition, or not addressed at all. Speaking about expanding on ideas, perhaps we can discuss the title? When I initially called to ask about your interest in working with me on this exhibition at the National Portrait Gallery, we soon realized this could be an opportunity to expand on some of the ideas brought forward in your 2019 exhibition at David Zwirner Gallery, *God Made My Face: A Collective Portrait of James Baldwin.* For the exhibition here, we decided to incorporate a title from the essay Baldwin wrote in the *Atlantic* in 1960, a short story titled "This Morning, This Evening, So Soon."

HA: Which was great. It's a great story but it is one of the works of his that doesn't get a lot of critical attention. It's a story about an expatriate actor who is returning to America with his son. And on the journey to America, he begins to feel and experience the claustrophobia, the suffocation of racial difference coming to haunt him again, to kill him. And I think one of the things that Baldwin is doing in that story, of course, is talking about returning to America himself, this idea that you can go home again.

RLC: Exactly, yes, you can return home again, but it is not always a simple proposition. Home, but at what cost?

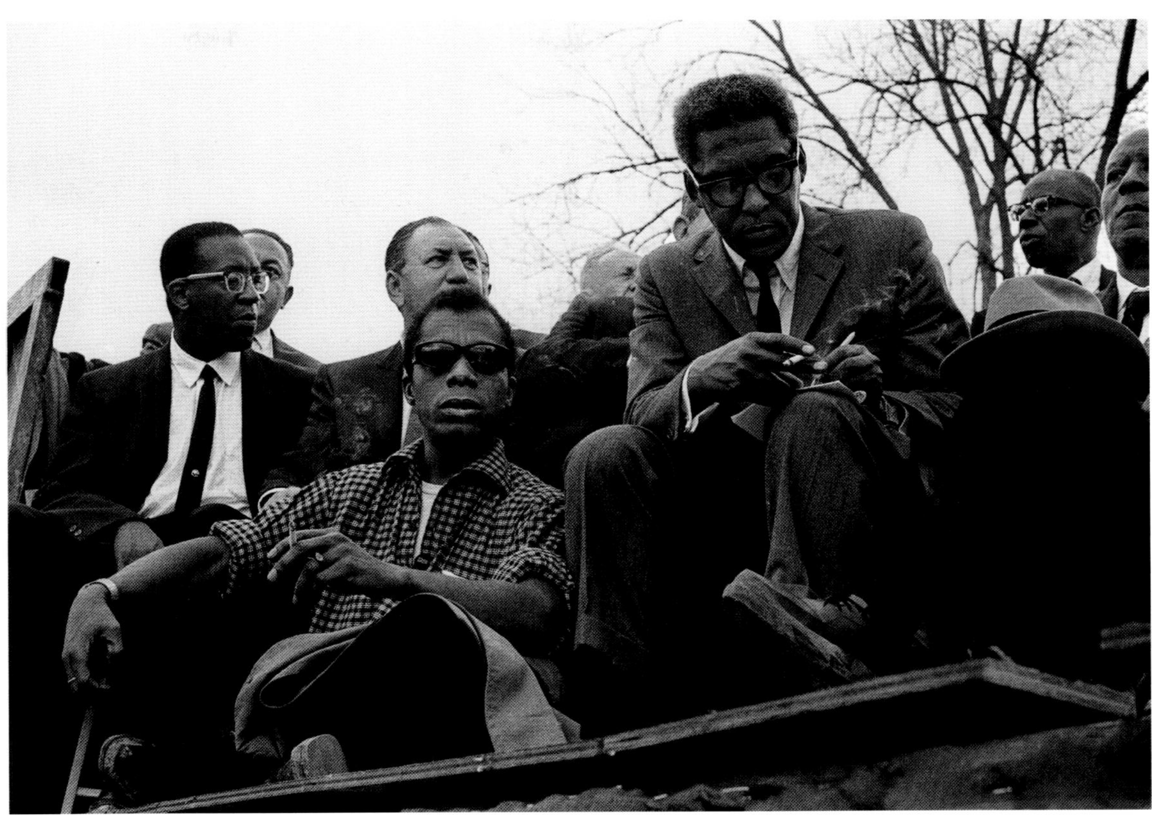

HA: One of the reasons I was keen to use that title was that it was about a return. And it was about the prodigal son who doesn't leave because of the father, but he leaves because of the cruelty of patriarchy, of white patriarchy, in particular. And one of the things so extraordinary about the piece is that you can feel Baldwin's own fears and trepidation but also his desire to come through, to push forward. So, I felt that this title would be fantastic for our show because, again, it's about a return, but it's also about why somebody had to leave, right?

RLC: Yes. It is poetic, and for me it embodies many of the ideas that Baldwin grappled with in his public writing and in his personal reflections.

HA: Why does the expatriate have to leave in the first place? And so, with the title we get two feelings: we get expatriation and we get return. I also felt that we needed a title that was evocative and connected to where he was personally and what he was doing as a creative.

RLC: Can you describe what about this circle of friends that we've included in this show enchants you?

HA: That's a lovely question. Well, they're all people who achieved but who may not be as well known to many as Baldwin is. I think it's a wonderful celebration of people who have had an enormous influence on our culture and on our politics without necessarily being public figures who would be collectively remembered or naturally affiliated with one another, even though we know there is a throughline between these individuals. I also think that in this act of

James Baldwin sits next to Bayard Rustin (seen taking notes) on the speakers platform in Montgomery, Alabama, on the final day of the Selma-to-Montgomery Civil Rights March, led by Martin Luther King, Jr., March 25, 1965
Photo by Stephen F. Somerstein
Getty Images

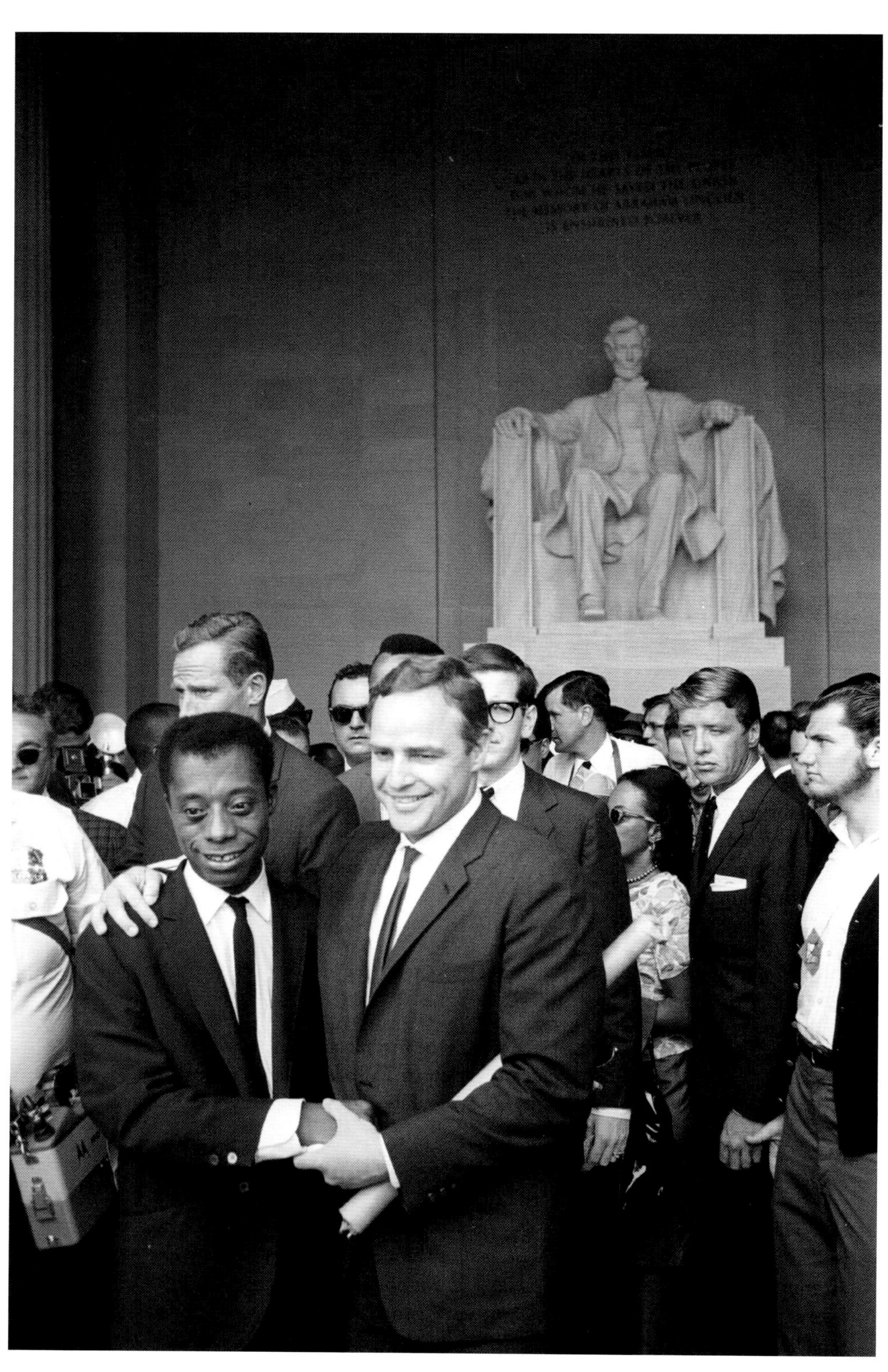

James Baldwin and Marlon Brando at the Lincoln Memorial during the March on Washington for Jobs and Freedom, August 28, 1963
Photo by Paul Slade
Paris Match via Getty Images

remembrance, we're not only remembering Baldwin as an activist but also as an artist. We're emphasizing the ways in which storytellers bring people together.

RLC: And I also appreciate, Hilton, the fact that in this exhibition, there is this sense of creating a portrait of someone but removing this deification of a singular figure and instead underscoring the variety of experiences and interactions and loves and relationships that make up the totality of a person.

HA: That's exactly right. What's also really important is that the actual layout of the show allows for the literal transmogrification of these personas so that there is a beginning and an end but also a center. Therefore architecturally, we are recognizing the circularity of a life.

RLC: I imagine there will be quite a few celebrations around the centennial of Baldwin's life. So, coming at it from this perspective, by honoring him through the circle of friends who meant a lot to him, is a wonderful way of approaching a person's biography. That said, we have also included people who were not part of his immediate friendship group. Can you speak about the artists who are featured in the show that Baldwin may not have known very well, like Essex Hemphill or Marlon Riggs, or even Lyle Ashton Harris, whose work of Hemphill and Riggs is represented in the show?

HA: Yes, it was important for us to have people who would've sat at Baldwin's feet to hear the story. We wanted younger artists included who didn't make it because of AIDS, and because of the horrifying ways in which AIDS was treated at that time. But we also wanted to have artists who were really in that legacy of people that Baldwin had left in his wake. So, I think, in terms of us including those younger members of the tribe, we were saying that the tribe continues and that the exhibition itself is evidence of the ways in which the tribe continues.

RLC: Considering this notion of continuance, there's not a day I don't see in social media a quote or reference to Baldwin. There are dedicated websites and Instagram feeds that feature only James Baldwin. How do you think he would respond and react to this interest in his work and dedication to him?

HA: He was a very modest person, from what I understand, and I think he would've been greatly amused from the distance of that little village [St. Paul de Vence, in the South of France], which I've been to. It's charming and beautiful, and it's very remote, and he would've just, I think, been deeply humbled. Because remember, something that people don't want to talk about are the ways in which we ignored Baldwin in the seventies and eighties, right? The ways in which he was lambasted by the critics for his later books, such as *The Devil Finds Work* or *No Name in the Street*. He was not a darling anymore after about 1968, so we didn't treat him very well. And I think that if there can be such a thing as an exhibition having a healing effect, I think we can take that idea and apply it to this one. Because, again, we're using the space to—in a funny way, ask for forgiveness for the collective amnesia when it came to his work in those decades. And it's a way of owning up to the significance despite the critical marginalization of how he kept growing.

RLC: And it's a healing in the sense—I think you and I talked about this before—that his ascension eclipsed other people's ability to speak about their queer identity, right? But at the same time, he was able to speak about queerness in ways others were not. One had to choose the fight for the cause of civil rights at the sacrifice of one's own self.

HA: Right.

RLC: It was a sacrifice, and maybe one that had something to do with why he was not necessarily the darling that he has become posthumously. Was he taking the hits for others? Or was his outspokenness being looked upon as a fool's errand that made others do the calculation and decide to stay quiet about certain things, particularly around race and sexuality. You know, there's a tension there.

HA: Right, and I think that's a good point to make. People like Essex and Marlon are the "out" voices of that legacy, the voices who were not conflicted about speaking given that Baldwin not only came of age during a time when one could be arrested for being Black, but one could also be arrested for being queer; it was sort of a double weight. I think that moving to France allowed him a certain amount of freedom as a gay man and a certain amount of freedom as a man of color.

It's weird to have to leave your home country to become yourself. That's such a painful thing to acknowledge. It is also the truth when thinking about Baldwin. He had to leave the place that shaped his understanding of life and carry it across the sea in order to understand himself. It was also the only way he would not be endangered for being who he was, Black and queer. This took daring, and I think Marlon and Essex are the children who benefited from that act.

RLC: Absolutely. At the time that Baldwin was acknowledging his queerness, medical guides were calling it a—

HA: psychosis.

RLC: . . .pathology, yes.

HA: Yes.

RLC: If we ponder that: medical book pathologized sexual identity. Couple that with also being a Black person, and also poor, so leaving became a matter of life or death.

HA: That's right. And I think that another one of the poignant parts of the show is that Barbara Jordan died young, Marlon and Essex also died young.

RLC: Lorraine died young.

HA: Lorraine died young. What I feel when I think about the exhibition, I feel the ways in which we get pulverized by our culture. The very culture that we're trying to help build and the very culture that we are all spearheading, let alone creating, doesn't accept you. And that the psychic damage that does to your body is untold, and physical damage that it does to your body is untold. And I think this show tells it by implication when we have dates for people's lives. If I were a kid walking into the show and I saw those dates, I'd be like, what happened, why did they die so young? And I think that we need to leave that question to America and to Americans who are seeing exhibitions like this, and say why did he have to move away, why was he so young? I think this show puts us in a very interesting position of showing power, but also showing the personal cost of race and queer life.

RLC: Speaking of race and queer life, at one point, you wrote that you had an ambivalence toward Baldwin. Can you explain what you meant?

HA: That's a great quote, and I think it had everything to do with how overwhelming he was for me. And that one of the ways in which we get to survive our parents and our elders is to become ambivalent about them, right? We love them but maybe we don't like them or. . . [Laughter]

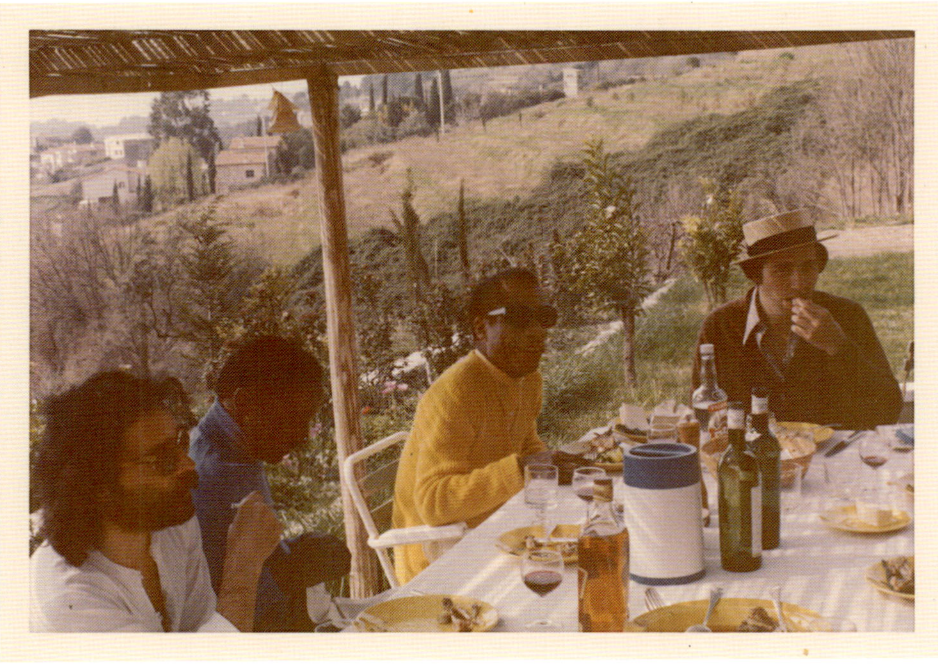

RLC: Yes.

HA: We love them, but we need distance. I think when I said that, and that was a while ago, I think what I was saying was that I needed to establish distance in order to find my own voice as a Black man. I had to find my own way, and he would've seconded that, and he did in his essays about Richard Wright, right? That he had to love him and be ambivalent about him at the same time in order to clear the desk so that he could sit down and have his word. Maybe looking back it was a bad word choice, but it was a very similar feeling that I had to have—I have to love him, but I had to be wary of his voice creeping into my voice.

RLC: I think that that is a very prudent and honest way to describe those we admire. I think that it would be refreshing to have more artists do that. I think sometimes one may see an artist's work, whatever the medium and you're like, okay, they're trying to be like this person as opposed to finding their own voice. And it sounds like you were saying, okay, I appreciate and I'm really connecting to what he's grappling with, but I cannot allow that reverence to overshadow so much that I don't find my own way.

HA: Right, you have to figure out a good way to minimize the elder without hurting them, and it's not their fault that they're powerful in your life. You have to find a way to minimize them in order to step up to your own voice and to your own life. I had to do that in order to have my own seat at my own table.

RLC: And so, speaking of your own table, in your curatorial work as well as your writings, what role do you feel or see the archive playing?

HA: Oh, my God, they're essential to storytelling. The archives are the alphabet that you need to make the sentences, you know? You need that archival information to make the narrative,

James Baldwin (center) and three friends sitting outside around a table in St. Paul de Vence, France,
July 1973

National Museum of African American History and Culture, Smithsonian Institution; gift of the Baldwin Family

and so you're taking from the archive, and you're putting together elements that are really paragraphs, letters, sentences in order to make the story.

RLC: In other words, you may have a morsel of an idea, but the archives make sense of that idea?

HA: Or the archive makes it three-dimensional, right? For example, it's one thing to remember pictures of Nina Simone and Baldwin that give the feeling of joy but also camaraderie. That's different than me saying I'll write the sentence that says that. We need to make the sentences of joy through the photographs, through the vitrines, through the archives, so that the audience can experience the various dimensions and see that the narrative has three dimensions as opposed to a sentence. Writing about Baldwin's friendship with Nina Simone, that's one thing, but when you show Baldwin's relationship to Nina Simone, what you're doing, in a funny way, is the work of cinema, right? You're giving visual evidence and credence something.

RLC: If we continue with the cinematic analogy do you believe the power of the archive also aids with understanding the motivation of that character?

HA: What you're doing is the work of a great editor working in cinema, which is that you are taking the pieces of these stories and you're putting them together to cohere to the story that you want to tell as opposed to these fragments that may not make sense individually, but together, they make a very powerful narrative.

RLC: Yes, for example, it was quite remarkable to find notes from Bayard Rustin and to see the ways in which he's mapping out some ideas around civil rights, Gandhi but then also making connections with Stonewall and queer identity. So, to your point, there's a concept, but then the archives provide the scaffolding behind that concept, yes.

HA: Right, like you need a bulwark for the evocation.

RLC: Yes, and that's the role you see archives playing?

HA: Archives are facts, right, you can't alter them. You're dealing with factual information, and what you're doing in the exhibition space is you're giving those facts a form. It's a literal and figurative form that you're giving to archival material.

RLC: In terms of the form in which we're looking at this work, there's a theme that we talked about earlier, civil rights. I would love for you to discuss some of the artwork that was selected that speaks to civil rights, but also to queer identity. Since some of the artworks featured are not obviously representational portraits of Baldwin, speak about some of the selections that were included.

HA: Of course, I mean to begin with, there is Glenn Ligon's *Untitled (Hands/Stranger in the Village)*, which takes part of its name from a Baldwin essay. And again, if we're talking about Marlon and Essex being the children of Baldwin, and then Glenn is the symbolic grandchild of Baldwin and the child of Marlon and Essex (even though he's born only a few years after they were), it was important for us to have a living representation of that legacy. And the work that Glenn does is always evidence of the ways in which the political and the personal converge, and how do you make politics visual information? How do you tell a story of a people in a static medium? So those are the intellectual and metaphysical challenges in Glenn's work that were perfect for what we had in mind in terms of helping us frame these ideas.

I think also someone like Donald Moffett is very important because to go back to the point about integration, Don is a gay white artist who made a piece about Barbara Jordan. And it was very important for us to have that kind of inclusivity in this show but also to show that Barbara

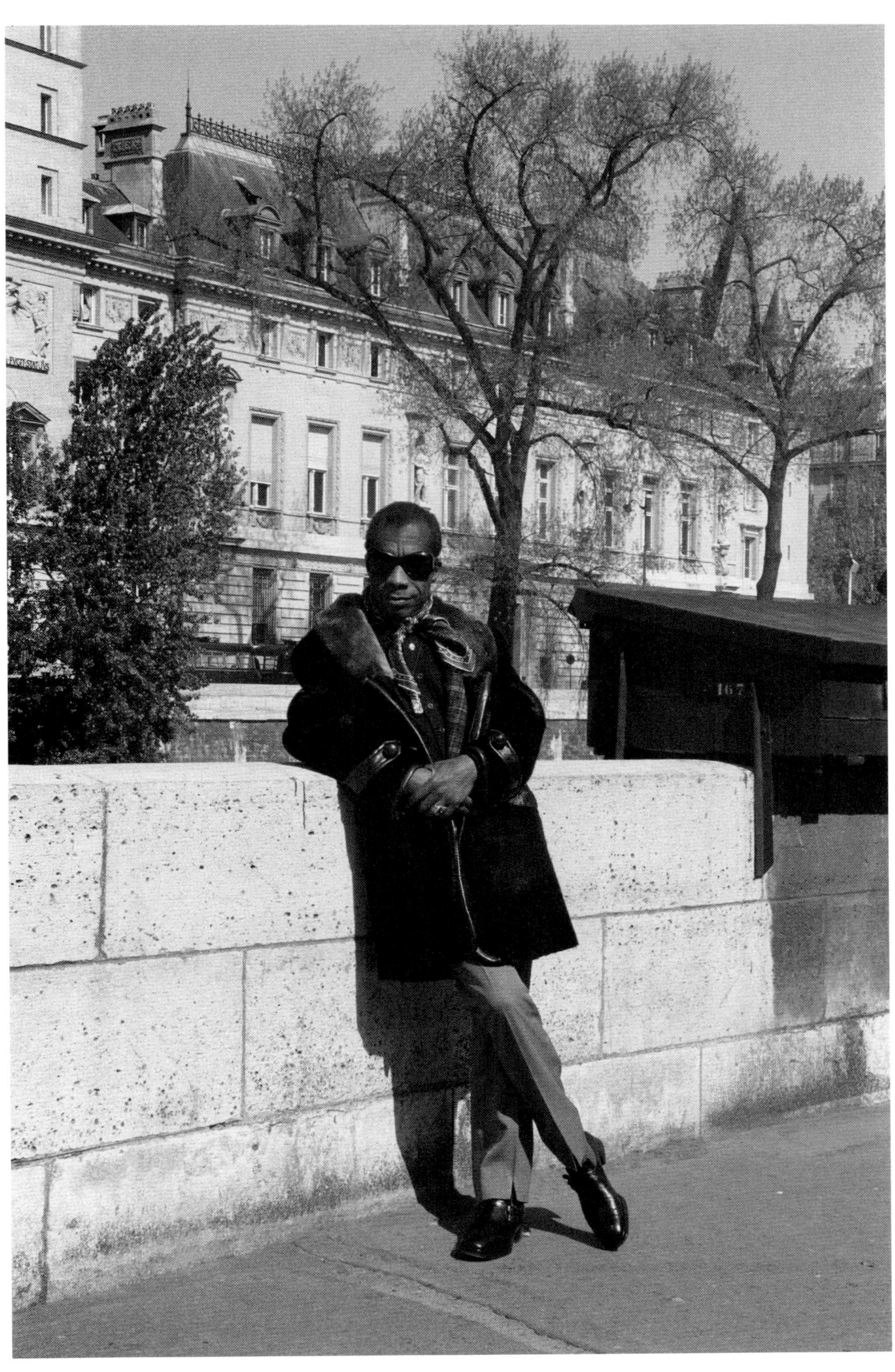

James Baldwin in Paris, April 1972
Photo by Sophie Bassouls
Sygma via Getty Images

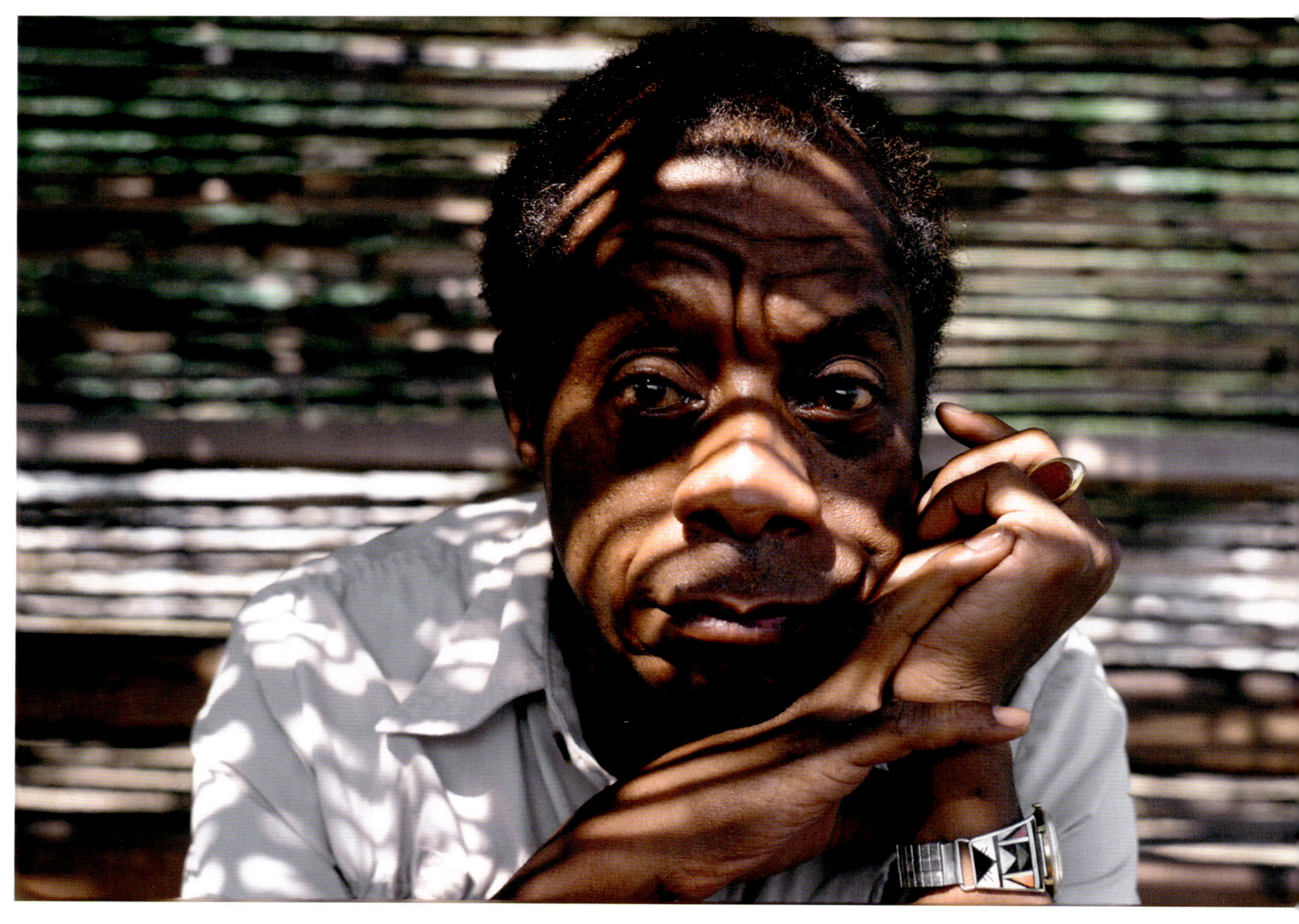

James Baldwin at home in Saint Paul de Vence, France,
September 1985
Photo by Ulf Andersen
Getty Images

had great resonance for folks. And even if they didn't remember how effective she had been in her home state of Texas, we would have evidence of that, along with Richard Avedon's great portrait. Then there is the quilt. If we have someone like Faith Ringold, we're not only talking about someone who was a near contemporary of Baldwin's, we're talking about the ways in which civil rights not only resonate for the artist but also change the artist's point of view and give it a kind of focus.

RLC: And Ringgold's work focuses on Marlon Riggs. She's examining queer identity. She's looking at AIDS and how it devastated the Black community, the queer Black community. And like you said, she's a near contemporary of Baldwin, so for someone to be speaking about these ideas from his generation is also critical.

HA: I think it is critical to our discussion, and, of course, there is also the great American Jack Whitten, who is asking, how do we talk about these seismic events in Black life through visual culture? I love that this show has a lot of questions in it. I believe it is important to leave a lot of questions in the show and not have an overwhelming series of answers because we're still in progress as a nation. And if we are in progress as a nation, we can't stop it or stop ourselves by giving a definitive answer about anything.

RLC: I also appreciate the fact that we have work that is figurative as well as abstract in this space.

HA: Yes.

RLC: I think this acknowledges that things are constantly in a changing state. There are things one is very clear about, and then there are other things that are, as you just mentioned, in process. I find human beings, just in general, to be very abstract. [Laughter]

HA: I would say most human beings feel that about other people, yes.

RLC: Yes, so, that play of the personal and the political, that idea of having more questions than answers, and looking at how visual artists are representing individuals both figuratively and abstractly offers a dynamism that allows people to understand the kaleidoscopic nature of human beings—and human nature.

HA: I agree.

RLC: Are there other things you would like visitors to take away from this experience?

HA: How much we love him and how much we love the people he loved. They were extraordinary humans, who contributed greatly to the progress of this nation. And I think there is so much that we need to thank people for as we move forward. I think we concentrate a lot in this country on failure.

RLC: And canceling people, right?

HA: And segregating. I think it's time we learn a little humility. This is a very humble show about someone—and a bunch of people in his orbit—to whom we owe a great deal of gratitude.

RLC: Humble but also with an outsized impact.

HA: Again, going back to this idea of bodies and how young a lot of these people were when they passed—and there is a reason for that. I think we need to answer to that as a nation but also be grateful for what they went through in order to become themselves, you know?

RLC: Absolutely. Thank you, Hilton. It's been a pleasure.

HA: Thank you. I enjoyed this.

Catalogue

Subjects

James Baldwin
(1924–1987)

Beauford Delaney
(1901–1979)

Lorraine Hansberry
(1930–1965)

Essex Hemphill
(1957–1995)

bell hooks
(1952–2019)

Barbara Jordan
(1936–1996)

Martin Luther King Jr.
(1929–1968)

Burgess Meredith
(1907–1997)

Toni Morrison
(1931–2019)

Bertice Reading
(1933–1991)

Marlon Riggs
(1957–1994)

Bayard Rustin
(1912–1987)

Diana Sands
(1934–1973)

Nina Simone
(1933–2003)

Evan Winfield
(1906–1984)

Orilla "Bill Miller" Winfield
(1912–1990)

Artists/ Photographers

David Attie
(1920–1982)

Richard Avedon
(1923–2004)

Anthony Barboza
(b. 1944)

Dan Budnik
(1933–2020)

Beauford Delaney
(1901–1979)

Bernard Gotfryd
(1924–2016)

Lyle Ashton Harris
(b. 1965)

Glenn Ligon
(b. 1960)

Helen Marcus
(1925–2023)

Donald Moffett
(b. 1955)

Hakim Mutlaq
(b. 1955)

Sedat Pakay
(1945–2016)

Faith Ringgold
(1930–2024)

Lorna Simpson
(b. 1960)

Jack Whitten
(b. 1939)

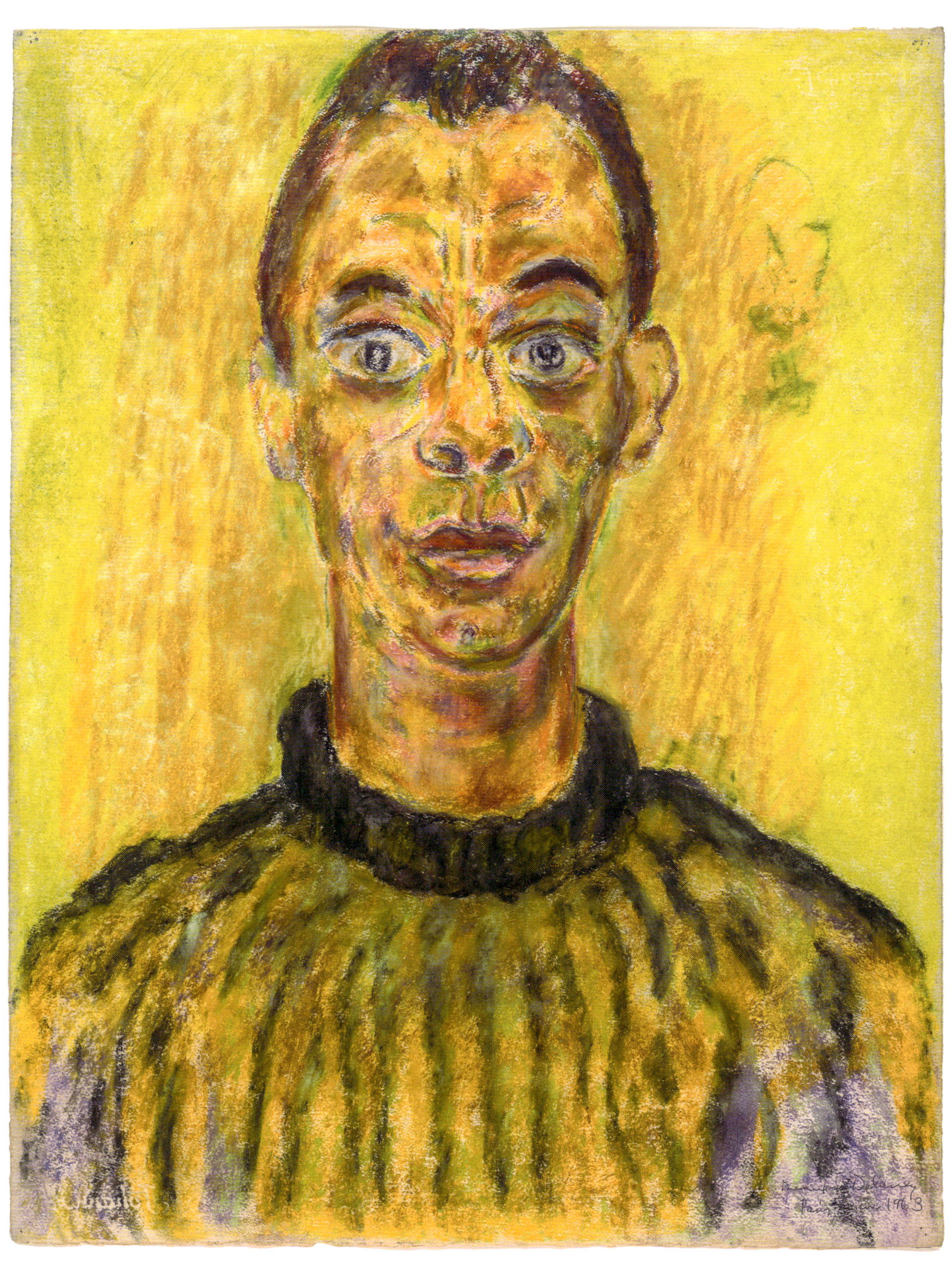

James Baldwin, 1963
Beauford Delaney
pastel on paper, 25 ½ × 19 ⅝ in. (64.8 × 49.8 cm)
National Portrait Gallery, Smithsonian Institution

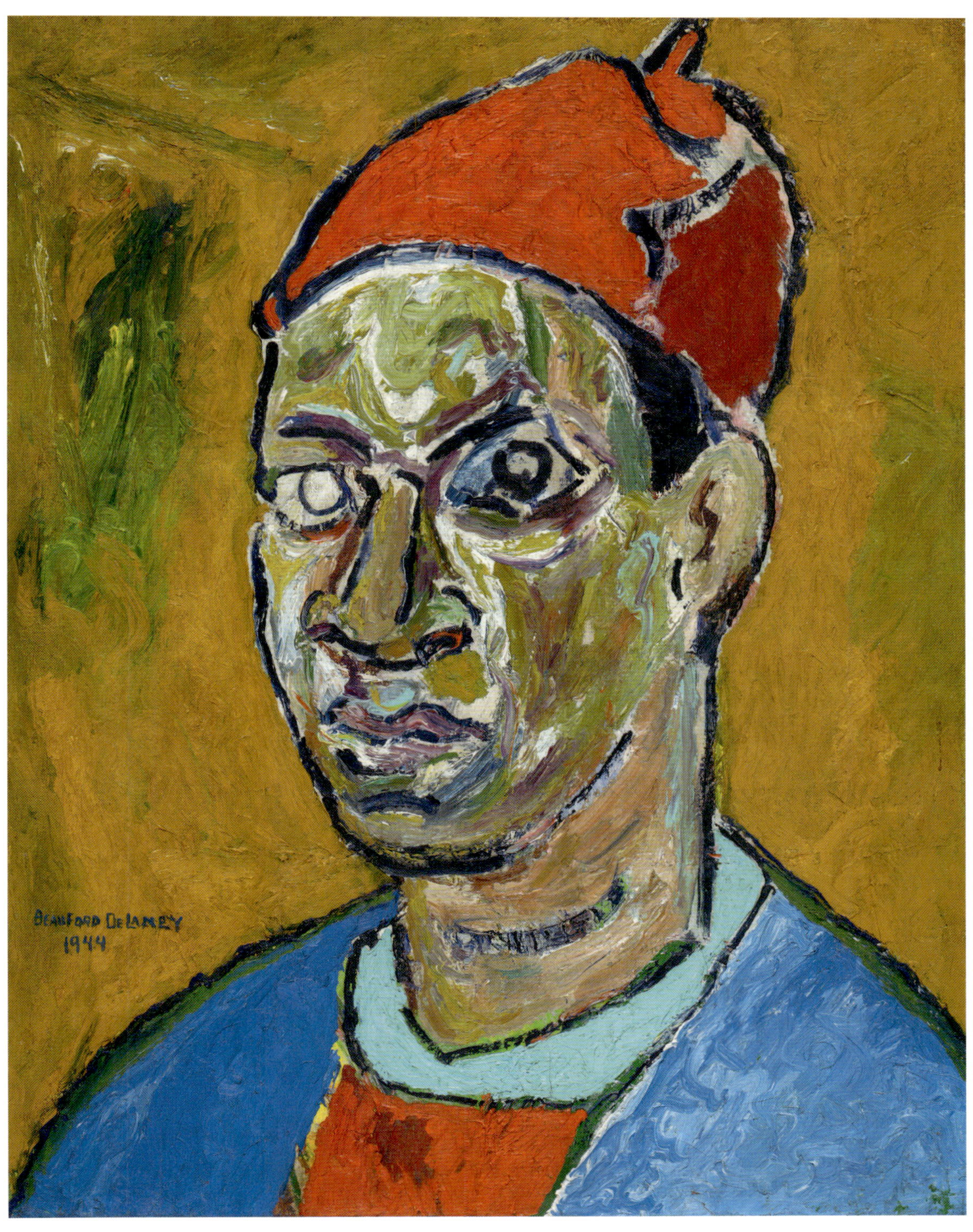

Self-Portrait, 1944

Beauford Delaney

oil on canvas, 27 × 22 ½ in. (68.6 × 57.2 cm)

The Art Institute of Chicago; purchased with funds provided by Alexander C. and Tillie S. Speyer Foundation; Samuel A. Marx Endowment

ed (Hands/Stranger in the Village), 1999
Ligon
een ink, coal dust, and glue on paper mounted on
s, 40 ½ x 45 ½ in. (102.9 x 115.6 cm)
Museum of Art, The University of Texas at Austin,
er Acquisitions Fund

In 1996, the American artist Glenn Ligon, who often incorporates text into his work, began to pull from writings by Baldwin, specifically those centering on questions of identity. For this piece, he took lines from Baldwin's 1953 essay "Stranger in the Village" to address the Black presence in Western culture. The text rests on top of Black hands raised in protest—or benediction.

Using silkscreen ink, coal crystals, and glue, Ligon created a dense, layered image that stands as a metaphor for the fragility of Black American life. The artist considered both the coal dust's irrefutable blackness as well as its relationship to chance. Whenever the piece is moved or shifted, even incrementally, some of the dust is dislodged, a reminder of what Baldwin explained in his essay: "There is a dreadful abyss between the streets of this village and the streets of the city in which I was born."

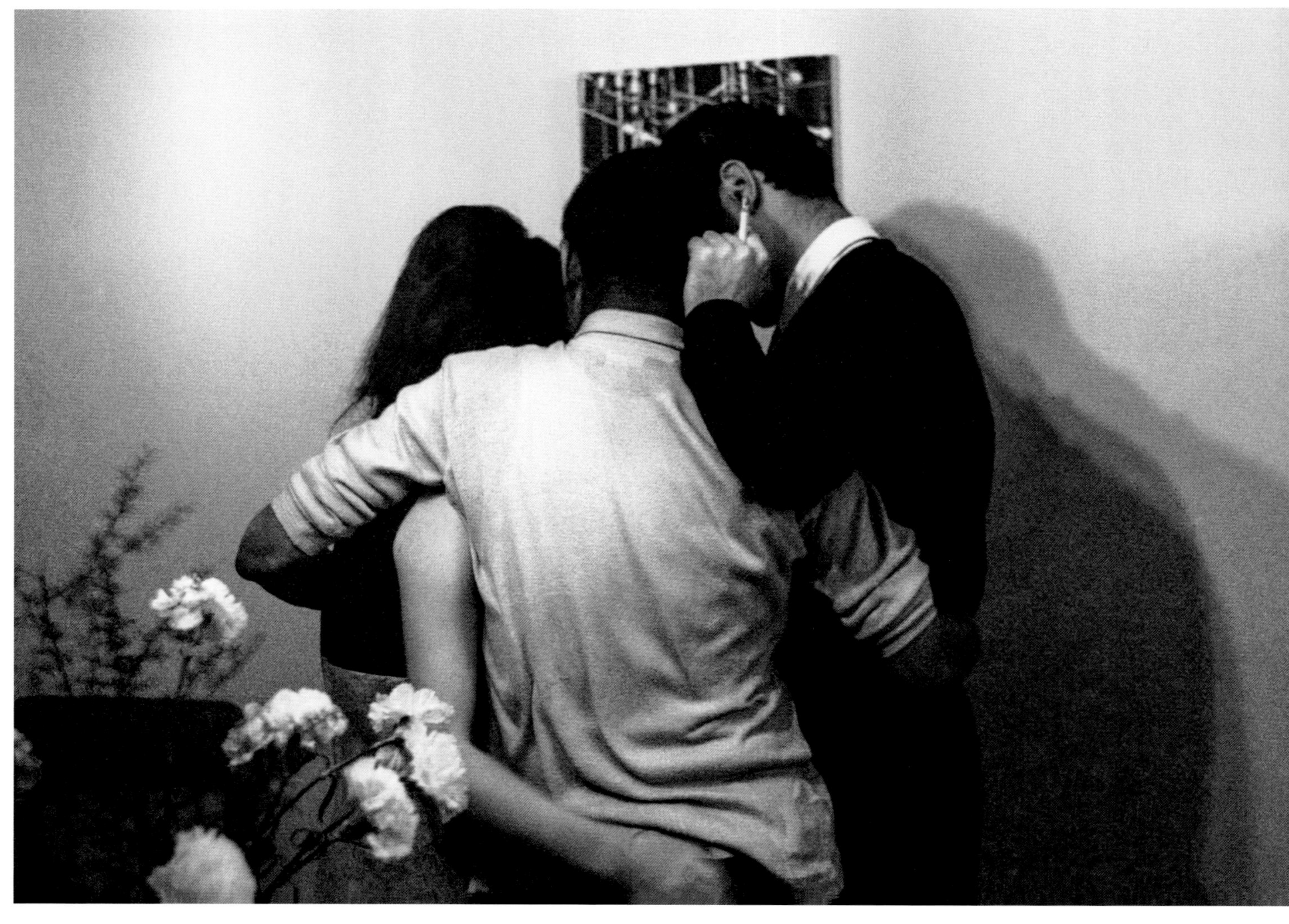

James Baldwin with Gülriz Sururi and Engin Cezzar, Istanbul, 1965
Sedat Pakay
gelatin silver print, dimensions variable
Courtesy of the Estate of Sedat Pakay

In 1970, the Turkish-born photographer and filmmaker Sedat Pakay premiered a short black-and-white documentary about Baldwin, who spent a significant part of the 1960s in Istanbul. Titled *James Baldwin: From Another Place* and shot in the author's home and in the streets and souks of the fabled city, Pakay's documentary includes the still images that are shown here in slideshow form. Poetic and rich in detail, Pakay's pictures offer a moving record of a writer living in a culture that is not his own, of someone hoping to gain perspective on his native land.

Istanbul was fertile ground for Baldwin. In 1961, he completed his third novel, *Another Country* (1962), there. Inspired by his life in New York's bohemian world, *Another Country* openly addresses miscegenation and gay desire—a groundbreaking book that went on to become the author's first bestseller.

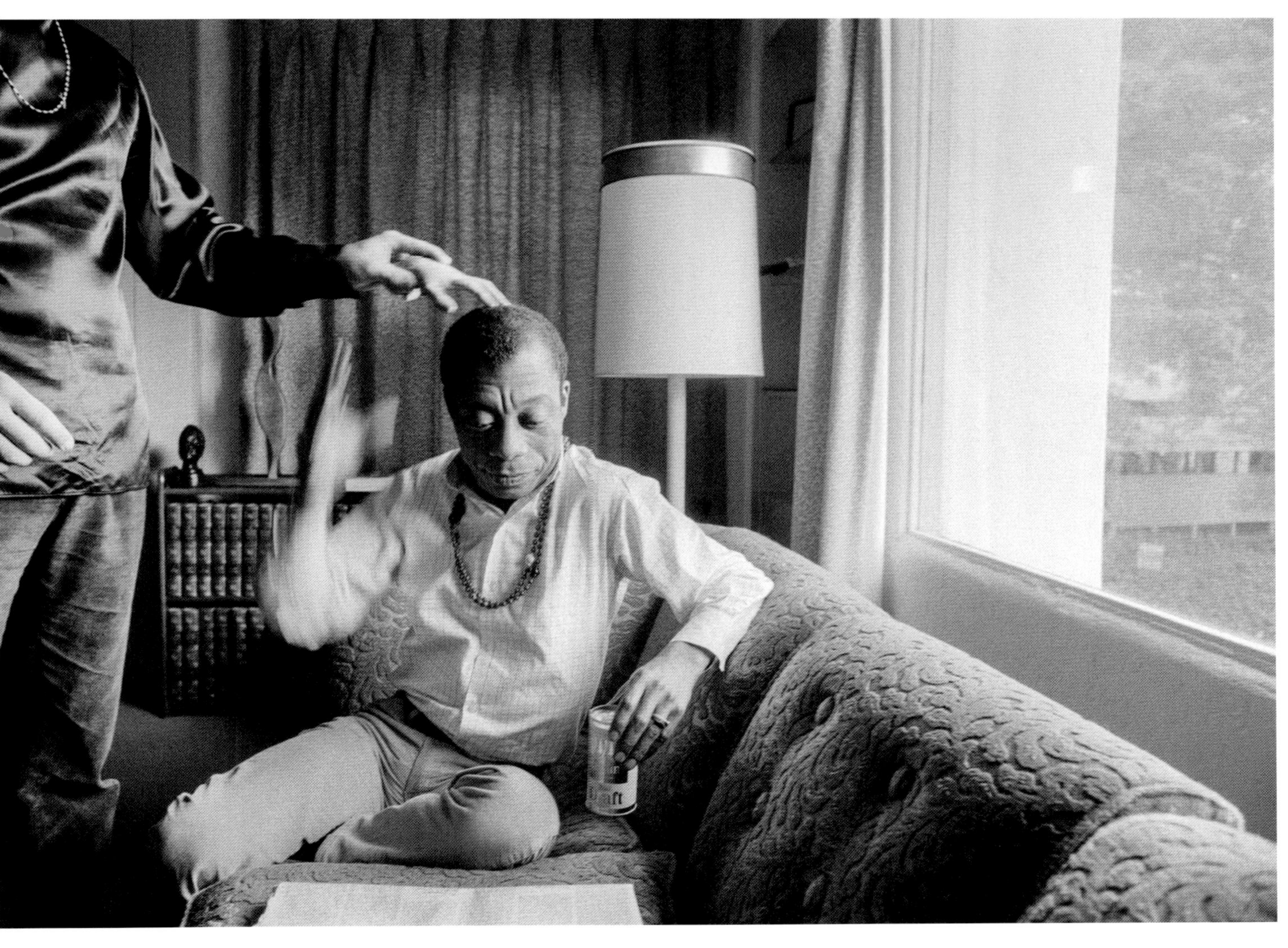

James Baldwin and friend in Los Angeles, 1969
Sedat Pakay
gelatin silver print, dimensions variable
Courtesy of the Estate of Sedat Pakay

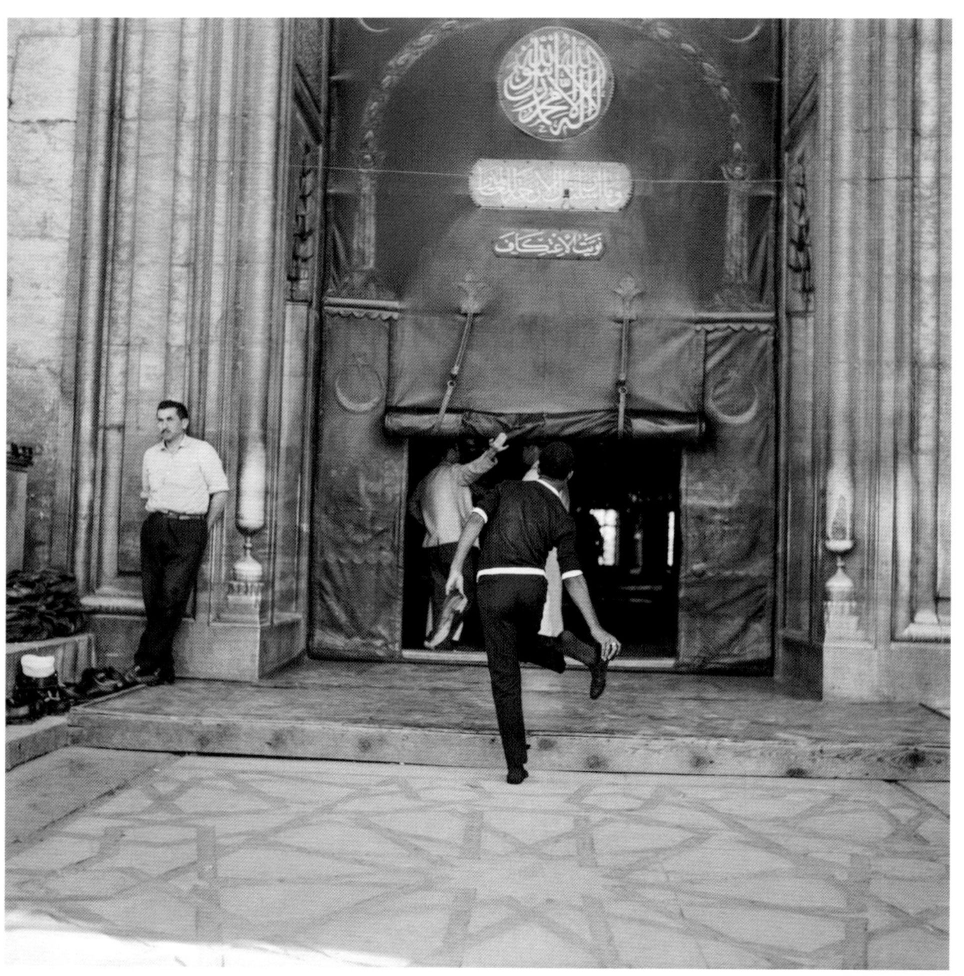

James Baldwin removing his shoes before ente
the Blue Mosque, Istanbul, 1965
Sedat Pakay
gelatin silver print, dimensions variable
Courtesy of the Estate of Sedat Pakay

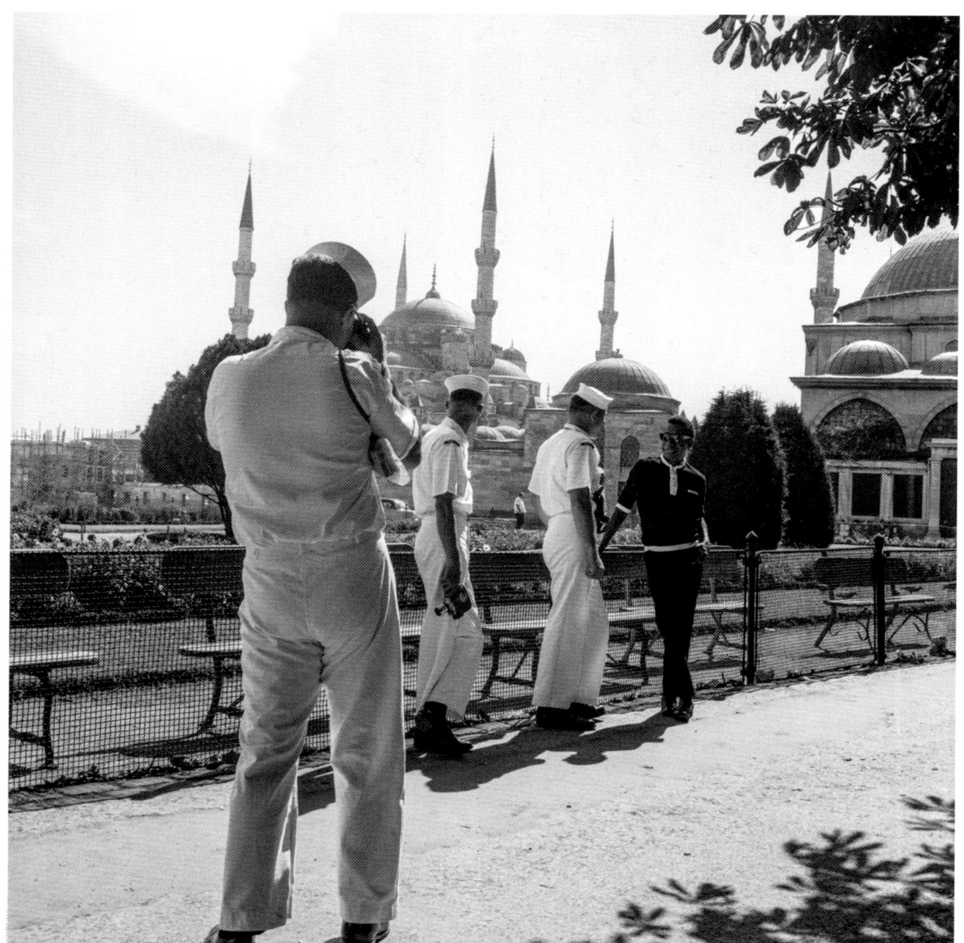

James Baldwin conversing with sailors from the
Sixth Fleet in front of the Blue Mosque, Istanb
Sedat Pakay
gelatin silver print, 13 $\frac{15}{16}$ x 10 $\frac{15}{16}$ in.
(35.4 x 27.8 cm)
Courtesy of the Estate of Sedat Pakay

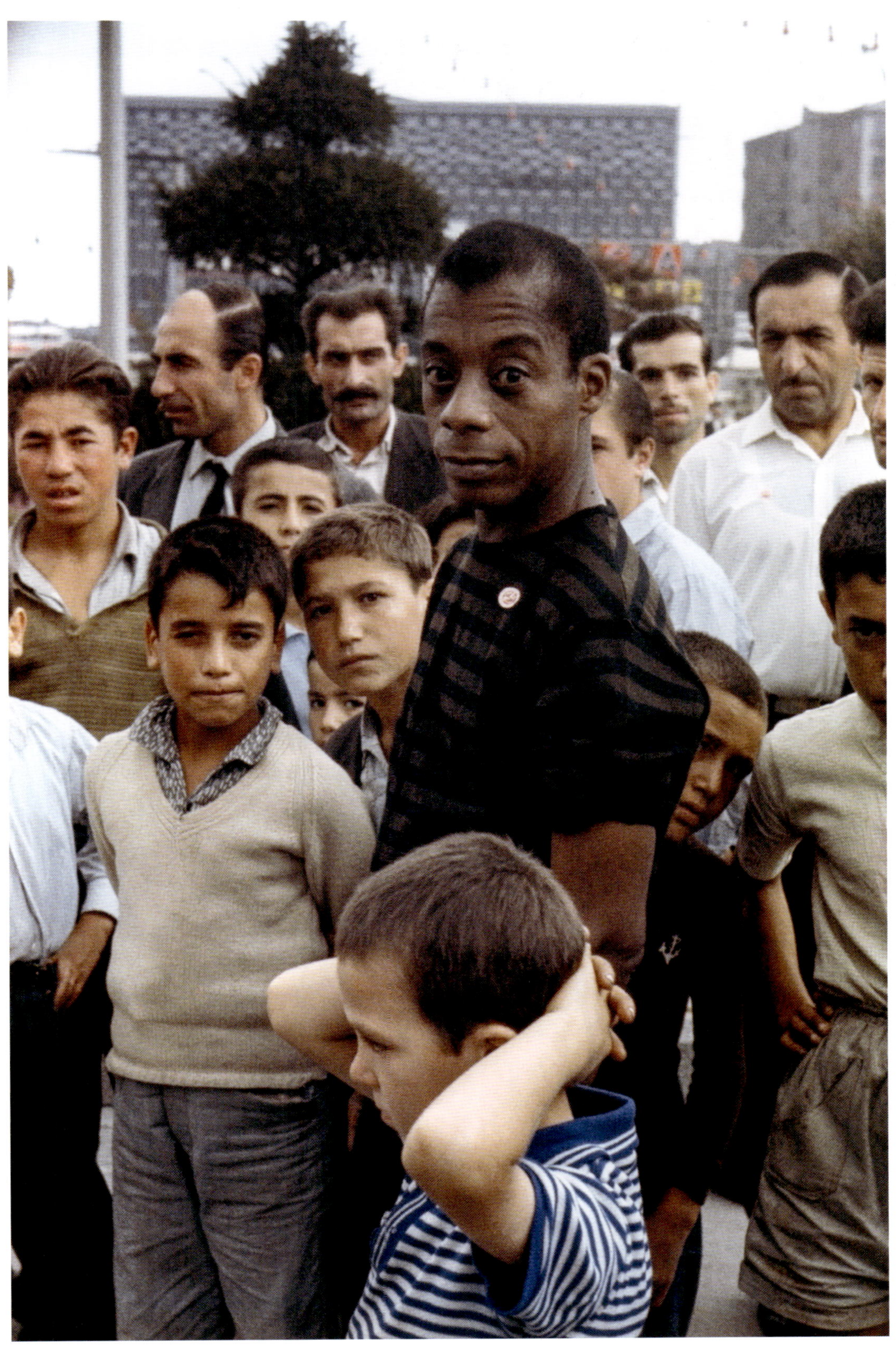

James Baldwin and crowd, Taksim Square, Istanbul,
1965
Sedat Pakay
chromogenic print, dimensions variable
Courtesy of the Estate of Sedat Pakay

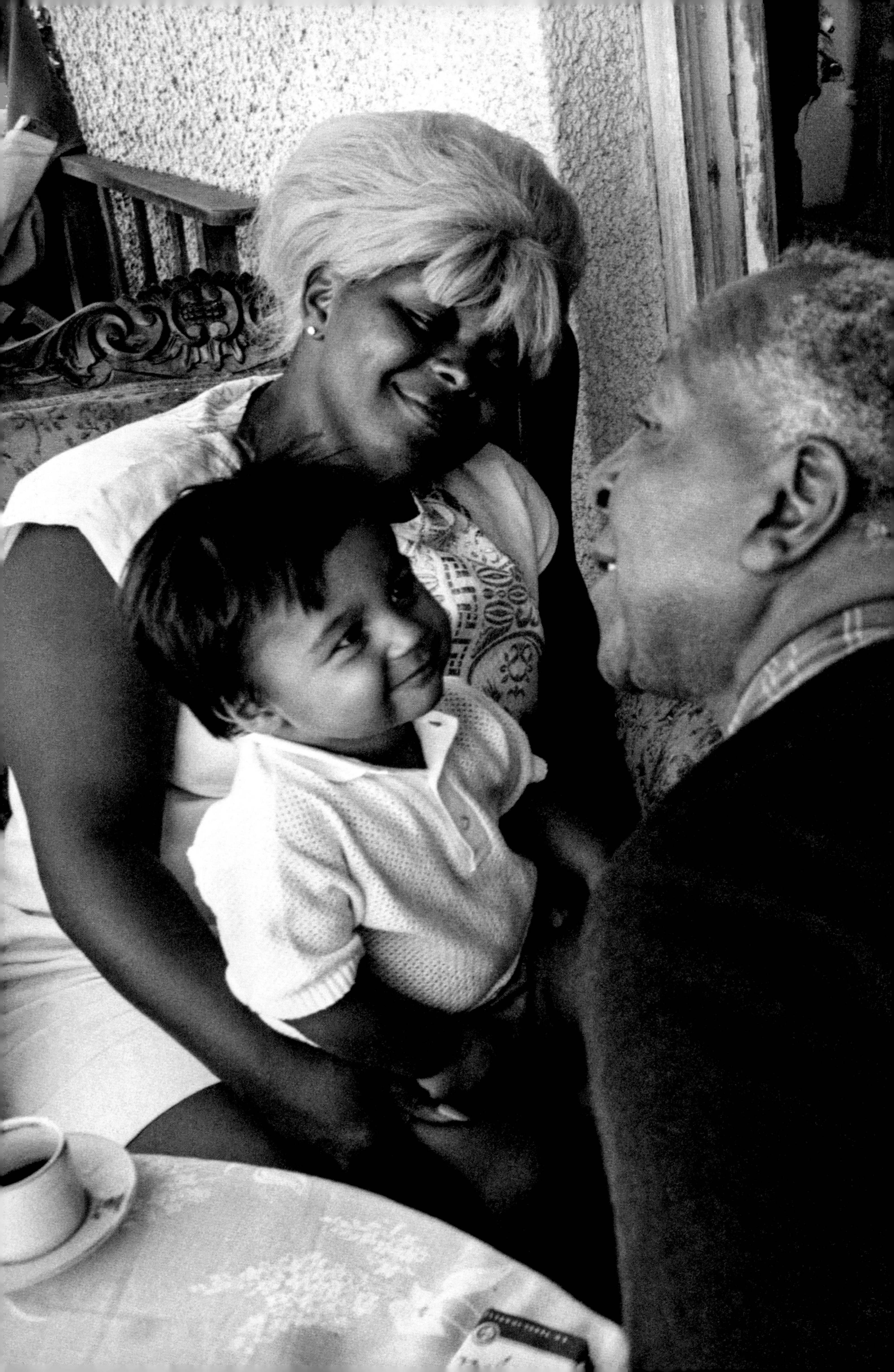

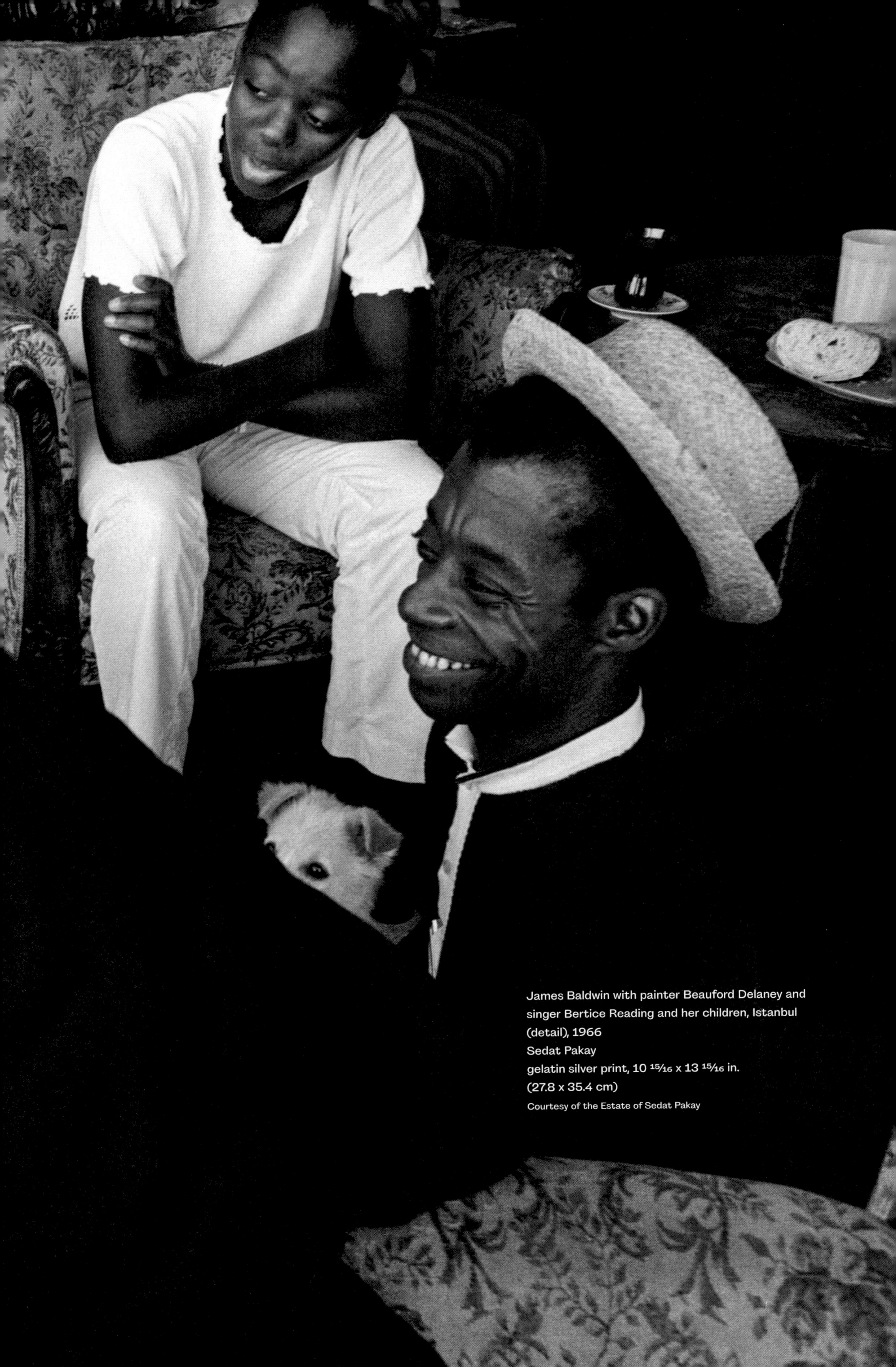

James Baldwin with painter Beauford Delaney and singer Bertice Reading and her children, Istanbul (detail), 1966
Sedat Pakay
gelatin silver print, 10 15⁄16 x 13 15⁄16 in. (27.8 x 35.4 cm)
Courtesy of the Estate of Sedat Pakay

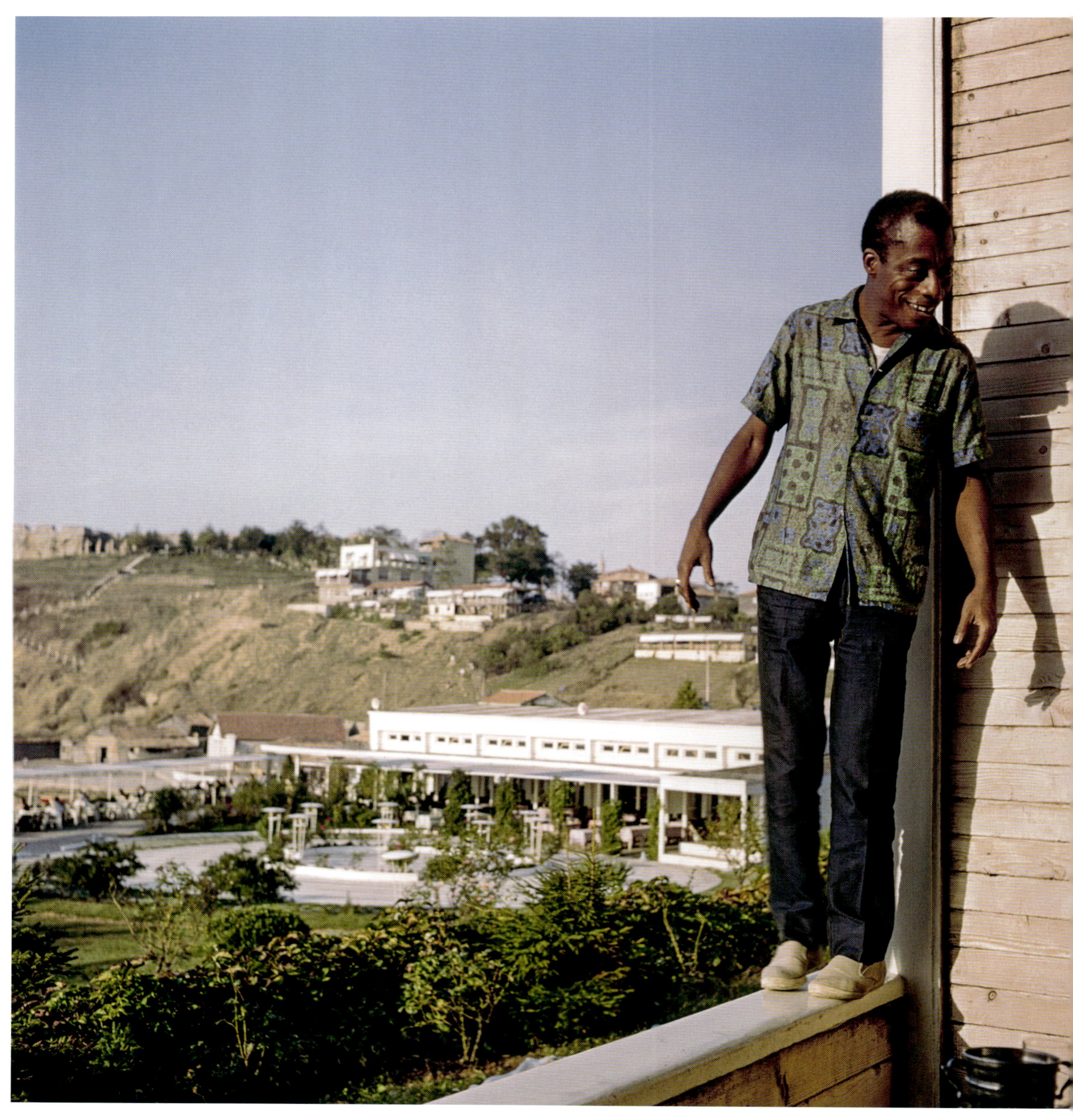

James Baldwin at Kilyos, Turkey, 1965
Sedat Pakay
chromogenic print, dimensions variable
Courtesy of the Estate of Sedat Pakay

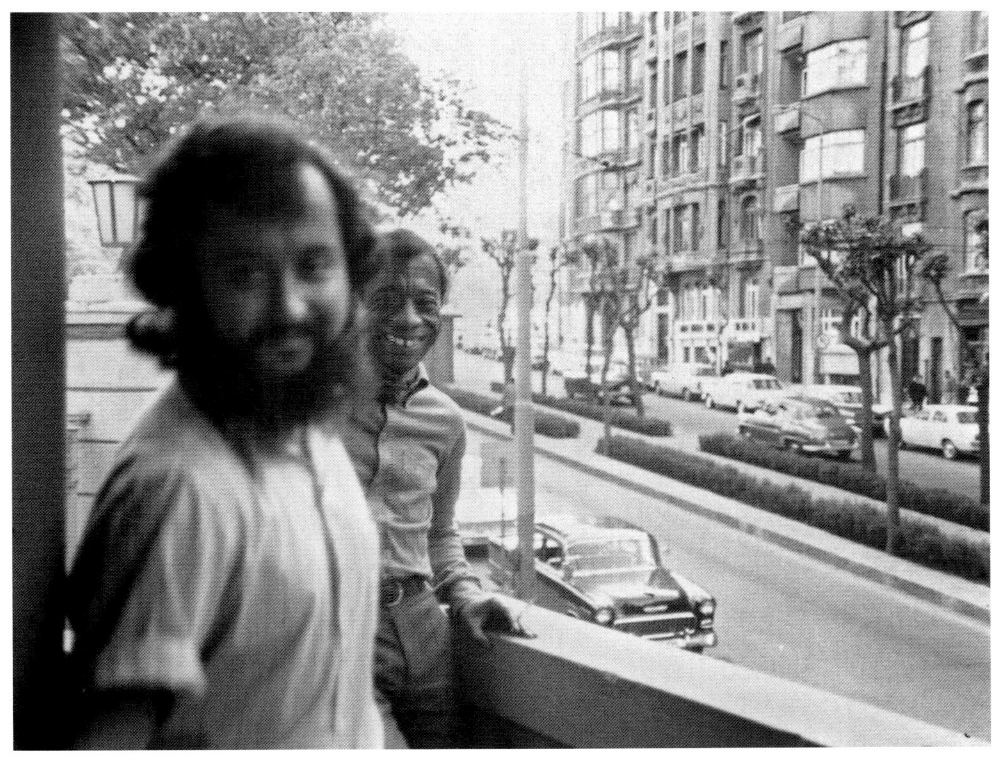

Sedat Pakay at James Baldwin's apartment while filming <u>James Baldwin: From Another Place</u>, 1970
Sedat Pakay
gelatin silver print, dimensions variable
Courtesy of the Estate of Sedat Pakay

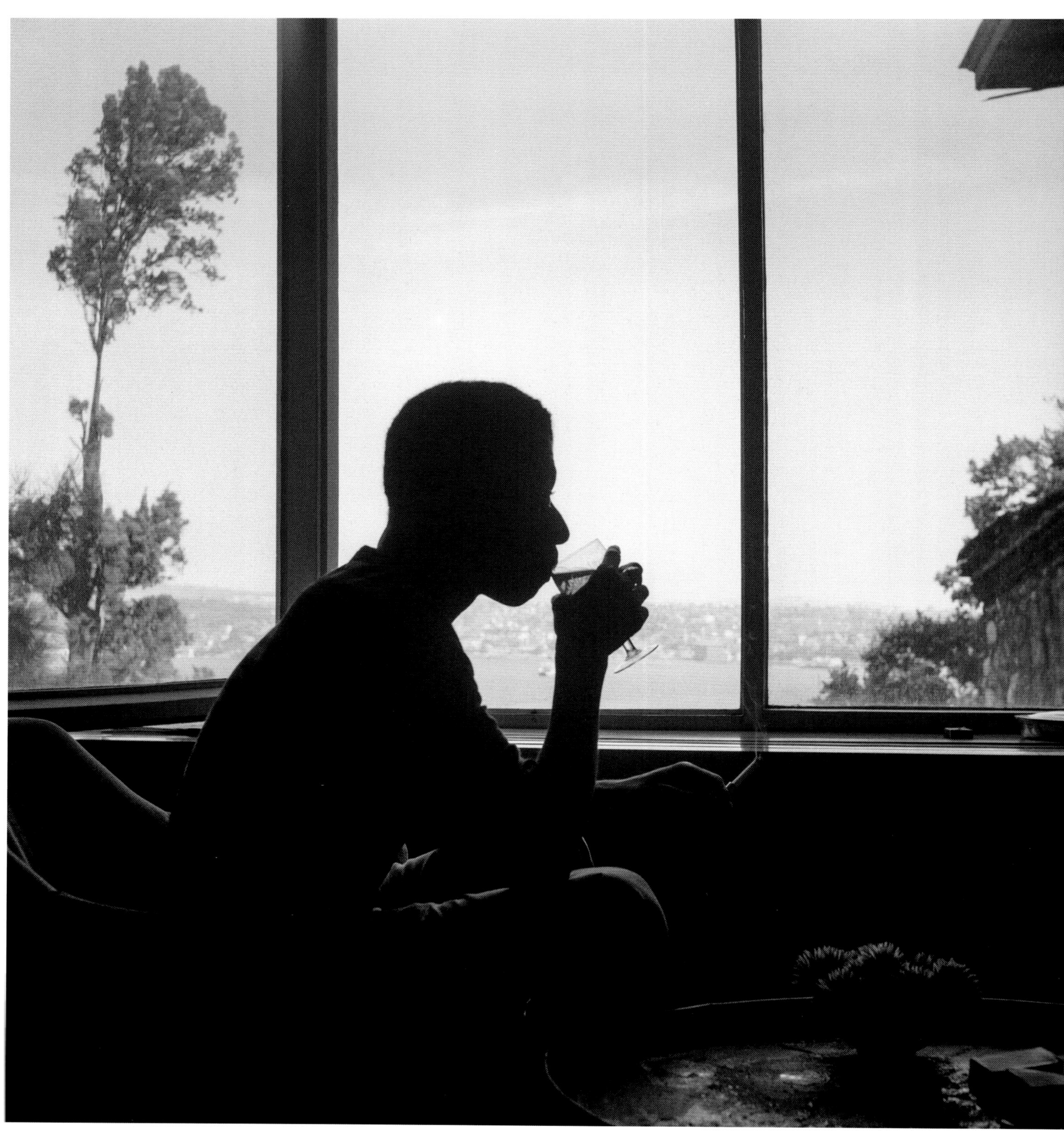

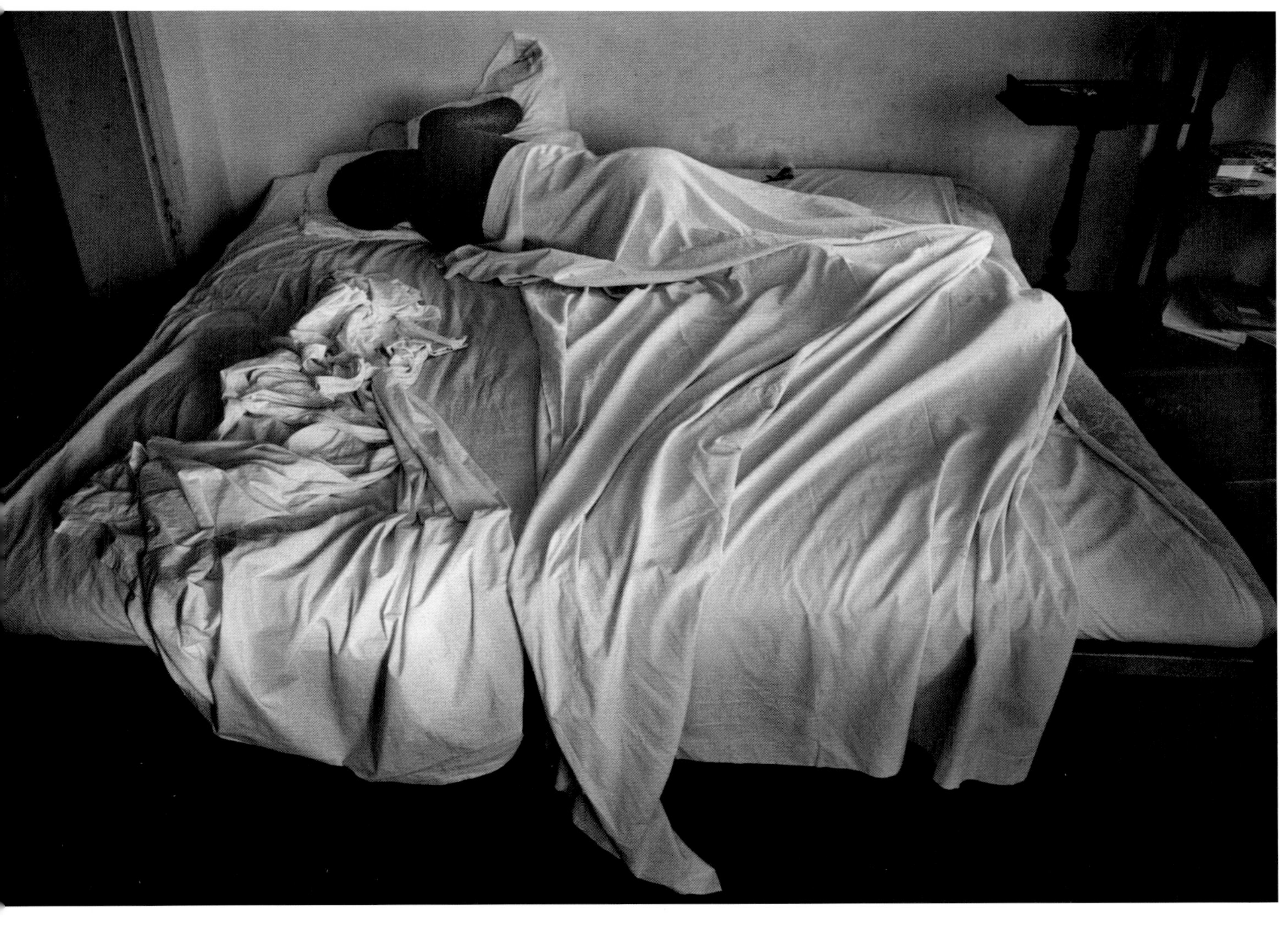

es Baldwin, Istanbul, c. 1965
t Pakay
in silver print, dimensions variable
esy of the Estate of Sedat Pakay

James Baldwin asleep in Istanbul, 1966
Sedat Pakay
gelatin silver print, dimensions variable
Courtesy of the Estate of Sedat Pakay

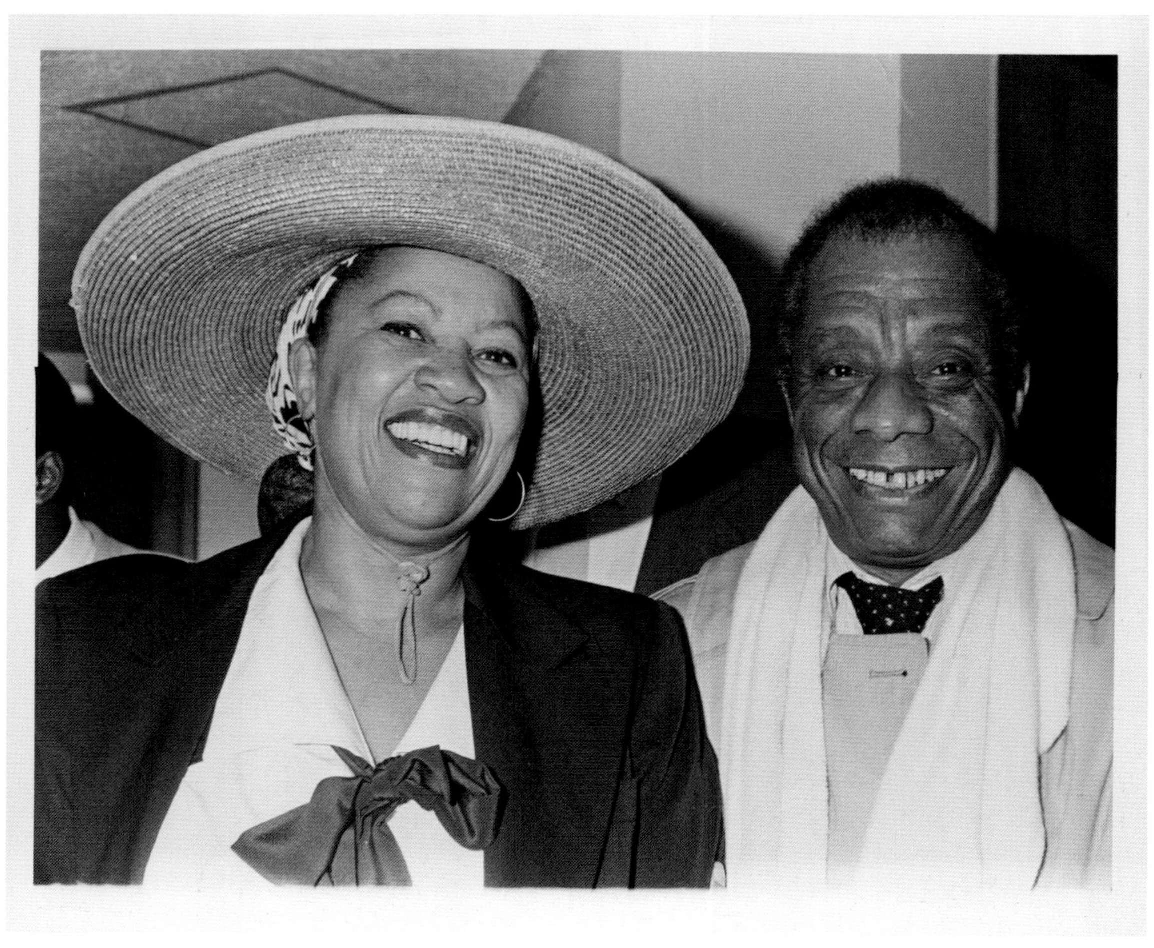

Toni Morrison and James Baldwin celebrate Founder's Day at the Schomburg Center for Research in Black Culture, New York, 1986
Hakim Mutlaq
gelatin silver print, 8 ¼ x 10 ¼ in. (21 x 26 cm)

Schomburg Center for Research in Black Culture, Photographs and Prints Division. The New York Public Library, Astor, Lenox, and Tilden Foundations

From 1967 to 1983, Toni Morrison served as a senior editor at Random House, editing books by Angela Davis and Muhammad Ali, among oth During this period, the future Pulitzer Prize winner paved her way as an author as well. Morrison frequently wrote to James Baldwin, both personally and in her capacity as editor. In a letter from 1973, Morrison expresses her regrets for having to notify Baldwin of Random House's decision not to buy his fifth novel, *If Beale Street Could Talk* (1974). "It beautiful that I wanted to cover it, touch it, promote it, be knowledgea about it," she remarked. Over the years, Morrison and Baldwin remain close. This photograph shows the pair together in 1986, the year before Morrison delivered a eulogy at Baldwin's funeral, where she recalled sc of his powerful words: "'Our crown has already been bought and paid All we have to do,' you said, 'is wear it.' And we do, Jimmy. You crowne

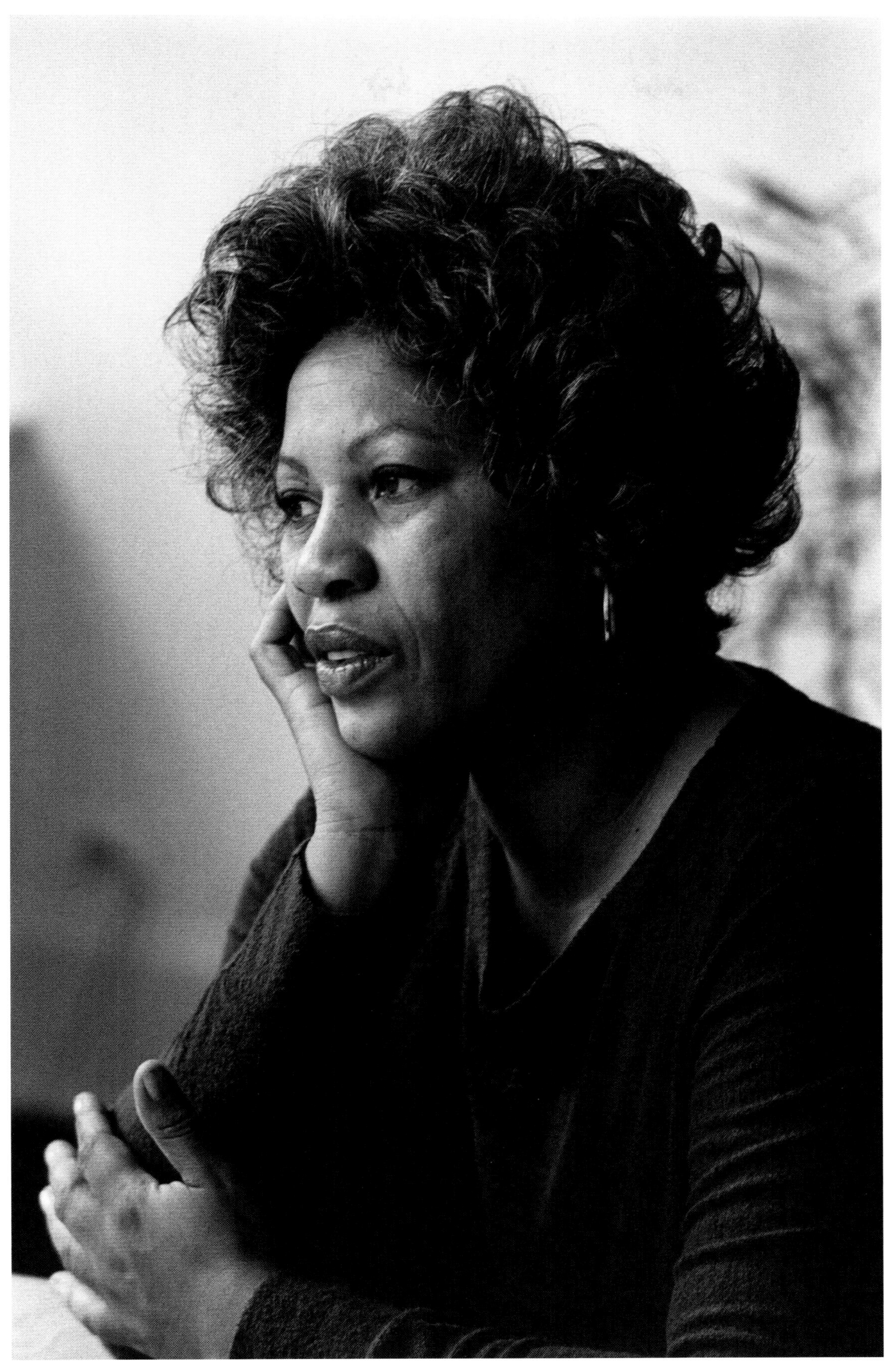

Toni Morrison, 1978
Helen Marcus
gelatin silver print, 11 ¾ x 7 ¾ in. (29.8 x 19.7 cm)
National Portrait Gallery, Smithsonian Institution; gift of Helen Marcus

1

1955

Dear Bill :

I don't know if people call you that anymore. I certainly hope you don't mind my using it, just this once. I suppose, in those days, I always called you 'Miss Miller', but I knew that other people called you 'Bill' and that was the way I thought of you, I guess it's still the way I think of you.

It's very good to find you again. I've wondered many times what had happened to you and Evan and Henrietta, what you were doing, where you were. And I wanted you to know what I was doing. You probably don't remember it, but the last time we saw each other was that stormy summer I joined the church. You and Evan were living downtown, near the Village. I remember I had to come downtown to tell you that, since I was a church-boy now, I couldn't go to movies anymore, or read as much as I had, or go to the theatre. It was one of the hardest things I'd ever had to do in my life till then and I'll never forget, as I stumbled out of the house, your last words to me. Which were :'I've lost a lot of respect for you'. Well, I guess I'd lost a lot of respect for myself - insofar as I had a self that summer -but I had to go through all that, I guess, in order to be free of it. And, years later, when God had died, and I'd left home, I wanted to let you know about

Letter from James Baldwin to Orilla "Bill Miller" Winfield, 1955 (p. 1)

James Weldon Johnson Collection in the Yale Collection of American Literature, Beinecke Rare Book and Manuscript Library, Yale University

it. Well. That was almost seventeen years ago. More. I was around fourteen then and I'll be thirty-two this summer.

I've seen a lot of movies since then - to put it that way - and, of course, more things have happened than I'll ever be able to tell. As you know, my father's dead but my mother is still alive, thank God, and quite well, and, in many ways, better and younger than she was when you knew her. The kids are all grown. Out of five girls, three are married, one with three children, one with two, one with one - the one with two children(Gloria) is expecting a third, and the one with one child (Ruth) is expecting a second. You see. The boys are considerably less productive; my baby brother, David, is married, but childless, my other two brothers are bachelors. I am, too, in spite of a couple of close calls. They are all in Harlem and we get on very well, which doesn't always happen.

After my father died, I bounced around in the classic bohemian fashion,messed around in politics- made it all the way from the Stalinists to the Anarchists in what I think must be record time. Obviously, after the Anarchists, there was no place to go but out, so that's what I did. And I started to write again, and did all kinds of odd jobs - you know - and did all the other things young people are supposed to do, like drinking

Letter from James Baldwin to Orilla "Bill Miller" Winfield, 1955 (p. 2)

James Weldon Johnson Collection in the Yale Collection of American Literature, Beinecke Rare Book and Manuscript Library, Yale University

too much and having unhappy love affairs. (I probably thought it would be unpoetical to have any other kind). After several years of this delightful misery, I crossed the ocean. Got to Paris broke. But stayed here for nearly four years without going home and I suppose, after all, in spite of everything, that thosefour years were the best and the most important years of my life. I went back home for awhile, came back to Paris and stayed here until early '54, and have now been back in Paris now for about four months.

Paris is a dreadful city in exactly the way all great cities are dreadful; but it's a good city for the eye, it's a good city for me. I can reflect, I can work, and I understand my country better when I'm out of it. Which is very important for me. I sometimes regret, perhaps, that I had to travel so far in order to feel in any way at home; but I also rather suspect that this is but a prolonged moment, since becoming an expatriate is not one of my ambitions. But it is one of my ambitions to become a good writer and I hope I will always do whatever this seems to demand. At the moment it seems to demand distance from the USA.

Am working; have a play going the rounds, which was done at Howard U. the summer of '54, have a new novel coming out in the Fall, am working on another one. Don't make much of a living but this, too, I trust, will change. Have had, as who has not? a very hard time. Am still, I guess, but don't feel

Letter from James Baldwin to Orilla "Bill Miller" Winfield, 1955 (p. 3)

James Weldon Johnson Collection in the Yale Collection of American Literature, Beinecke Rare Book and Manuscript Library, Yale University

driven toward the river or the oven. I think that I have probably not changed very much, am simply rather older than I was.

I plan to come home again when I have my new novel finished, which will probably be about a year from now. In the meantime, I'd like very much to keep in touch. Perhaps, when I come home again, we can see each other. I'd love to see Evan again, and I want to meet your children.

I hope it doesn't sound too silly to say that I wonder what you look like now . I wish you'd send me a photograph. I don't have any right now, but I'll get some snapshots made right away and send a couple. You were very important to me, you know, and I've held your face in my mind for many years.

Please write me when you can.

Very sincerely,
James Baldwin
James Baldwin

119 Ave. de Versailles,
Paris, 16e,
France

Letter from James Baldwin to Orilla "Bill Miller" Winfield, 1955 (p. 4)

James Weldon Johnson Collection in the Yale Collection of American Literature, Beinecke Rare Book and Manuscript Library, Yale University

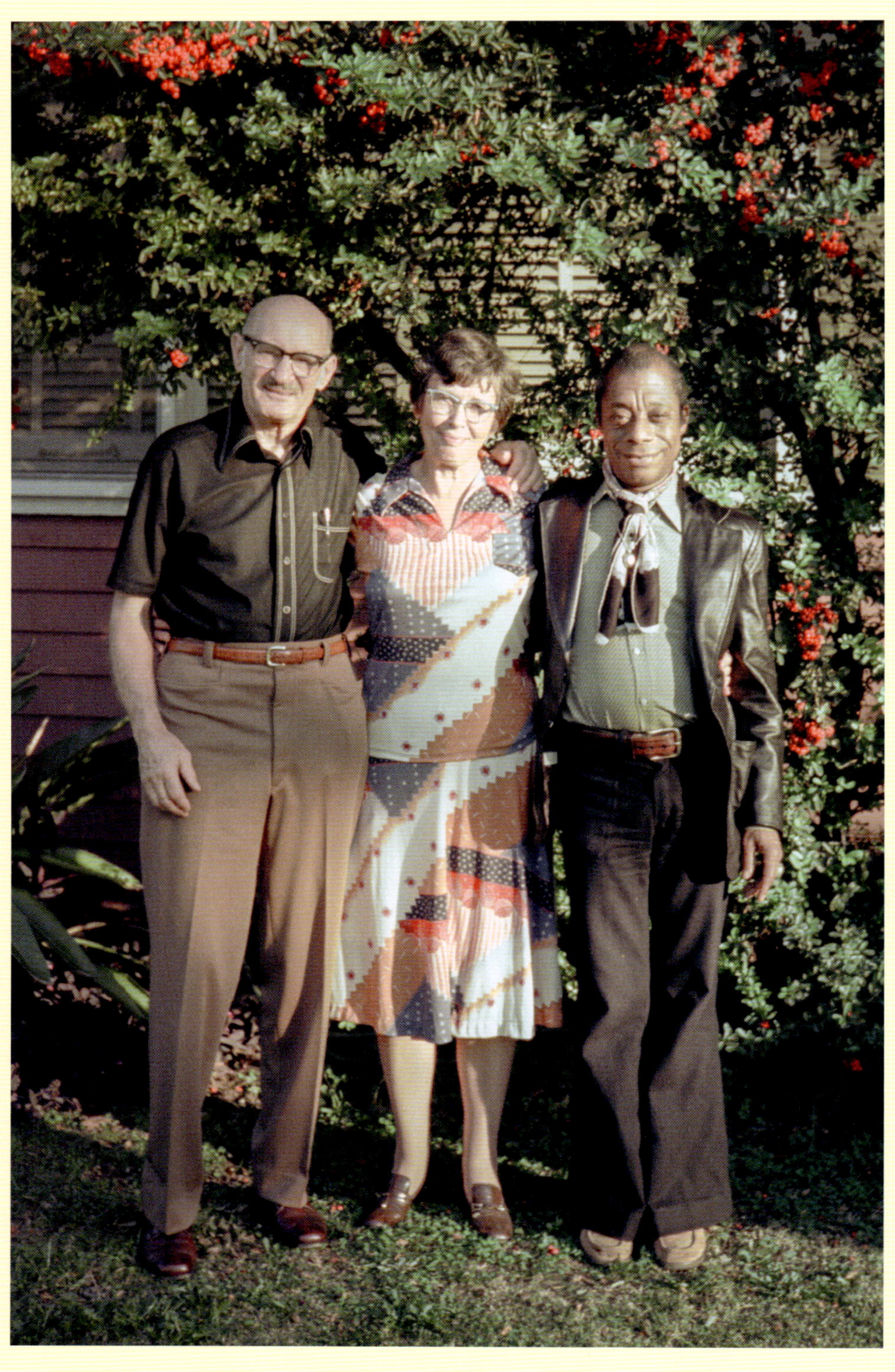

Orilla "Bill Miller" Winfield, Evan Miller, and James Baldwin, 1976
Unidentified photographer
chromogenic print, 9 ¼ x 6 in.
(23.5 x 15.2 cm)
Courtesy of Lynn Orilla Scott and Ken Winfield

As an elementary school student at Harlem's P.S. 24 (now Harlem Renaissance High School), James Baldwin was mentored by Orilla "Bill Miller" Winfield, a young teacher and activist. Deeply encouraging of Baldwin's interest in all forms of writing, Miller loaned him books and to[ok] him to the theater—activities that were forbidden in Baldwin's strict Bap[tist] household, particularly by his father, David, a lay minister in the church.

Baldwin lost touch with Miller at age fourteen, when he began bri[efly] serving as a preacher. But in 1955, while on a speaking tour in California, the two reunited. Their friendship continued uninterrupted thereafter u[ntil] Baldwin's death.

July 5th '82

Dear Bill, and Evan :

I am sorry to have been so derelict for so long, but I am sure, on the other hand, that you understand : hard trials, great tribulations, and what else is new? Am still here, am back in France, that is, trying to finish a book, and will be coming to California from here, God willing, around Labor Day.

Have more to say than can possibly be said. Am still going to become a great writer when I grow up (and, as my Mama said, boy, that's more than a notion!) which probably - hopefully -/tells you all you need to know concerning my stubborn morale.

I was talking about the two of you to a couple of my students the other day, and it was strange to recognize, again, how much you helped prepare me for these present stormy days.

my love,

Jimmy B.

Letter from James Baldwin to Orilla "Bill Miller" Winfield and Evan Winfield, July 5, 1982

James Weldon Johnson Collection in the Yale Collection of American Literature, Beinecke Rare Book and Manuscript Library, Yale University

July 29, 1982

Dear James, It was so good to hear from you and if "thoughts" could pull you towards So-calif, you will arrive. I felt good to see June 30th on Public TV - via "I heard it thru the Grapevine". You looked well, handsome and relaxed. And there was our young James listening carefully; thinking; the familiar tilt of the head. Talk about vivid old memories! Some are very clear.

Now the problem! I am simply devastated by my youngest sister's sudden cancer operation. Two weeks before, she was in N.Y.C. demonstrating for peace and then back to Michigan to be "Struck" Down! So my September schedule includes your visit and a visit to her.

If by any chance your schedule should change, is there any ~~chance~~ one in N.Y.C. who

Letter from Orilla "Bill Miller" Winfield and Evan Winfield to James Baldwin, July 29, 1982

James Weldon Johnson Collection in the Yale Collection of American Literature, Beinecke Rare Book and Manuscript Library, Yale University

Knows your schedule - day by day? I would appreciate just a card with the phone number on it. If I should not hear anything further do we expect you around Labor Day?

I realize you have friends everywhere - probably a L.A headquarters. Our house is your house (simple as it may be) and we'd like to have you come to Ojai, one of the most desirable small communities near L.A. However, we can offer better transportation than the last time you were coming, and James, we think of you as family, and will even come to LA to see you!

Our love as always,

Bill and Evan

December 27 '84

My dear Bill :

I have been trying to write you - and, also, been trying to see you - for a very long time,now. This will not be the letter I have been meaning to write. I have had some hard trials, but the good Lord knows that I don't want to bore you with any of that.

I have been unforgivably busy and grimly unhappy - : sometimes, the water seems to close over one's head. But none of that means anything compared to your loss of Evan - and I didn't want to write you about that, I wanted to come and see you.

I don't know if there is anything to be said concerning the passage of someone one loved - loves, for love does not exist in the past tense. I can say only that I was very happy for you - in the way of the child that I was then - when he came into your life. I remember you, in the 12th Street apartment, in my memory, at dusk, silhouetted against the windows (I think you lived on the ground floor) talking to each other, face to face, and the light in his face, and in yours. I felt very shy about being there, but enormously privileged, too. You hid nothing from me : it was very beautiful, and it helped me, later, when such a moment came, for the first time, for me.

And Evan released me from a recurrent nightmare I had had for years - which I thought came from A Tale Of Two Cities. In this nightmare, I am about to be trampled by a horse : the horse's head is in the air, against the sky, and the hooves are above my face, coming down. At the moment the hooves come down, I woke up.

Evan said that that was no dream. We marched together,in a May Day parade, when I was thirteen, and, around Fiftieth Street

Letter from James Baldwin to Orilla "Bill Miller" Winfield, December 27, 1984

James Weldon Johnson Collection in the Yale Collection of American Literature, Beinecke Rare Book and Manuscript Library, Yale University

and Eighth Avenue, the cops charged us. The horse was real and I WAS ABOUT TO GO BENEATH IT when Evan scooped me up and carried me away. He says that he was scared shitless, which I don't doubt, and he carried me to the subway station and gave me fifty cents or a quarter, and sent me home. And it's funny - I mean, I remember Evan's face at the top of the subway steps, but I didn't remember that he dragged me out of the shadow of death.

You were very very important to me - and neither does what I am/now trying to say exist in the past tense - very very very important. Both of you, for me, were models of courage and integrity and love. You do not know, my friend, how much that example meant to me, later, when my time for choices came. You do not know how much you helped me to get beyond the trap of color - and, once beyond that trap, so many others! You fault yourself, you told me once, for having said to me, when I came to 12th Street and told you that I was 'saved' and would not be going to the movies or seeing you anymore, that you had lost a lot of respect for me. Thank God you said it. I loved you so deeply and trusted you so much that it rang in my head and it helped me when my hour came and my faith pulverized and I knew I had to move.

Do you see - which is no excuse - why it has taken me so long to write you? I wanted to see you and kiss your eyes and take you to dinner and a movie and spoil you with champagne.

Which I can still do. If the segregationists don't get you, you once yelled to me from a balcony (watching me being hurtled off to yet another rally) the integrationists will! How right you were - yet, I think, on the whole, that I can lay claim to having (narrowly) survived both delusions. Will be home (!) in February, if not before. Please take a number - my baby brother, David, is my best friend and knows who my friends are, and, also, always knows where I am. His number : 212 / 865 2948.

And my mother (who has never forgotten you) : 212 / 873 0401.

And my number, for that matter, here, in my home away from home : 32 87 90 area code 93 country code 33. Call collect.

Sorrow wears and uses us - says Henry James - but we wear and use it, too, and it is blind, whereas we, after a manner, see.

But that is colder comfort than I thought. There is much much more than that to see. - Enough. I love you and will see you soon.

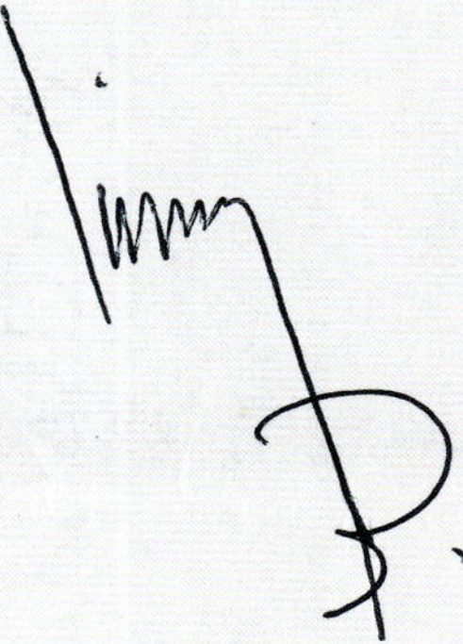

April 12th, 1985

Dear James, wherever you are –

I have just finished writing your mother and want to thank you for your very beautiful and loving letter which came in time to really lift my spirits. I was not able to come to L.A. to the library meeting because I was in the process of recovering from a leg operation.

Incredible as it seemed, I developed a rare cancer of the bone; so rare at my age that there are approximately two hundred cases a year in the entire USA, in my age bracket (73 years). This is not so rare in young people under the age of forty. It was the same type as the young Kennedy boy had and lost his leg. The treatment is now changed; so with chemotherapy, radiation and an operation, I now feel very optomistic. However, I had to spend time in the UCLA hospital and I am rather in terror of Los Angeles and big hospitals. But I managed with the aid of Steve who came out from Boston and my sister Henrietta from Illinois plus good LA friends!

When the LA library association phoned me and I inquired about your stay here, I was stunned by your schedule in and out of LA; to Berkeley; to where and where? I had hoped after the Birthday Celebration and your illness that you would be able to take life easier and think in terms of health. Of course, there is so much you want to _write_ and _do_ that it is very understandable! Please take care of yourself

Is the Scholarship Fund an on-going effort? I would like to make another contribution small as it may be; and of course, I always hope that you will have time to visit this small, small, quiet California town.

In closing –

"Time's winged chariot rushes near" – (I believe from King Lear) Do you remember Orson Wells "MacBeth" with the Harlem theater? I remember taking you – but not the movies so clearly.

Love as always,

Orilla (Bill Miller)

rn letter from Orilla "Bill Miller" Winfield to es Baldwin after the passing of Evan Miller, 12, 1985

Weldon Johnson Collection in the Yale Collection of American ture, Beinecke Rare Book and Manuscript Library, Yale University

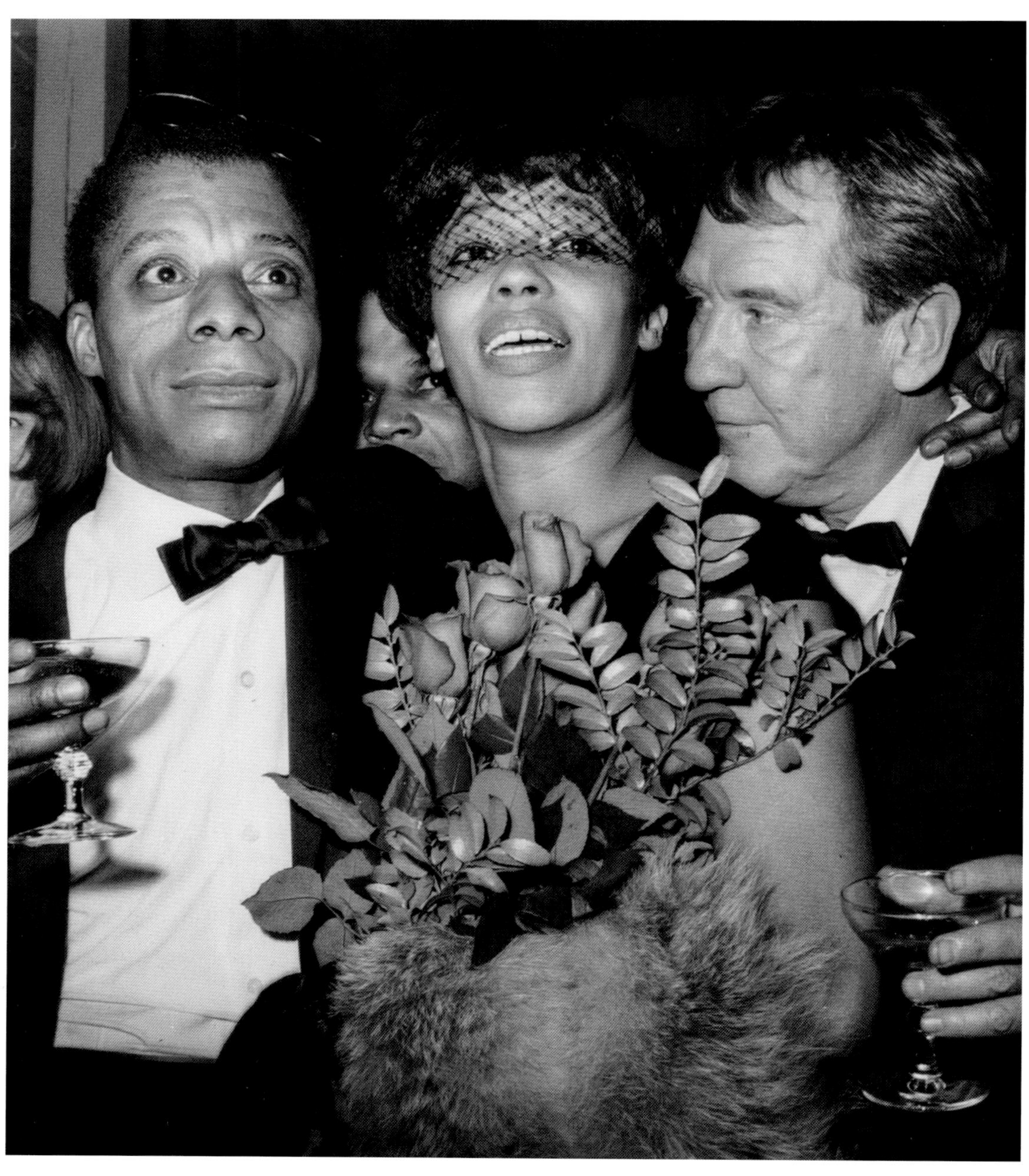

James Baldwin with Diana Sands and Burgess Meredith, opening night of Blues for Mister Charlie,
1964
Unidentified photographer
gelatin silver print, 9 1⁄8 x 7 in (23.2 x 17.8 cm)
Prints and Photographs Division, Library of Congress, Washington, D.C.

"You have to go the way your blood beats. If you don't live the only life you have, you won't live some other life, you won't live any life at all."

—James Baldwin

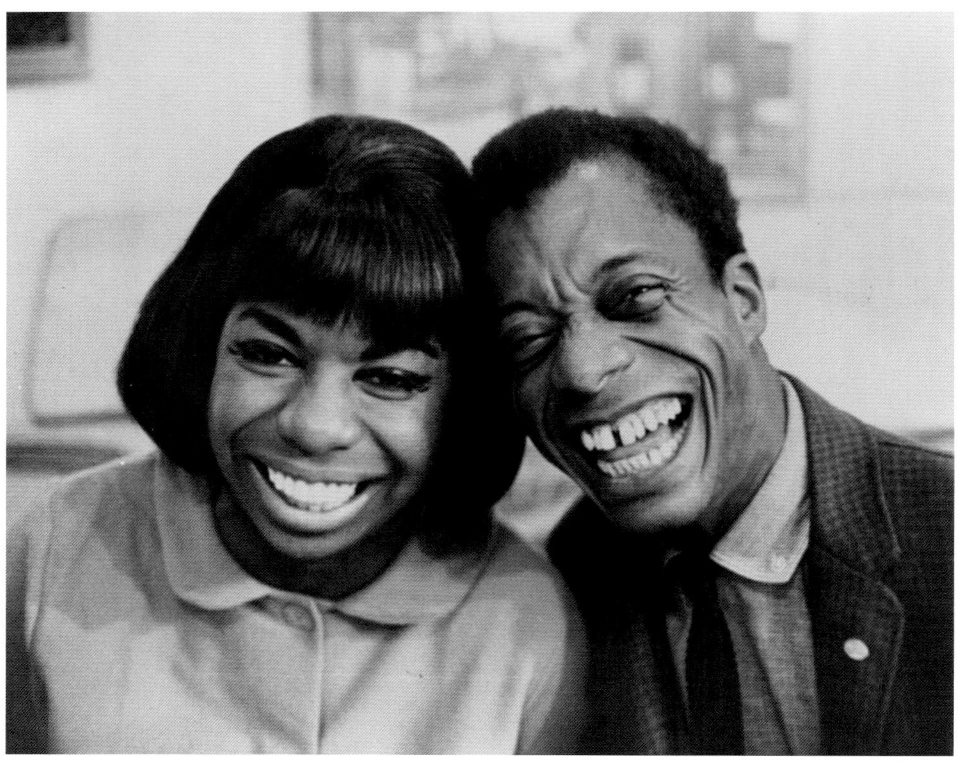

Nina Simone with James Baldwin, 1965
Bernard Gotfryd
gelatin silver print, 8 x 10 in. (20.3 x 25.4 cm)

Schomburg Center for Research in Black Culture, Photographs and Prints Division. The New York Public Library, Astor, Lenox, and Tilden Foundations

"Picket lines, school boycotts, they try to say it's a communist plot. All I want is equality for my sister, my brother, my people, and me."
—Nina Simone

The musician Nina Simone met James Baldwin through their mutual friend Lorraine Hansberry. Following the success of her groundbreaking play *A Raisin in the Sun* (1959), Hansberry had committed herself to educating others she felt could contribute to raising awareness about the cause of equal rights.

By introducing Simone to Baldwin and the poet Langston Hughes, Hansberry ensured her close friend would be embraced by other queer writers who understood something about difference. Simone would feel empowered to honestly express herself in the early 1960s, when she began penning and performing more political songs. The charged song "Mississippi Goddamn" (1964), with lyrics like those seen at the top of this entry, grew out of Simone's despair and rage over the killings of young Emmett Till and the civil rights leader Medgar Evers, and the Sixteenth Street Baptist Church bombings in Birmingham, Alabama, in 1963. Baldwin and Simone shared a great bond: the desire to marry anger to lyricism while refusing to separate the personal from the political.

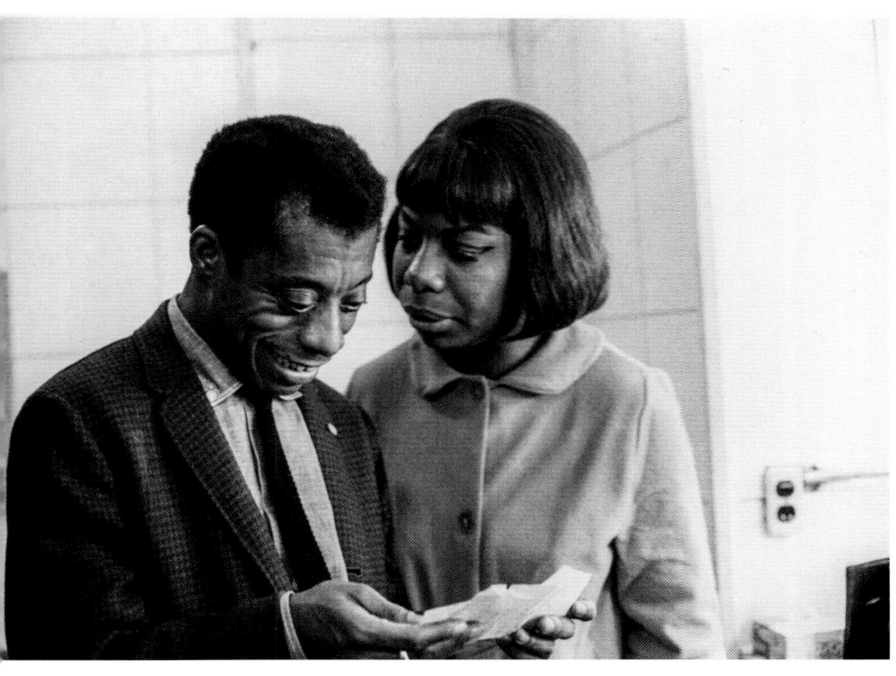

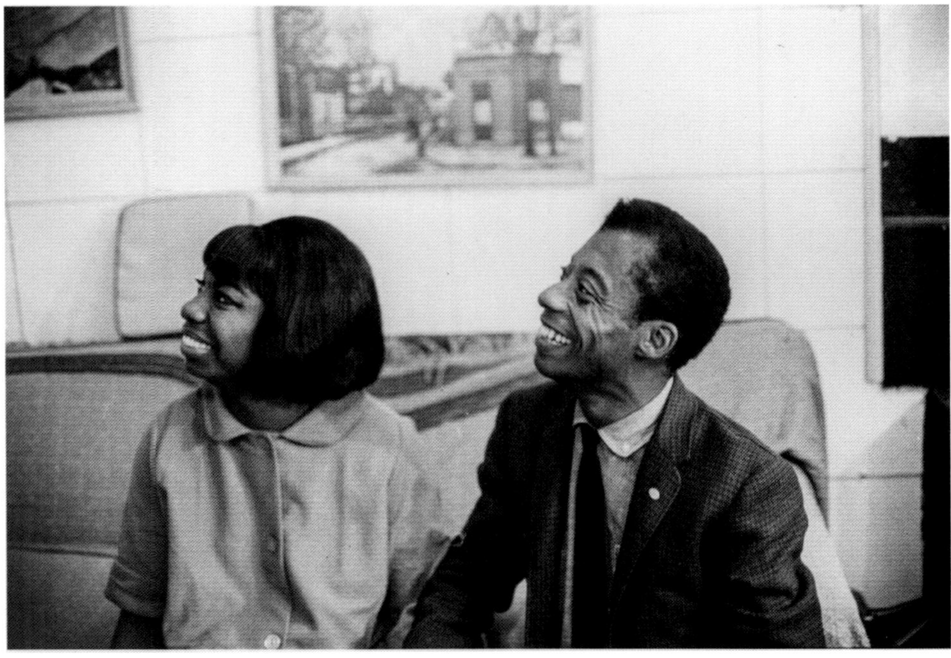

Nina Simone with James Baldwin, 1965
Bernard Gotfryd
gelatin silver prints, each: 8 x 10 in. (20.3 x 25.4 cm)
National Museum of African American History and Culture, Smithsonian Institution

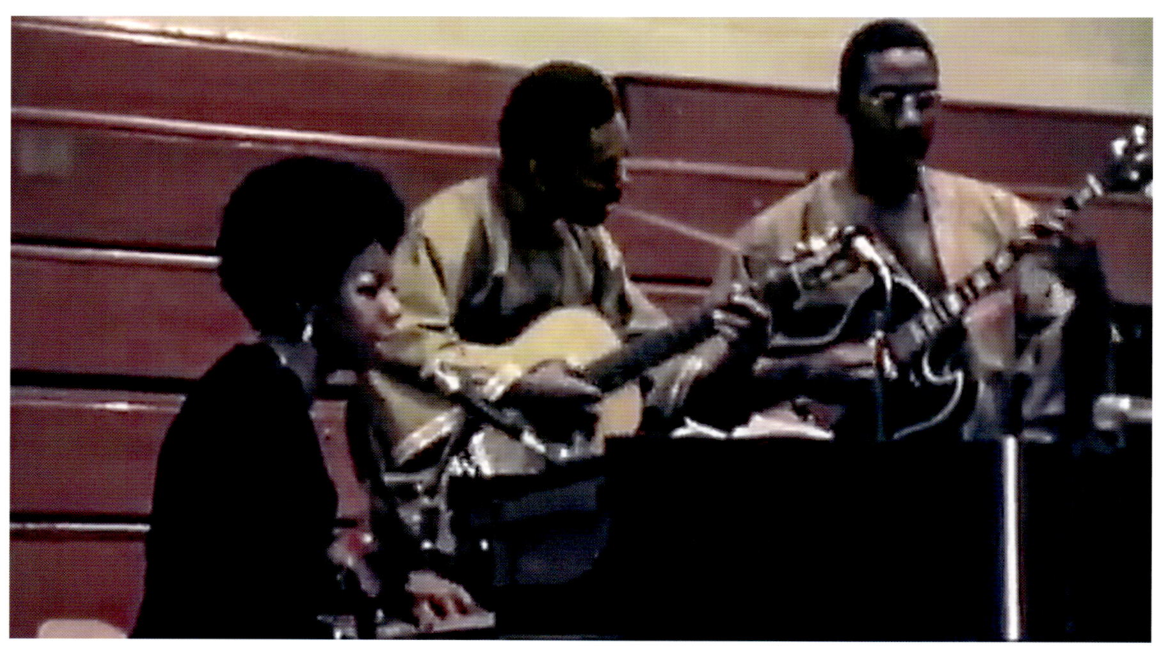

Still from Nina Simone's Performance of "To Be Young, Gifted and Black," Live at Morehouse College, Atlanta, June 1969

Under license from the Nina Simone Charitable Trust and Rich & Famous Records, Ltd., courtesy of Steven Ames Brown

When the musician and activist Nina Simone performed at Morehous College in 1969, she was earning a reputation for her protest songs and close relationship to Lorraine Hansberry, who had died in 1965.

Simone's "To Be Young, Gifted and Black" was based on a play adapted from Hansberry's speeches and writing. The play had been a success, in part because it evoked the radicalism of the times. Simone's with lyrics by the brilliant composer Weldon Irvine, had a similar pow Defiant and strong, the opening chords and language are a declaration of one's Blackness being a source of power—and possibility. In time, it only became the official Black anthem for many but was also covered swath of musicians ranging from Aretha Franklin to Meshell Ndegeoc all of whom imbued the tune with their own meaning.

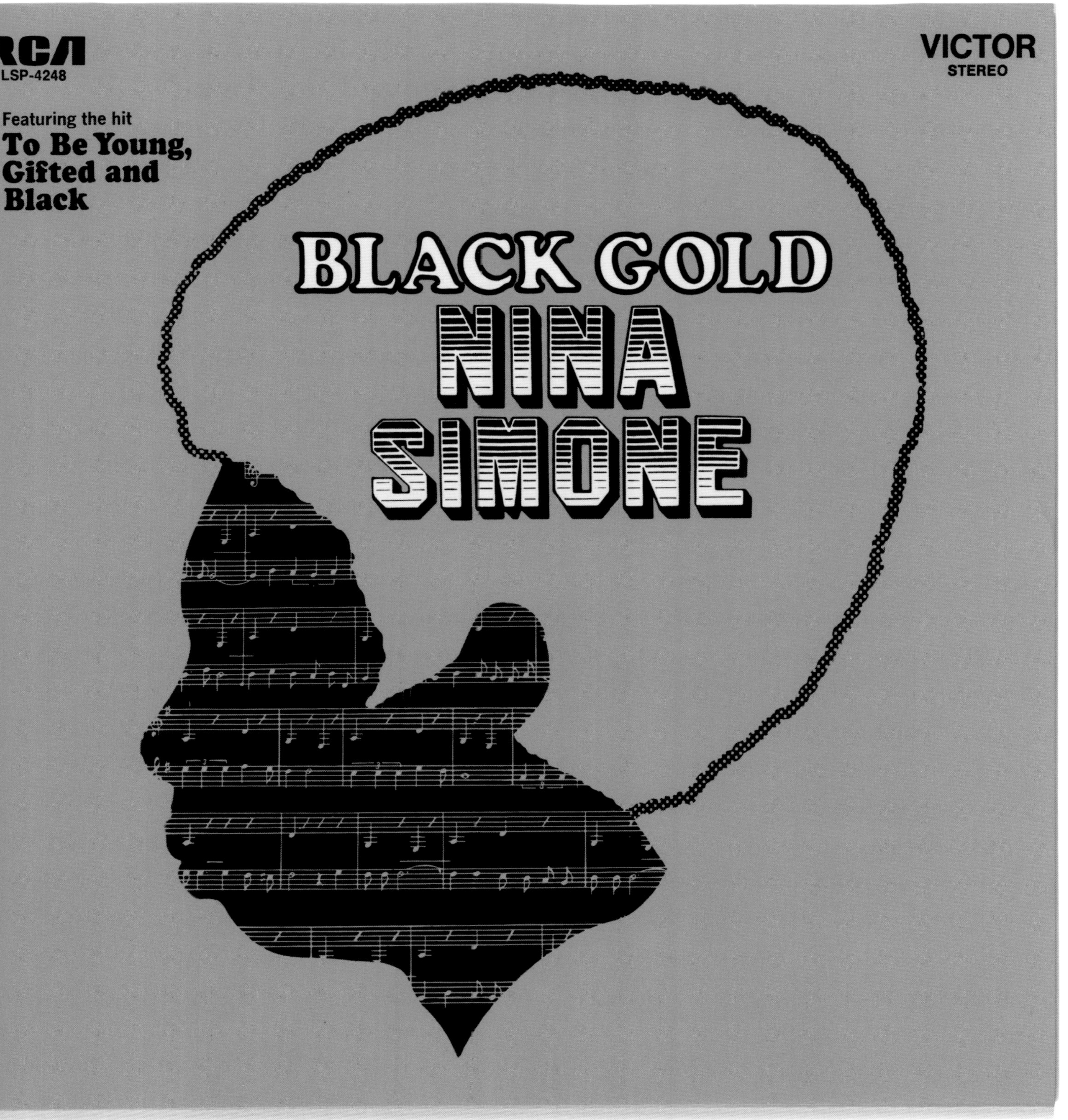

Black Gold

Nina Simone

RCA Records, 1970

Collection of Hilton Als

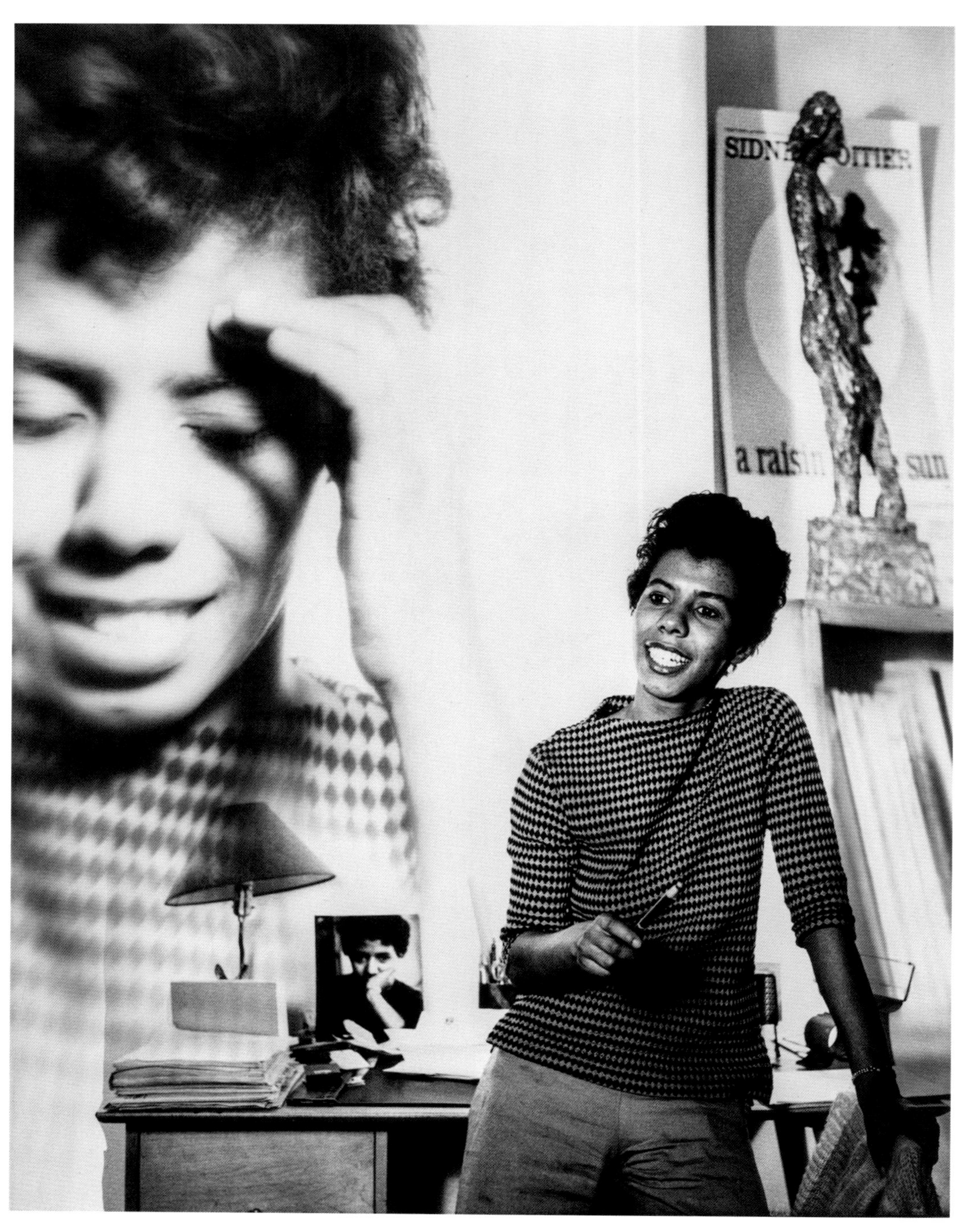

Lorraine Hansberry, 1959
David Attie
gelatin silver print, 13 5/8 x 10 3/4 in. (34.6 x 27.3 cm)
National Portrait Gallery, Smithsonian Institution

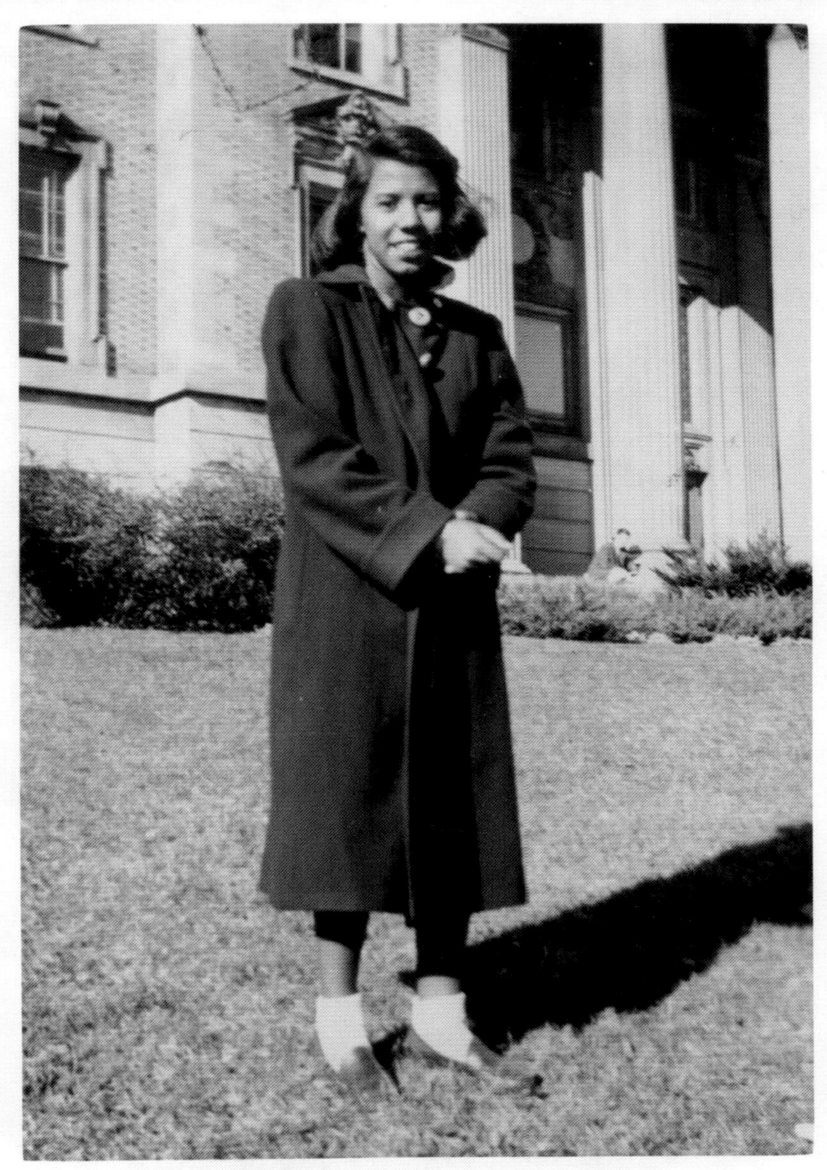

Lorraine Hansberry in front of academic building at the University of Wisconsin–Madison, 1948
Unidentified photographer
gelatin silver print, dimensions unknown
Courtesy of Joi Gresham and the Lorraine Hansberry Literary Trust

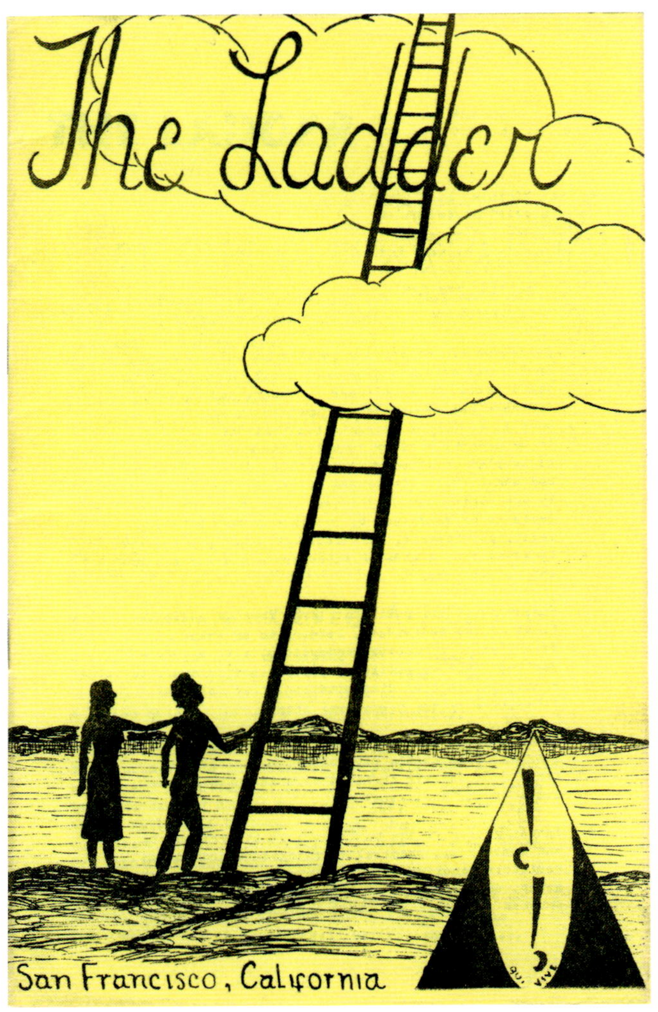

The Ladder, established by the Daughters of Bilitis in 1956 and publi monthly for nearly fifteen years, is regarded as one of the earliest les serial publications in the United States. Subject to discrimination, public scrutiny, and few opportunities for lesbians to meet, contributors often signed their names using initials or a pseudonym to prot their identities. Lorraine Hansberry signed her letter in a 1957 issue, "L.N., New York, N.Y.," recognizing her then-married name Nemiro while passionately responding to an article on heterosexually marri lesbians. Hansberry's words, while supportive of women's causes, reveal how race intersects with feminism, pointing to a new way of thinking about both.

The Ladder
Daughters of Bilitis, August 1957
Gay Lesbian Bisexual Transgender (GLBT) Historical Society

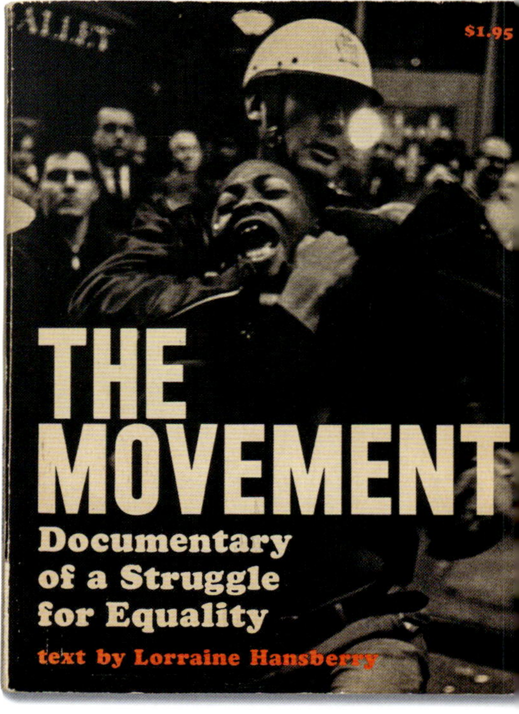

Like her dear friend "Jimmy" Baldwin, Lorraine Hansberry felt a deep commitment to justice and was unafraid to address difficult topics through her writings. *The Movement*, published the year before she died, was developed in collaboration with the Student Nonviolent Coordinating Committee (SNCC), a civil rights organization. Written during the height of the civil rights movement, Hansberry's searing, poetic words document "the struggle for humanization of our country." An unvarnished look at African American history and the civil rights movement, Hansberry's texts are accompanied by more than one hundred photographs from Bob Adelman, Frank Dandridge, Roy DeCarava, Danny Lyon, and other notable photographers.

The Movement: Documentary of a Struggle for Equality
Lorraine Hansberry
Simon and Schuster, 1964
Private collection

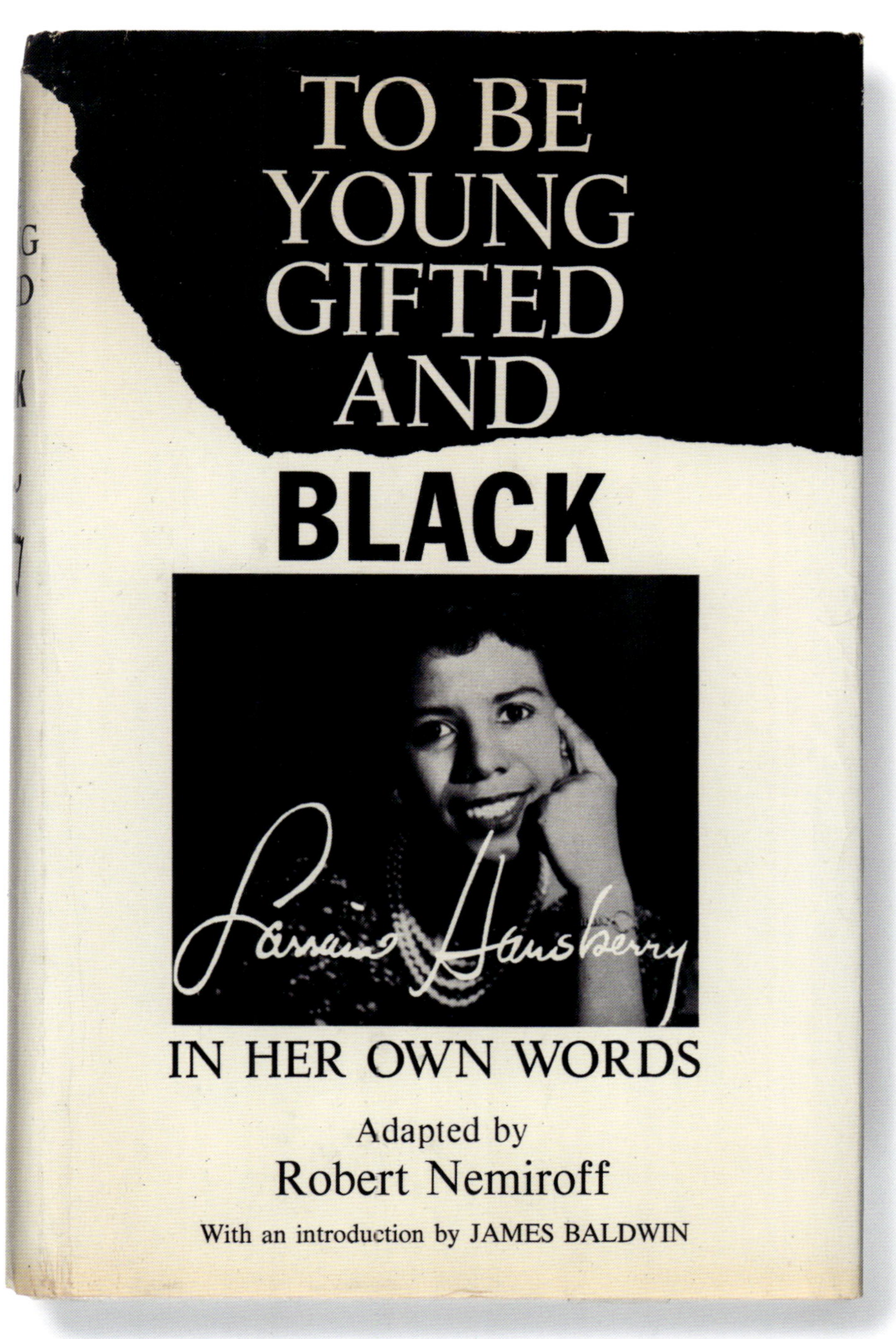

Young, Gifted and Black: Lorraine Hansberry
Own Words
e Hansberry and Robert Nemiroff
e Hall, 1969
ollection

With an introduction by James Baldwin and original art by Lorraine Hansberry, this memoir incorporates Hansberry's perspectives on gender and racial equality, family, and politics. Originally an off-Broadway play created and developed by Hansberry's ex-husband, Robert Nemiroff, the book comprises interviews, letters, and journal entries that paint a layered portrait of a young artist and activist. As the first Black woman to have a play produced on Broadway, with *A Raisin in the Sun* (1959), Hansberry's autobiography embodies her motivations and work: to be young, gifted, and Black. Hansberry's dear friend Nina Simone penned a song with this title.

Throughout her decades-long career, Lorna Simpson has addressed the ways in which gender intersects with race. In *Three Figures*, she draws on an archival image from a painful past. Here, we see three young people from the civil rights era being hosed down. What makes the image particularly poignant is that despite the water's force, none of the figures are letting go— showing resilience and fortitude despite troubling circumstances.

By layering the main picture on top of other panels that replicate the same image, Simpson calls our attention to moving pictures, specifically television, where so much of the turbulent civil rights period was publicly disseminated. *Three Figures* may also evoke the imagery of Andy Warhol's *Race Riot* series (1963–64). Warhol's large-scale silkscreen paintings were among the various postwar pictures confronting violence in the United States.

Three Figures, 2014
Lorna Simpson
ink and screenprint on Claybord, 116 ¾ x 96 in. (296.5 x 243.8 cm)
Forman Family Collection

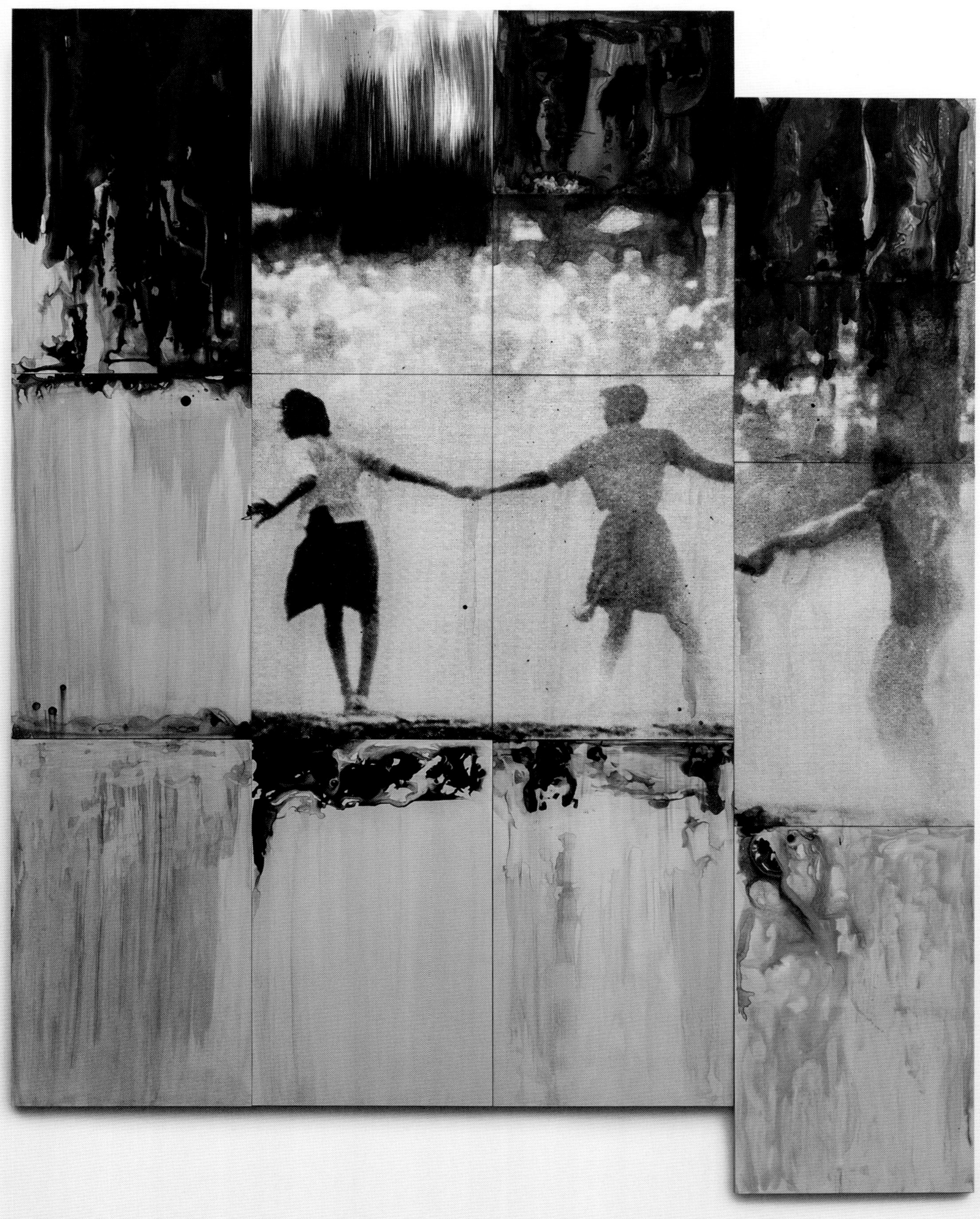

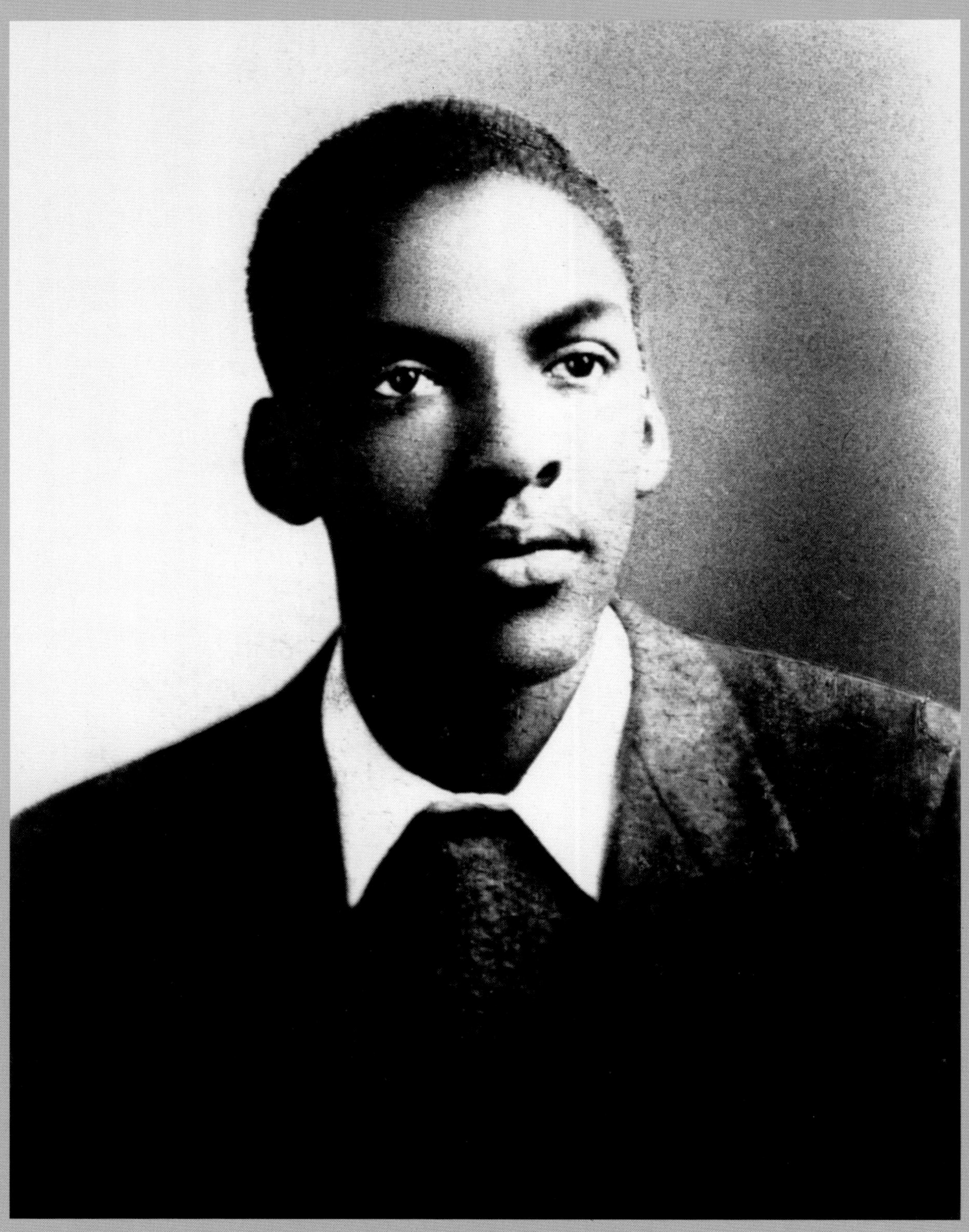

Young Bayard, date unknown
Unidentified photographer
gelatin silver print, 10 x 8 in.
(25.4 x 20.3 cm)

Prints and Photographs Division, Library of Congress, Washington, D.C.

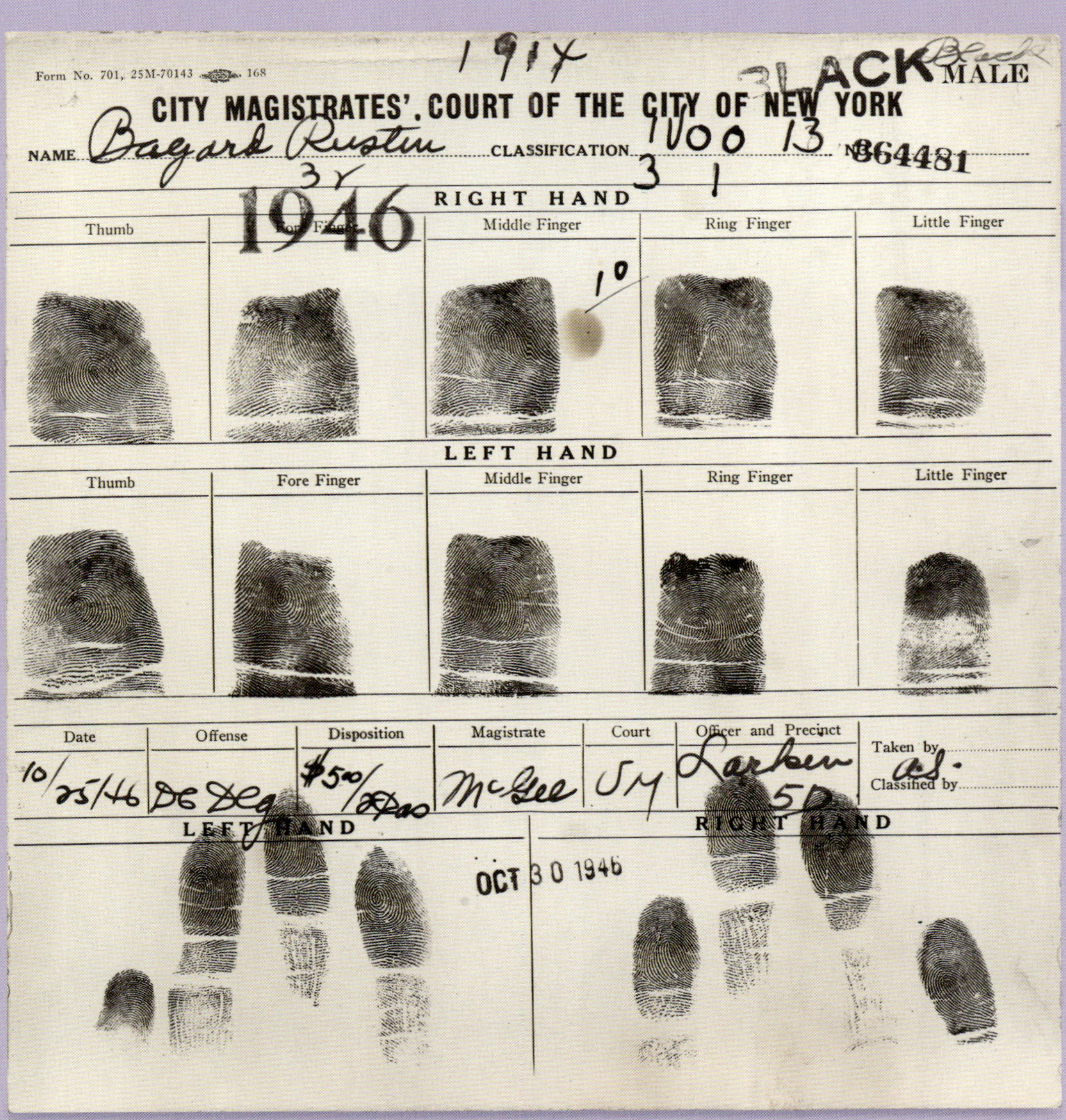

Form No. 701, 25M-70143 168

1914

BLACK MALE

CITY MAGISTRATES'. COURT OF THE CITY OF NEW YORK

NAME Bayard Rustin CLASSIFICATION 1 U OO 13 / 3 1 No. 364481

1946

RIGHT HAND

Thumb	Fore Finger	Middle Finger	Ring Finger	Little Finger

LEFT HAND

Thumb	Fore Finger	Middle Finger	Ring Finger	Little Finger

Date	Offense	Disposition	Magistrate	Court	Officer and Precinct	
10/25/46	De Deg	$500/	McGee	UM	Larkin 5P	Taken by Classified by

LEFT HAND RIGHT HAND

OCT 30 1946

Being a queer man almost derailed Bayard Rustin's career. This original set of fingerprints, from October 25, 1946, shows that Rustin was arrested by the New York City Police Department for allegedly violating Section 722 of the Penal Code (offering to commit a lewd or indecent act). In 1953, he would be arrested again, in California, and sentenced to sixty days in jail on suspicion of "lewd vagrancy." Rustin's identity troubled some civil rights activists, who encouraged Martin Luther King Jr. to distance himself from his friend and ally. Despite being outcast, Rustin was instrumental in organizing the historic 1963 March on Washington for Jobs and Freedom.

Bayard Rustin's fingerprints, 1946

National Portrait Gallery, Smithsonian Institution

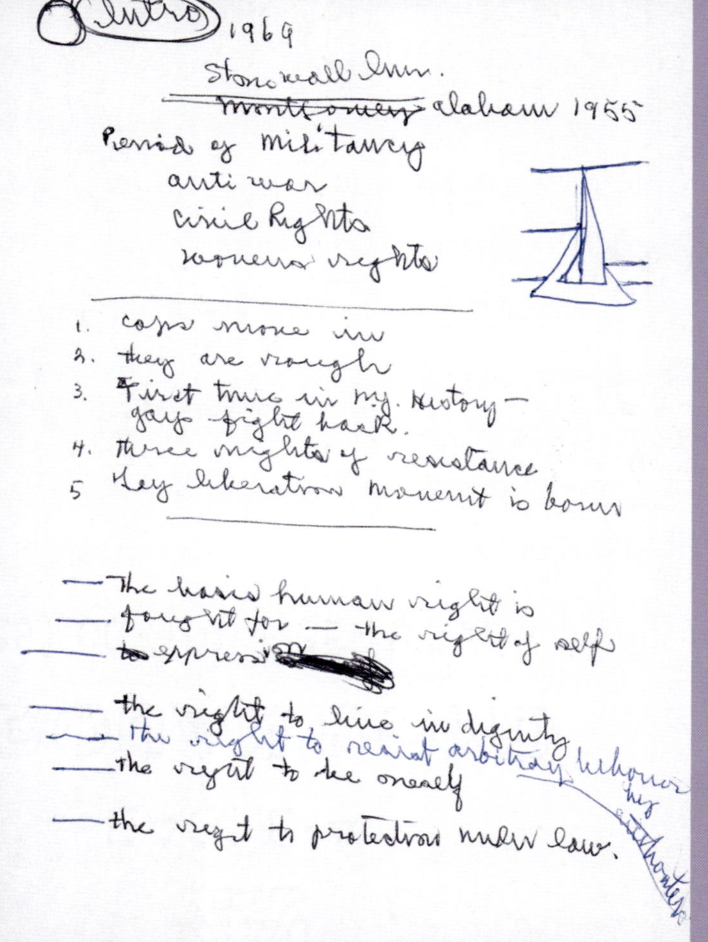

Intro 1969

Stonewall Inn.

~~Montgomery~~ alabam 1955

Period of Militancy

anti war

civil Rights

womens rights

1. cops move in
2. they are rough
3. First time in my history — gays fight back.
4. three nights of resistance
5 Gay liberation movement is born

— The basic human right is
— fought for — the right of self
— ~~to~~ expression

— the right to live in dignity
— the right to resist arbitrary behavior by authorities
— the right to be oneself

— the right to protection under law.

(a) Human Rights important moral Problem of our Time

(b) negative human Rights must preceed positive ones. why? change related to Elementary democracy.

(c) Gay rights litmus paper why so. Because

(d) Respect for all Human personality core of human rights — Gays most easily + frequently rejected

(e) Danger — This rejection of Democracy — where "all are free for full self expression and individual self expression."

(f) Yet Homosexuality is the one area where the "we - they" concept is still morally acceptable

(g) what that means.

(2)

) The formula for Breaking the we - they

) Rabbi Hillel
"If I am not for myself who am I
But if I am only for myself, what am I
and if not now, when"

) all morality concerns Liberation of Self / others / Society

who am I

1. over coming fear
2. over coming self hate
3. over coming self denial:

coming out of closet

lf acceptance requires engaging in gay activity ~ ~ -
and such activity is essential to move on the other issues of human liberation.

s by Bayard Rustin on civil rights and gay ity, c. 1986

Rustin Papers, Manuscript Division, Library of Congress, gton, D.C.

Bayard Rustin, the close advisor, mentor, and principal strategist to Martin Luther King Jr. on issues of nonviolent protest, was also the architect and main organizer of the 1963 March on Washington for Jobs and Freedom. Despite his contributions to the civil rights movement, Rustin was marginalized in large part due to his sexuality.

These handwritten musings, which Rustin penned toward the end of his life, outline his perspectives on the civil rights of gay people. An ally of Baldwin, Rustin believed homophobia limited democracy. The profound, outspoken thinker argued that basic human rights allow for the "right of self-expression, the right to live in dignity, and the right to be oneself."

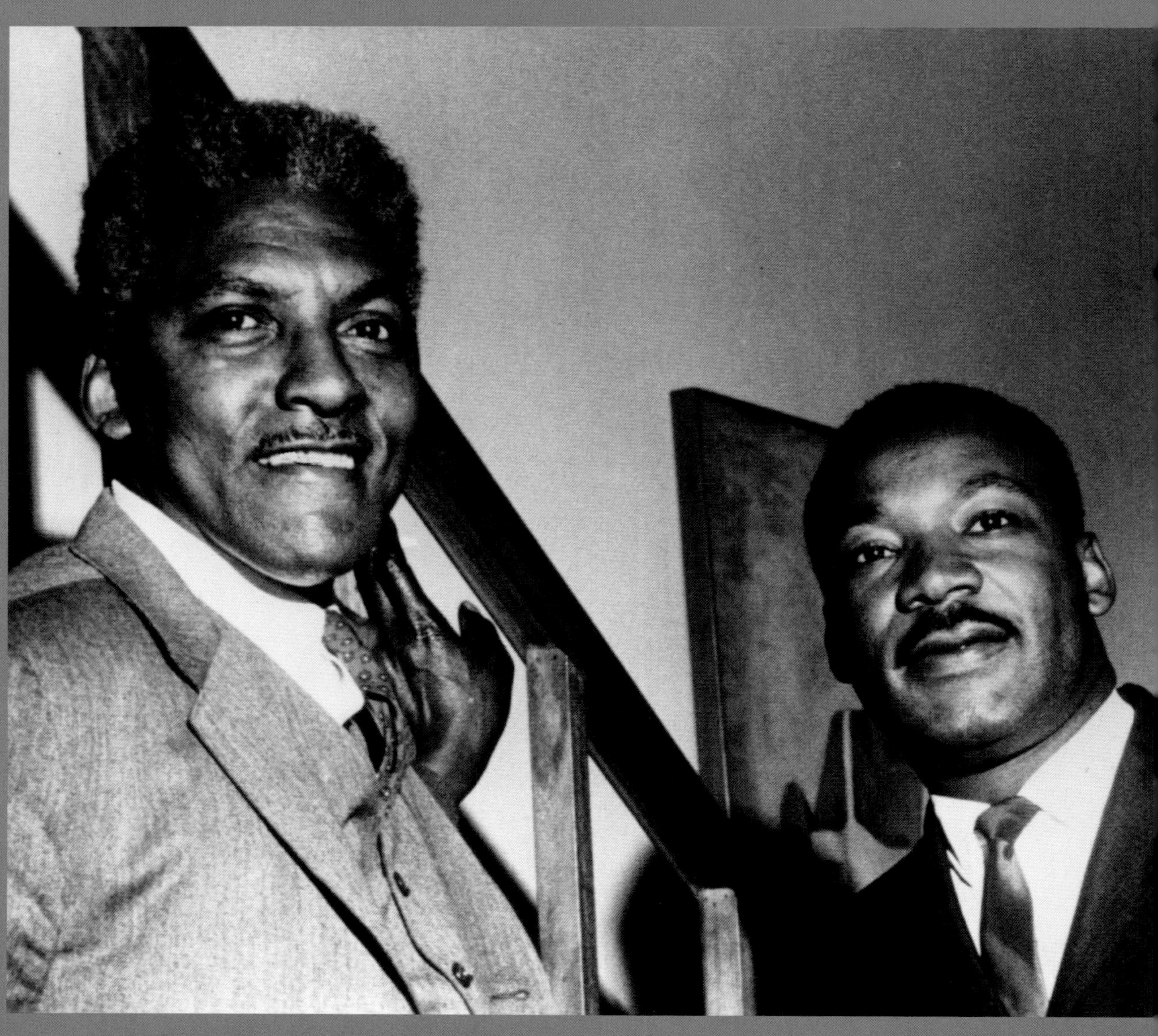

Bayard Rustin and Martin Luther King Jr., 1962
Unidentified photographer
gelatin silver print, 8 x 10 in. (20.3 x 25.4 cm)
Prints and Photographs Division, Library of Congress, Washington, D.C.

"Let us be enraged about injustice, but let us not be destroyed by it."

—Bayard Rustin

American painter Jack Whitten was born into a segregated world. A native of Bessemer, Alabama, he met the Reverend Martin Luther King Jr. in 1957, when King was organizing the seminal bus boycott in Montgomery. King's teachings of nonviolence informed Whitten's life. By 1964, the young artist had graduated from one of the most prestigious art schools in the country—the Cooper Union. (He was the only Black student in his class.) Nevertheless, Whitten rejected the popular rules of the predominant art movement, Abstract Expressionism, and instead experimented with figuration and dimensionality.

Whitten found his own style with paintings such as this one, which gives shape to grief and chaos. The sunbursts of red and yellow, and frenzied pinks, speak not only to King's violent death but also to Whitten's dream of nonviolence.

USA Oracle (Assassination of M.L. King), 1968
Jack Whitten
oil on canvas, 55 ⅞ x 50 in. (141.9 x 127 cm)
Courtesy of the Jack Whitten Estate and Hauser & Wirth

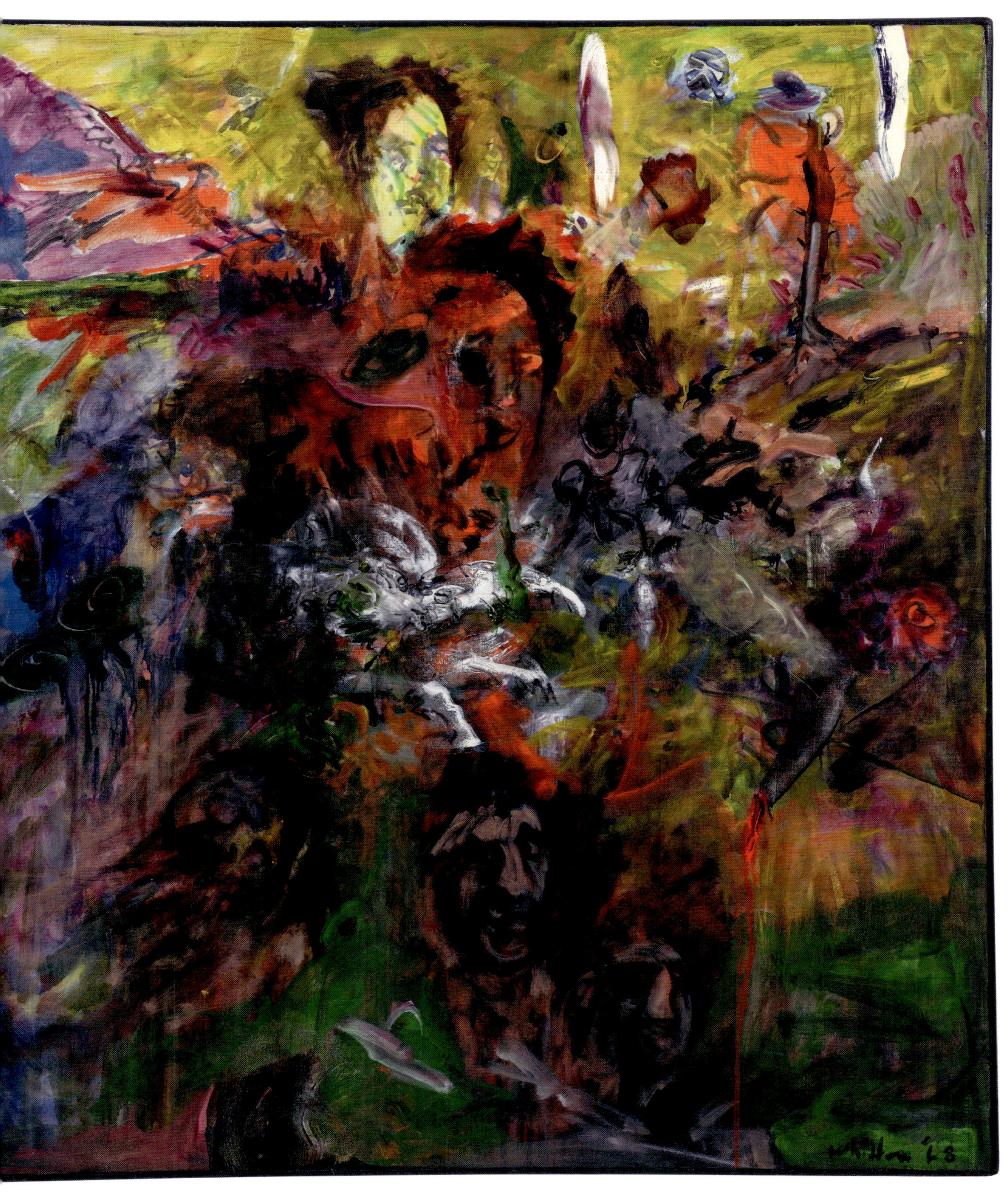

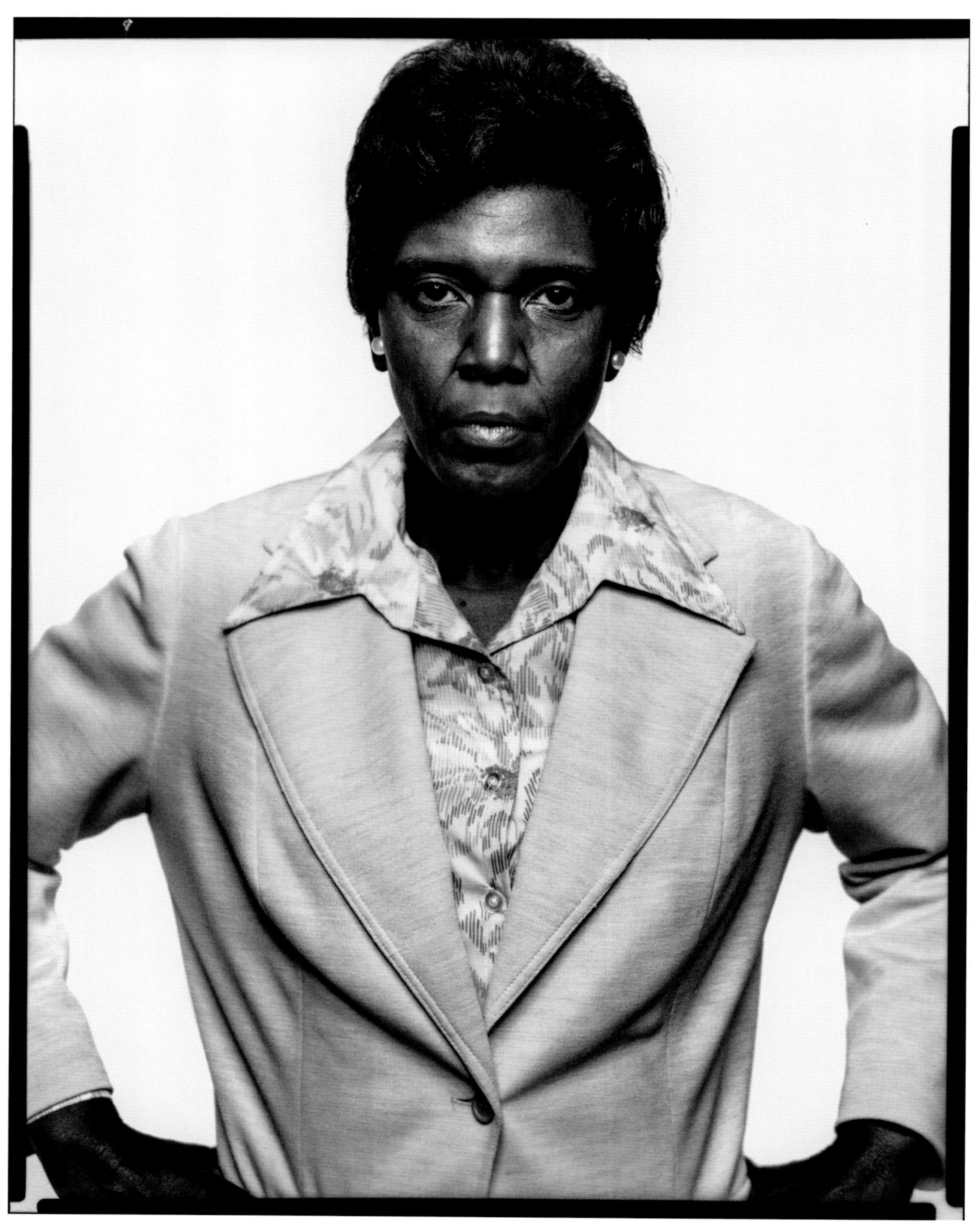

Barbara Jordan, U.S. Congresswoman, Texas, 1976

Richard Avedon

gelatin silver print, 9 15⁄16 x 8 in. (25.3 x 20.3 cm)

National Portrait Gallery, Smithsonian Institution; this acquisition was made possible by generous contributions from Jeane W. Austin and the James Smithson Society

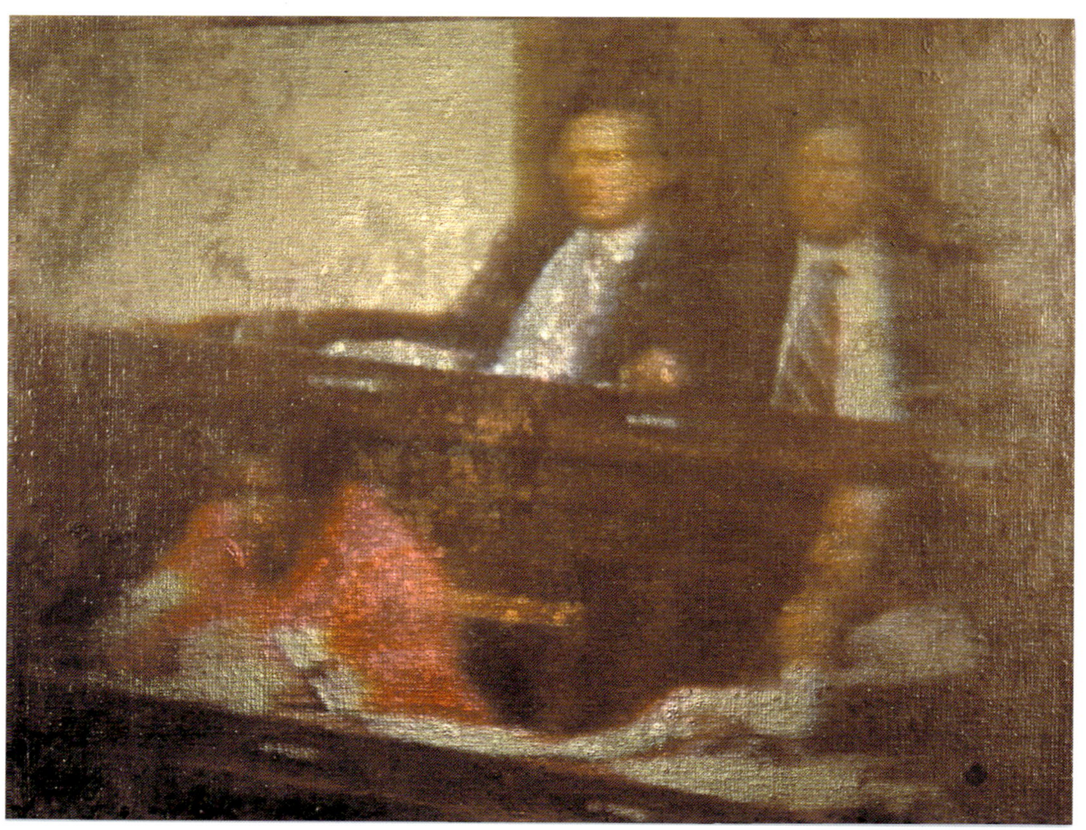

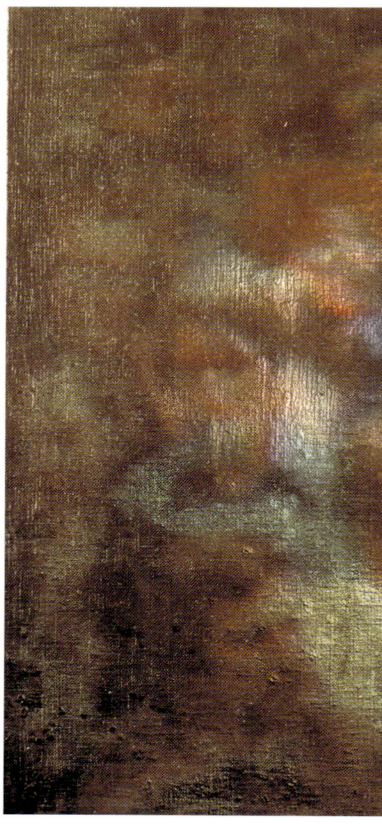

What Barbara Jordan Wore, 2002
Donald Moffett
oil and enamel on linen with video projection,
three panels, each: 45 x 60 in. (114.3 x 152.4 cm)

Museum of Contemporary Art Chicago; restricted gift of Nancy A. Lauter and Alfred L. McDougal, Judith Neisser, Barbara and Thomas Ruben, Faye and Victor Morgenstern Family Foundation, and Ruth Horwich

This work is about perception and how we both saw and did not see th late great Congresswoman Barbara Jordan. Early in her career, Jordan helped organize a get-out-the-vote program that served Houston's for Black precincts. Then, in 1966, she became the first Black woman elect to the Texas Senate after Reconstruction, and in 1977, she was elected t U.S. House of Representatives. An advocate for the poor and for wome Jordan delivered a historic speech in 1974, supporting the impeachmer President Nixon.

Moffett's portrait shows a close-up of Jordan, who spoke whi surrounded and scrutinized by a sea of mostly white men. The Texas-b artist mixed painting and video, and also played with sound so that Jordan's message, along with her image—including her queer history— remains legible within the haze of memory. When Jordan died, she left behind her companion of more than two decades, educational psychol Nancy Earl.

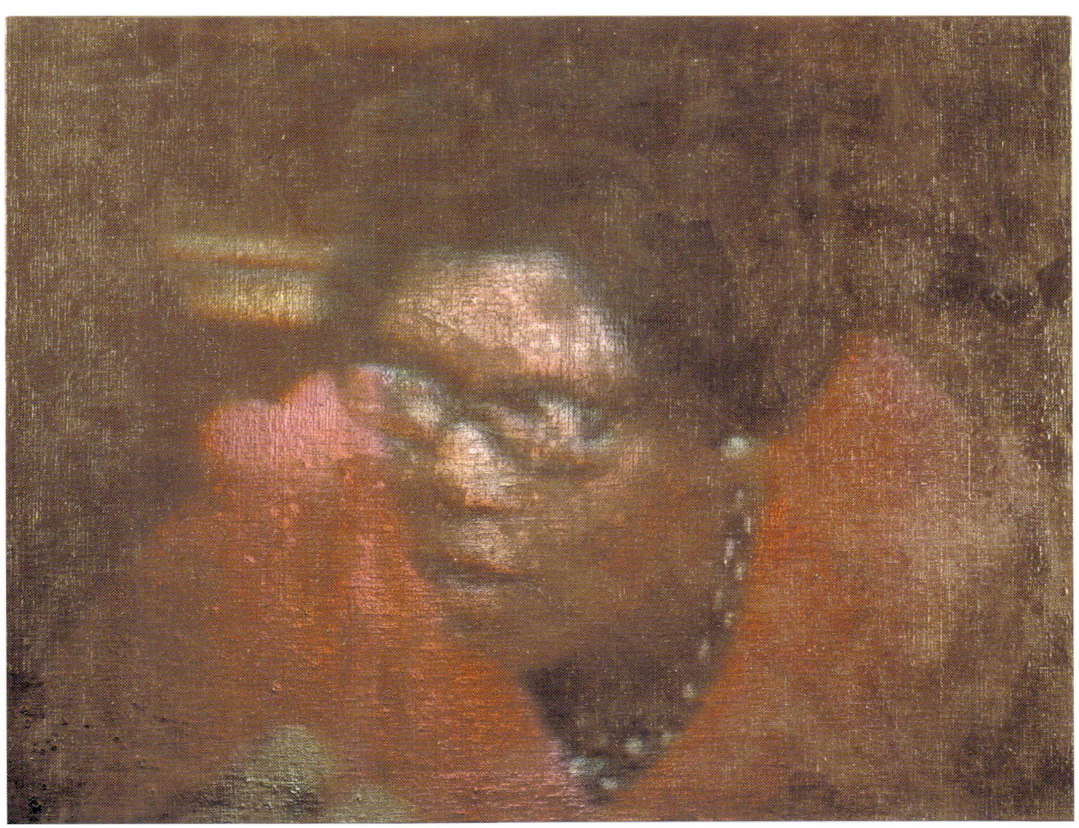

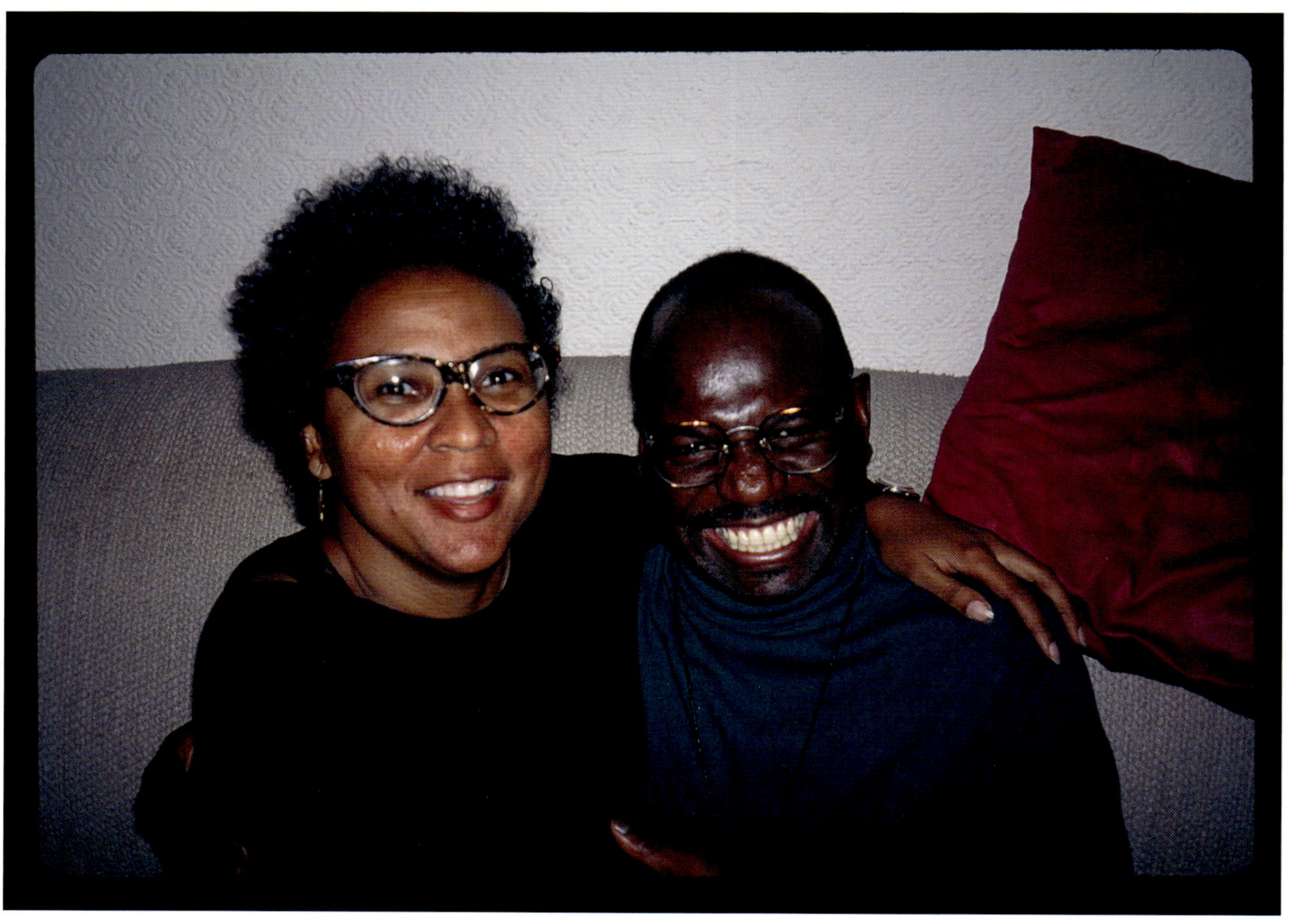

bell hooks and Marlon Riggs, New York, early 1990s,
(printed 2019)
Lyle Ashton Harris
chromogenic print from slide, 15 x 20 ½ in.
(38.1 x 52.1 cm)
Courtesy of the artist and Salon 94, New York

The extraordinary joy one finds in Lyle Ashton Harris's informal portrai of the feminist writer and educator bell hooks and her friend, filmmaker Marlon Riggs, speaks not only of their close relationship but also of a ver fertile time in American culture. Taken in the early 1990s, Harris's photo graph reminds us of the many ways race and gender were being reconsic by hooks and Riggs (as in hooks's 1981 landmark study of race and femin *ain't i a woman*), and by their contemporaries, or near contemporaries, including the critic Greg Tate, the feminist scholar Gina Dent, and the curator Thelma Golden. Together and separately, these thinkers, all of w were influenced by James Baldwin, have changed not only the way Blacl sees itself but also its role in the making of all Americans.

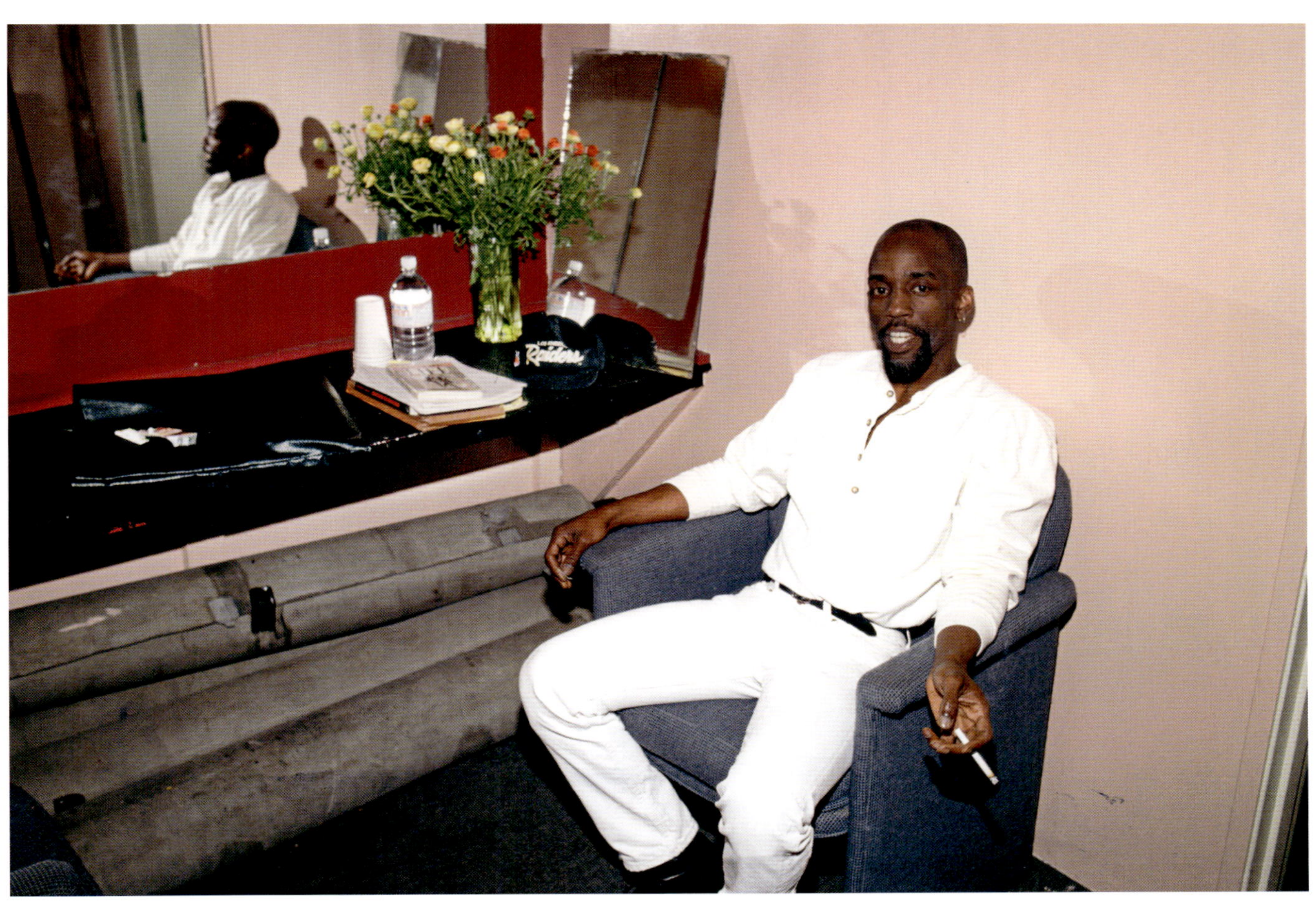

Essex, LA Contemporary Exhibitions, Los Angeles, 1992,
Photograph of Essex Hemphill (printed 2015)
Lyle Ashton Harris
chromogenic print from slide, 11 x 16 ½ in.
(27.9 x 41.9 cm)
Whitney Museum of American Art, New York; gift of the artist and Miyoung Lee and Neil Simpkins in honor of Thelma Golden

Marlon Riggs: Tongues Untied, 1994
Faith Ringgold
acrylic on canvas with printed and pieced fabric,
90 ¼ x 59 ⅝ in. (226.1 x 151.1 cm)
Private collection

In 1994, the American artist Faith Ringgold made a piece in the spirit of the AIDS Memorial Quilt Project, which she dedicated to the late poet, filmmaker, and activist Marlon Riggs. Riggs, born in Fort Worth, Texas, graduated *magna cum laude* from Harvard University in 1978. From the start, he sought to tell a different kind of story—of a Black queer man not necessarily at home in Black or white society—that was redolent of Baldwin's experiences in New York and Paris. Cinema was Riggs's métier, and in works such as *Tongues Untied* (1989), he radicalized the form in essay-films that mixed footage with poetry by Essex Hemphill, who also perished from AIDS. One can view Riggs and Hemphill as Baldwin's queer progeny, each working in a different genre than their mentor, certainly, but carrying Baldwin's message about the importance of connection.

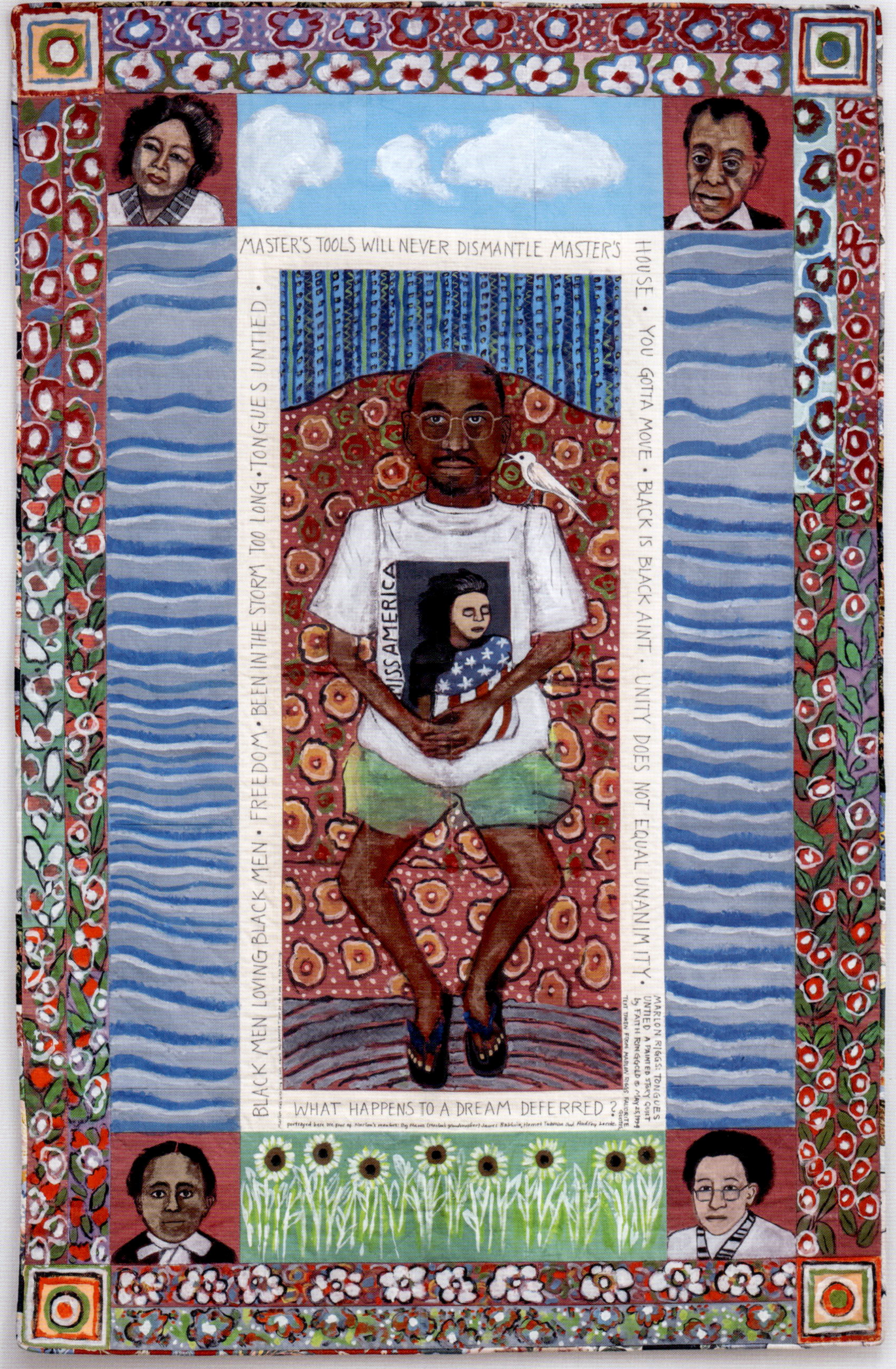
MASTER'S TOOLS WILL NEVER DISMANTLE MASTER'S
HOUSE • YOU GOTA MOVE • BLACK IS BLACK AINT • UNITY DOES NOT EQUAL UNANIMITY •
BLACK MEN LOVING BLACK MEN • FREEDOM • BEEN IN THE STORM TOO LONG • TONGUES UNTIED •
WHAT HAPPENS TO A DREAM DEFERRED ?
MISS AMERICA
MARLON RIGGS: TONGUES UNTIED A PAINTED STORY QUILT by FAITH RINGGOLD © MAY 25 1994
TEXT TAKEN FROM MARLON RIGGS FAVORITE QUOTES.

Selected Writings

James Baldwin

The following writings by James Baldwin were selected for their marked relevance to the themes in *This Morning, This Evening, So Soon: James Baldwin and the Voices of Queer Resistance.* These selections are not necessarily his most known works. Of these, "Freaks and the American Ideal of Manhood" is likely most familiar. The essay was reproduced as "Here Be Dragons" in the anthology *Price of the Ticket: Collected Nonfiction 1948–1985,* but it originally appeared in *Playboy Magazine* in 1985. "To Crush the Serpent" was also featured in *Playboy*, in 1987. There is a wonderful irony to see Baldwin writing in *Playboy,* a magazine dedicated to male heteronormativity. Here he is challenging cis masculinity and the pitfalls of religious zealots in the mid-1980s, when AIDS was ravaging the gay community. These works, along with the short story that gives this exhibition its title, are still germane—perhaps now it's time for them to share their rightful place among the compendium of his other highly regarded materials.

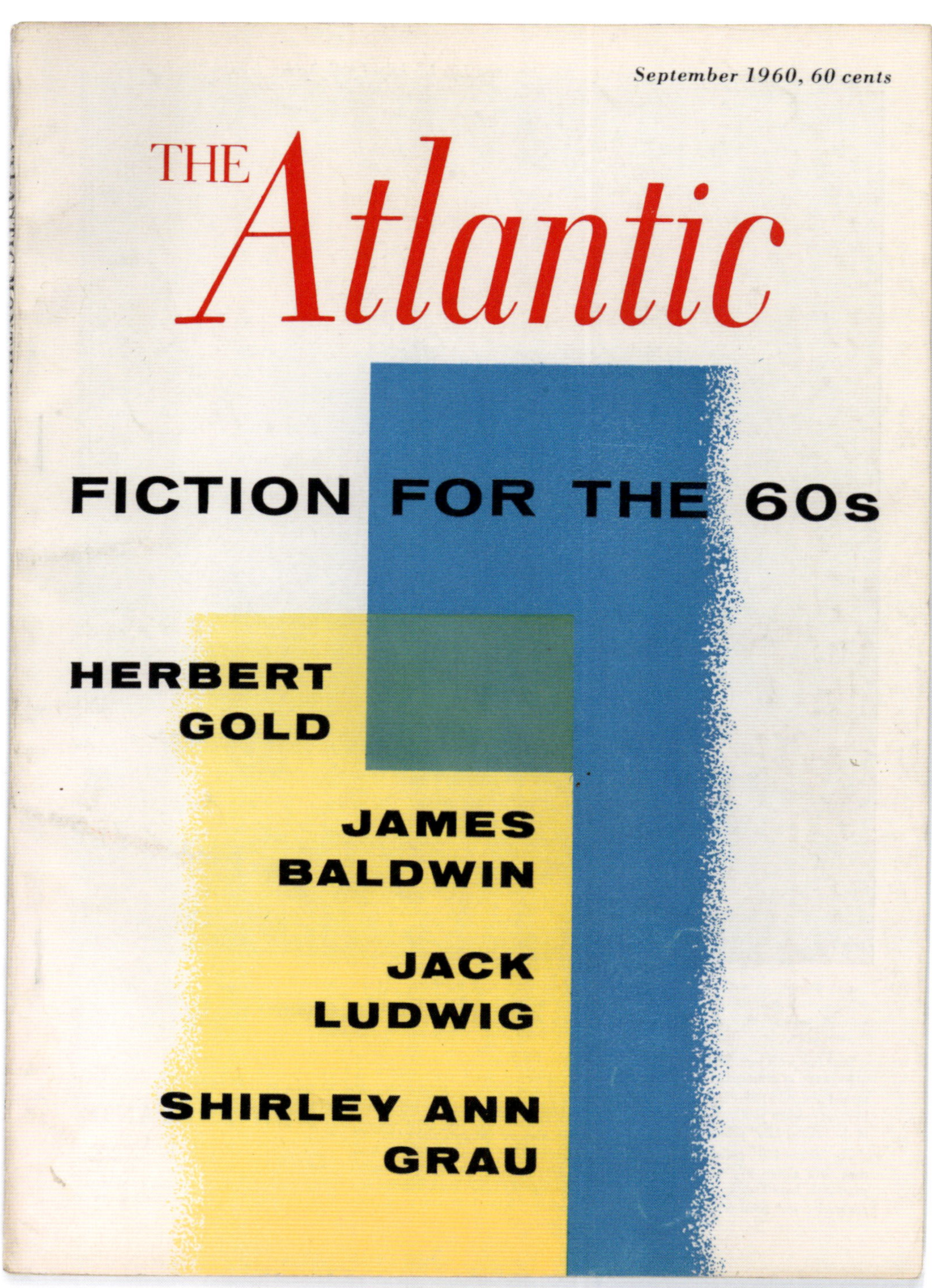

Cover of **The Atlantic**, September 1960

This Morning, This Evening, So Soon

The Atlantic, September 1960

JAMES BALDWIN was born in New York City in 1924 and as a boy first tasted the poverty and discrimination of a Negro in Harlem. In 1945 a Eugene Saxon Fellowship enabled him to free-lance, and the stories, plays, and novels which followed established him as a young writer of extraordinary power. After living and writing in England and on the Continent, he has returned to this country and now makes his home in Greenwich Village.

"You are full of nightmares," Harriet tells me. She is in her dressing gown and has cream all over her face. She and my older sister, Louisa, are going out to be girls together. I suppose they have many things to talk about — they have *me* to talk about, certainly — and they do not want my presence. I have been given a bachelor's evening. The director of the film which has brought us such incredible and troubling riches will be along later to take me out to dinner.

I watch her face. I know that it is quite impossible for her to be as untroubled as she seems. Her self-control is mainly for my benefit — my benefit, and Paul's. Harriet comes from orderly and progressive Sweden and has reacted against all the advanced doctrines to which she has been exposed by becoming steadily and beautifully old-fashioned. We never fought in front of Paul, not even when he was a baby. Harriet does not so much believe in protecting children as she does in helping them to build a foundation on which they can build and build again, each time life's high-flying steel ball knocks down everything they have built.

Whenever I become upset, Harriet becomes very cheerful and composed. I think she began to learn how to do this over eight years ago, when I returned from my only visit to America. Now, perhaps, it has become something she could not control if she wished to. This morning, at breakfast, when I yelled at Paul, she averted Paul's tears and my own guilt by looking up and saying, "My God, your father is cranky this morning, isn't he?"

Paul's attention was immediately distracted from his wounds, and the unjust inflicter of those wounds, to his mother's laughter. He watched her.

"It is because he is afraid they will not like his songs in New York. Your father is an *artiste, mon chou,* and they are very mysterious people, *les artistes.* Millions of people are waiting for him in New York, they are begging him to come, and they will give him a *lot* of money, but he is afraid they will not like him. Tell him he is wrong."

She succeeded in rekindling Paul's excitement about places he has never seen. I was also, at once, reinvested with all my glamour. I think it is sometimes extremely difficult for Paul to realize that the face he sees on record sleeves and in the newspapers and on the screen is nothing more or less than the face of his father — who sometimes yells at him. Of course, since he is only seven — going on eight, he will be eight years old this winter — he cannot know that I am baffled, too.

"Of course, you are wrong, you are silly," he said with passion — and caused me to smile. His English is strongly accented and is not, in fact, as good as his French, for he speaks French all day at school. French is really his first language, the first he ever heard. "You are the greatest singer in France" —sounding exactly as he must sound when he makes this pronouncement to his schoolmates — "the greatest *American* singer" — this concession was so gracefully made that it was not a concession at all, it added inches to my stature, America being only a glamorous word for Paul. It is the place from which his father came, and to which he now is going, a place which very few people have ever seen. But his aunt is one of them and he looked over at her. "Mme. Dumont says so, and she says he is a *great actor, too."* Louisa nodded, smiling. "And she has seen *Les Fauves Nous Attendent* — five times!" This clinched it, of course. Mme. Dumont is our concierge and she has known Paul all his life. I suppose he will not begin to doubt anything she says until he begins to doubt everything.

He looked over at me again. "So you are wrong to be afraid."

"I was wrong to yell at you, too. I won't yell at you any more today."

"All right." He was very grave.

Louisa poured more coffee. "He's going to knock them dead in New York. You'll see."

"Mais bien sûr," said Paul, doubtfully. He does not quite know what "knock them dead" means, though he was sure, from her tone, that she must have been agreeing with him. He does not quite understand this aunt, whom he met for the first time two months ago, when she arrived to spend the summer with us. Her accent is entirely different from anything he has ever heard. He does not really understand why, since she is my sister and his aunt, she should be unable to speak French.

Harriet, Louisa, and I looked at each other and smiled. "Knock them dead," said Harriet, "means *d'avoir un succès fou.* But you will soon pick up all the American expressions." She looked at me and laughed. "So will I."

"That's what he's afraid of." Louisa grinned. "We have *got* some expressions, believe me. Don't let anybody ever tell you America hasn't got a culture. Our culture is as thick as clabber milk."

"Ah." Harriet answered, "I know. I know."

"I'm going to be practicing later," I told Paul.

His face lit up. *"Bon."* This meant that, later, he would come into my study and lie on the floor with his papers and crayons while I worked out with the piano and the tape recorder. He knew that I was offering this as an olive branch. All things considered, we get on pretty well, my son and I.

He looked over at Louisa again. She held a coffee cup in one hand and a cigarette in the other; and something about her baffled him. It was early, so she had not yet put on her face. Her short, thick, graying hair was rougher than usual, almost as rough as my own — later, she would he going to the hairdresser's; she is fairer than I, and better-looking; Louisa, in fact, caught all the looks in the family. Paul knows that she is my older sister and that she helped to raise me, though he does not, of course, know what this means. He knows that she is a schoolteacher in the *American* South, which is not, for some reason, the same place as South America. I could see him trying to fit all these exotic details together into a pattern which would explain her strangeness — strangeness of accent, strangeness of manner. In comparison with the people he has always known, Louisa must seem, for all her generosity and laughter and affection, peculiarly uncertain of herself, peculiarly hostile and embattled.

I wondered what he would think of his Uncle Norman, older and much blacker than I, who lives near the Alabama town in which we were born. Norman will meet us at the boat.

Now Harriet repeats, "Nightmares, nightmares. Nothing ever turns out as badly as you think it will — in fact," she adds laughing, "I am happy to say that that would scarcely he possible."

Her eyes seek mine in the mirror — dark-blue eyes, pale skin, black hair. I had always thought of Sweden as being populated entirely by blondes, and I thought that Harriet was abnormally dark for a Swedish girl. But when we visited Sweden, I found out differently. "It is all a great racial salad, Europe, that is why I am sure that I will never understand your country," Harriet said. That was in the days when we never imagined that we would be going to it.

I wonder what she is really thinking. Still, she is right, in two days we will be on a boat, and there is simply no point in carrying around my load of apprehension. I sit down on the bed, watching her fix her face. I realize that I am going to miss this old-fashioned bedroom. For years, we've talked about throwing out the old junk which came with the apartment and replacing it with less massive, modern furniture. But we never have.

"Oh, everything will probably work out," I say. "I've been in a bad mood all day long. I just can't sing any more." We both laugh. She reaches for a wad of tissues and begins wiping off the cream. "I wonder how Paul will like it, if he'll make friends — that's all."

"Paul will like any place where you are, where we are. Don't worry about Paul."

Paul has never been called any names, so far. Only, once he asked us what the word *métis* meant and Harriet explained to him that it meant mixed blood, adding that the blood of just about everybody in the world was mixed by now. Mme. Dumont contributed bawdy and detailed corroboration from her own family tree, the roots of which were somewhere in Corsica; the moral of the story, as she told it, was that women were weak, men incorrigible, and *le bon Dieu* appallingly clever. Mme. Dumont's version is the version I prefer, but it may not be, for Paul, the most utilitarian.

Harriet rises from the dressing table and comes over to sit in my lap. I fall back with her on the bed, and she smiles down into my face.

"Now, don't worry," she tells me, "please try not to worry. Whatever is coming, we will manage it all very well, you will see. We have each other and we have our son and we know what we want. So, we are luckier than most people."

I kiss her on the chin. "I'm luckier than most men."

"I'm a very lucky woman, too."

And for a moment we are silent, alone in our room, which we have shared so long. The slight rise and fall of Harriet's breathing creates an intermittent pressure against my chest, and I think how, if I had never left America, I would never have met her and would never have established a life of my own, would never have entered my own life. For everyone's life begins on a level where races, armies, and churches stop. And yet everyone's life is always shaped by races, churches, and armies; races, churches, armies menace, and have taken, many lives. If Harriet had been born in America, it would have taken her a long time, perhaps forever, to look on me as a man like other men; if I had met her in America, I would never have been able to look on her as a woman like all other women. The habits of public rage and power would also have been our private compulsions, and would have blinded our eyes. We would never have been able to love each other. And Paul would never have been born.

Perhaps, if I had stayed in America, I would have found another woman and had another son. But that other woman, that other son are in the limbo of vanished possibilities. I might also have become something else, instead of an actor-singer, perhaps a lawyer, like my brother, or a teacher, like my sister. But no, I am what I have become and this woman beside me is my wife, and I love her. All the sons I might have had mean nothing, since I *have* a son, I named him, Paul, for my father, and I love him.

I think of all the things I have seen destroyed in America, all the things that I have lost there, all the threats it holds for me and mine.

I grin up at Harriet. "Do you love me?"

"Of course not. I simply have been madly plotting to get to America all these years."

"What a patient wench you are."

"The Swedes are very patient."

She kisses me again and stands up. Louisa comes in, also in a dressing gown.

"I hope you two aren't sitting in here yakking about the *subject*." She looks at me. "My, you are the sorriest-looking celebrity I've ever seen. I've always wondered why people like you hired press agents. Now I know." She goes to Harriet's dressing table. "Honey, do you mind if I borrow some of that *mad* nail polish?"

Harriet goes over to the dressing table. "I'm not sure I know *which* mad nail polish you mean."

Harriet and Louisa, somewhat to my surprise, get on very well. Each seems to find the other full of the weirdest and most delightful surprises. Harriet has been teaching Louisa French and Swedish expressions, and Louisa has been teaching Harriet some of the saltier expressions of the black South. Whenever one of them is not playing straight man to the other's accent, they become involved in long speculations as to how a language reveals the history and the attitudes of a people. They discovered that all the European languages contain a phrase equivalent to "to work like a nigger." ("Of course," says Louisa, "they've had black men working for them for a long time.") "Language is experience and language is power," says Louisa, after regretting that she does not know any of the African dialects. "That's what I keep trying to tell those dicty bastards down South. They get their own experience into the language, we'll have a great language. But, no, they all want to talk like white folks." Then she leans forward, grasping Harriet by the knee. "I tell them, honey, white folks ain't saying *nothing.* Not a thing are they saying — and *some* of them know it, they *need* what you got, the whole world needs it." Then she leans back, in disgust. "You think they listen to me? Indeed they do not. They just go right on, trying to talk like white folks." She leans forward again, in tremendous indignation. "You know some of them folks are *ashamed* of Mahalia Jackson? *Ashamed* of her, one of the greatest singers alive! They think she's common." Then she looks about the room as though she held a bottle in her hand and were looking for a skull to crack.

I think it is because Louisa has never been able to talk like this to any white person before. All the white people she has ever met needed, in one way or another, to be reassured, consoled, to have their consciences pricked but not blasted; could not, could not afford to hear a truth which would shatter, irrevocably, their image of themselves. It is astonishing the lengths to which a person, or a people, will go in order to avoid a truthful mirror. But Harriet's necessity is precisely the opposite: it is of the utmost importance that she learn everything that Louisa can tell her, and then learn more, much more. Harriet is really trying to learn from Louisa how best to protect her husband and her son. This is why they are going out alone tonight. They will have, tonight, as it were, a final council of war. I may be moody, but they, thank God, are practical.

Now Louisa turns to me while Harriet rummages about on the dressing table. "What time is Vidal coming for you?"

"Oh, around seven thirty, eight o'clock. He says he's reserved tables for us in some very chic place, but he won't say where." Louisa wriggles her shoulders, raises her eyebrows, and does a tiny bump and grind. I laugh. "That's right. And then I guess we'll go out and get drunk."

"I hope to God you do. You've been about as cheerful as a cemetery these last few days. And, that way, your hangover will keep you from bugging us tomorrow."

"What about *your* hangovers? I know the way you girls drink."

"Well, we'll be paying for our own drinks," says Harriet, "so I don't think we'll have that problem. But *you're* going to be feted, like an international movie star."

"You sure you don't want to change your mind and come out with Vidal and me?"

"We're sure," Louisa says. She looks down at me and gives a small, amused grunt. "An international movie star. And I used to change your diapers. I'll be damned." She is grave for a moment. "Mama'd be proud of you, you know that?" We look at each other and the air between us is charged with secrets which not even Harriet will ever know. "Now, get the hell out of here, so we can get dressed."

"I'll take Paul on down to Mme. Dumont's."

Paul is to have supper with her children and spend the night there.

"For the last time," says Mme. Dumont and she rubs her hand over Paul's violently curly black hair. "*Tu vas nous manquer, tu sais?*" Then she looks up at me and laughs. "He doesn't care. He is only interested in seeing the big ship and all the wonders of New York. Children are never sad to make journeys."

"I would be very sad to go," says Paul, politely, "but my father must go to New York to work and he wants me to come with him."

Over his head, Mme. Dumont and I smile at each other. "*Il est malin, ton gosse!*" She looks down at him again. "And do you think, my little diplomat, that you will like New York?"

"We aren't only going to New York," Paul answers, "we are going to California, too."

"Well, do you think you will like California?"

Paul looks at me. "I don't know. If we don't like it, we'll come back."

"So simple. Just like that," says Mme. Dumont. She looks at me. "It is the best way to look at life. Do come back. You know, we feel that you belong to us, too, here in France."

"I hope you do," I say. "I hope you do. I have always felt — always felt at home here." I bend down and Paul and I kiss each other on the cheek. We have always done so — but will we be able to do so in America? American fathers never kiss American sons. I straighten, my hand on Paul's shoulder. "You be good. I'll pick you up for breakfast, or, if you get up first you come and pick me up and we can hang out together tomorrow, while your *maman* and your Aunt Louisa finish packing. They won't want two men hanging around the house."

"*D'accord.* Where shall we hang out?" On the last two words he stumbles a little and imitates me.

"Maybe we can go to the zoo, I don't know. And I'll take you to lunch at the Eiffel Tower, would you like that?"

"Oh, yes," he says, "I'd love that." When he is pleased, he seems to glow. All the energy of his small, tough, concentrated being charges an unseen battery and adds an incredible luster to his eyes, which are large and dark brown — like mine — and to his skin, which always reminds me of the colors of honey and the fires of the sun.

"Okay, then." I shake hands with Mme. Dumont. "*Bonsoir, Madame.*" I ring for the elevator, staring at Paul. "*Ciao, Pauli.*"

"*Bonsoir, Papa.*"

And Mme. Dumont takes him inside.

Upstairs, Harriet and Louisa are finally powdered. perfumed, and jeweled, and ready to go: dry Martinis at the Ritz, supper, "in some *very* expensive little place," says Harriet, and perhaps the Folies Bergère afterwards. "A real cornball, tourist evening," says Louisa. "I'm working on the theory that if I can get Harriet to act like an American now, she won't have so much trouble later."

"I very much doubt," Harriet says, "that I will be able to endure the Folies Bergère for three solid hours."

"Oh, then we'll duck across town to Harry's New York bar and drink mint juleps," says Louisa.

I realize that, quite apart from everything else, Louisa is having as much fun as she has ever had in her life before. Perhaps she, too, will be sad to leave Paris, even though she has only known it for such a short time.

"Do people drink those in New York?" Harriet asks. I think she is making a list of the things people do or do not do in New York.

"*Some* people do." Louisa winks at me. "Do you realize that this Swedish chick's picked up an Alabama drawl?"

We laugh together. The elevator chugs to a landing.

"We'll stop and say good night to Paul," Harriet says. She kisses me. "Give our best to Vidal."

"Right. Have a good time. Don't let any Frenchmen run off with Louisa."

"I did not come to Paris to be protected, and if I had, this wild chick *you* married couldn't do it. I just *might* upset everybody and come home with a French count." She presses the elevator button and the cage goes down.

I walk back into our dismantled apartment. It stinks of departure. There are bags and crates in the hall, which will be taken away tomorrow, there are no books in the bookcases, the kitchen looks as though we never cooked a meal there, never dawdled there, in the early morning or late at night, over coffee. Presently, I must shower and shave but now I pour myself a drink and light a cigarette and step out on our balcony. It is dusk, the brilliant light of Paris is beginning to fade, and the green of the trees is darkening,

I have lived in this city for twelve years. This apartment is on the top floor of a corner building. We look out over the trees and the roof tops to the Champ de Mars, where the Eiffel Tower stands. Beyond this field is the river, which I have crossed so often, in so many states of mind. I have crossed every bridge in Paris, I have walked along every *quai.* I know the river as one finally knows a friend, know it when it is black, guarding all the lights of Paris in its depths, and seeming, in its vast silence, to be communing with the dead who lie beneath it; when it is yellow, evil, and roaring, giving a rough time to tugboats and barges, and causing people to remember that it has been known to rise, it has been known to kill; when it is peaceful, a slick, dark, dirty green, playing host to rowboats and *les bateaux mouches* and throwing up from time to time an extremely unhealthy fish. The men who stand along the *quais* all summer with their fishing lines gratefully accept the slimy object and throw it in a rusty can. I have always wondered who eats those fish.

And I walk up and down, up and down, glad to be alone.

It is August, the month when all Parisians desert Paris and one has to walk miles to find a barbershop or a laundry open in some tree-shadowed, silent side street. There is a single person on the avenue, a paratrooper walking toward École Militaire. He is also walking, almost certainly, and rather sooner than later, toward Algeria. I have a friend, a good-natured boy who was always hanging around the clubs in which I worked in the old days, who has just returned from Algeria, with a recurring, debilitating fever, and minus one eye. The government has set his pension at the sum, arbitrary if not occult, of fifty-three thousand francs every three months. Of course, it is quite impossible to live on this amount of money without working — but who will hire a half-blind invalid? This boy has been spoiled forever, long before his thirtieth birthday, and there are thousands like him all over France.

And there are fewer Algerians to be found on the streets of Paris now. The rug sellers, the peanut vendors, the post-card peddlers and moneychangers have vanished. The boys I used to know during my first years in Paris are scattered — or corralled — the Lord knows where.

Most of them had no money. They lived three and four together in rooms with a single skylight, a single hard cot, or in buildings that seemed abandoned, with cardboard in the windows, with erratic plumbing in a wet, cobblestoned yard, in dark, dead-end alleys, or on the outer, chilling heights of Paris.

The Arab cafés are closed — those dark, acrid cafes in which I used to meet with them to drink tea, to get high on hashish, to listen to the obsessive, stringed music which has no relation to any beat, any time, that I have ever known. I once thought of the North Africans as my brothers and that is why I went to their cafés. They were very friendly to me, perhaps one or two of them remained really fond of me even after I could no longer afford to smoke Lucky Strikes and after my collection of American sport shirts had vanished — mostly into their wardrobes. They seemed to feel that they had every right to them, since I could only have wrested these things from the world by cunning — it meant nothing to say that I had had no choice in the matter; perhaps I had wrested these things from the world by treason, by refusing to be identified with the misery of my people. Perhaps, indeed, I identified myself with those who were responsible for this misery.

And this was true. Their rage, the only note in all their music which I could not fail to recognize, to which I responded, yet had the effect of setting us more than ever at a division. They were perfectly prepared to drive all Frenchmen into the sea, and to level the city of Paris. But I could not hate the French, because they left me alone. And I love Paris, I will always love it, it is the city which saved my life. It saved my life by allowing me to find out who I am.

It was on a bridge, one tremendous, April morning, that I knew I had fallen in love. Harriet and I were walking hand in hand. The bridge was the Pont Royal, just before us was the great *horloge,* high and lifted up, saying ten to ten; beyond this, the golden statue of Joan of Arc, with her sword uplifted. Harriet and I were silent, for we had been quarreling about something. Now, when I look back, I think we had reached that state when an affair must either end or become something more than an affair.

I looked sideways at Harriet's face, which was still. Her dark-blue eyes were narrowed against the sun, and her full, pink lips were still slightly sulky, like a child's. In those days, she hardly ever wore make-up. I was in my shirt sleeves. Her face made me want to laugh and run my hand over her short dark hair. I wanted to pull her to me and say, *Baby, don't be mad at me*, and at that moment something tugged at my heart and made me catch my breath. There were millions of people all around us, but I was alone with Harriet. She was alone with me. Never, in all my life, until that moment, had I been alone with anyone. The world had always been with us, between us, defeating the quarrel we could not achieve, and making love impossible. During all the years of my life, until that moment, I had carried the menacing, the hostile, killing world with me everywhere. No matter what I was doing or saying or feeling, one eye had always been on the world — that world which I had learned to distrust almost as soon as I learned my name, that world on which I knew one could never turn one's back, the white man's world. And for the first time in my life I was free of it; it had not existed for me; I had been quarreling with my girl. It was our quarrel, it was entirely between us, it had nothing to do with anyone else in the world. For the first time in my life I had not been afraid of the patriotism of the mindless, in uniform or out, who would beat me up and treat the woman who was with me as though she were the lowest of untouchables. For the first time in my fife I felt that no force jeopardized my right, my power, to possess and to protect a woman; for the first time, the first time, felt that the woman was not, in her own eyes or in the eyes of the world, degraded by my presence.

The sun fell over everything, like a blessing, people were moving all about us, I will never forget the feeling of Harriet's small hand in mine, dry and trusting, and I turned to her, slowing our pace. She looked up at me with her enormous, blue eyes, and she seemed to wait. I said, "*Harriet. Harriet. Tu sais, il y a quelque chose de très grave qui m'est arrivé. Je t'aime. Je t'aime. Tu me comprends,* or shall I say it in English?"

This was eight years ago, shortly before my first and only visit home.

That was when my mother died. I stayed in America for three months. When I came back, Harriet thought that the change in me was due to my grief— I was very silent, very thin. But it had not been my mother's death which accounted for the change. I had known that my mother was going to die. I had not known what America would be like for me after nearly four years away.

I remember standing at the rail and watching the distance between myself and Le Havre increase. Hands fell, ceasing to wave, handkerchiefs ceased to flutter, people turned away, they mounted their bicycles or got into their cars and rode off. Soon, Le Havre was nothing but a blur. I thought of Harriet, already miles from me in Paris, and I pressed my lips tightly together in order not to cry.

Then, as Europe dropped below the water, as the days passed and passed, as we left behind us the skies of Europe and the eyes of everyone on the ship began, so to speak, to refocus, waiting for the first glimpse of America, my apprehension began to give way to a secret joy, a checked anticipation. I thought of such details as showers, which are rare in Paris, and I thought of such things as rich, cold, American milk and heavy, chocolate cake. I wondered about my friends, wondered if I had any left, and wondered if they would be glad to see me.

The Americans on the boat did not seem to be so bad, but I was fascinated, after such a long absence from it, by the nature of their friendliness. It was a friendliness which did not suggest, and was not intended to suggest, any possibility of friendship. Unlike Europeans, they dropped titles and used first names almost at once, leaving themselves, unlike the Europeans, with nowhere thereafter to go. Once one had become "Pete" or "Jane" or "Bill" all that could decently be known was known and any suggestion that there might be further depths, a person, so to speak, behind the name, was taken as a violation of that privacy which did not, paradoxically, since they trusted it so little, seem to exist among Americans. They apparently equated privacy with the unspeakable things they did in the bathroom or the bedroom, which they related only to the analyst, and then read about in the pages of best sellers. There was an eerie and unnerving irreality about everything they said and did, as though they were all members of the same team and were acting on orders from some invincibly cheerful and tirelessly inventive coach. I was fascinated by it. I found it oddly moving, but I cannot say that I was displeased. It had not occurred to me before that Americans, who had never treated me with any respect, had no respect for each other.

On the last night but one, there was a gala in the big ballroom and I sang. It had been a long time since I had sung before so many Americans. My audience had mainly been penniless French students, in the weird, Left Bank bistros I worked in those days. Still, I was a great hit with them and by this time I had become enough of a drawing card, in the Latin Quarter and in St. Germain des Prés, to have attracted a couple of critics, to have had my picture in *France-soir*, and to have acquired a legal work permit which allowed me to make a little more money. Just the same, no matter how industrious and brilliant some of the musicians had been, or how devoted my audience, they did not know, they could not know, what my songs came out of. They did not know what was funny about it. It was impossible to translate: It damn well better be funny, or Laughing to keep from crying, or What did *I* do to be so black and blue?

The moment I stepped out on the floor, they began to smile, something opened in them, they were ready to be pleased. I found in their faces, as they watched me, smiling, waiting, an artless relief, a profound reassurance. Nothing was more familiar to them than the sight of a dark boy, singing, and there were few things on earth more necessary. It was under cover of darkness, my own darkness, that I could sing for them of the joys, passions, and terrors they smuggled about with them like steadily depreciating contraband. Under cover of the midnight fiction that I was unlike them because I was black, they could stealthily gaze at those treasures which they had been mysteriously forbidden to possess and were never permitted to declare.

I sang *I'm Coming, Virginia*, and *Take This Hammer*, and *Precious Lord.* They wouldn't let me go and I came back and sang a couple of the oldest blues I knew. Then someone asked me to sing *Swanee River*, and I did, astonished that I could, astonished that this song, which I had put down long ago, should have the power to move me. Then, if only, perhaps, to make the record complete, I wanted to sing *Strange Fruit*, but, on this number, no one can surpass the great, tormented Billie Holiday. So I finished with *Great Getting Up Morning* and I guess I can say that if I didn't stop the show I certainly ended it. I got a big hand and I drank at a few tables and I danced with a few girls.

AFTER one more day and one more night, the boat landed in New York. I woke up, I was bright awake at once, and I thought, *We're here.*

I turned on all the lights in my small cabin and I stared into the mirror as though I were committing my face to memory. I took a shower and I took a long time shaving and I dressed myself very carefully. I walked the long ship corridors to the dining room, looking at the luggage piled high before the elevators and beside the steps. The dining room was nearly half empty and full of a quick and joyous excitement which depressed me even more. People ate quickly, chattering to each other, anxious to get upstairs and go on deck. Was it my imagination or was it true that they seemed to avoid my eyes? A few people waved and smiled, but let me pass; perhaps it would have made them uncomfortable, this morning, to try to share their excitement with me; perhaps they did not want to know whether or not it was possible for me to share it. I walked to my table and sat down. I munched toast as dry as paper and drank a pot of coffee. Then I tipped my waiter, who bowed and smiled and called me "sir" and said that he hoped to see me on the boat again. "I hope so, too," I said.

And was it true, or was it my imagination, that a flash of wondering comprehension, a flicker of wry sympathy, then appeared in the waiter's eyes? I walked upstairs to the deck.

There was a breeze from the water but the sun was hot and made me remember how ugly New York summers could be. All of the deck chairs had been taken away and people milled about in the space where the deck chairs had been, moved from one side of the ship to the other, clambered up and down the steps, crowded the rails, and they were busy taking photographs — of the harbor, of each other, of the sea, of the gulls. I walked slowly along the deck, and an impulse stronger than myself drove me to the rail. There it was, the great, unfinished city, with all its towers blazing in the sun. It came toward us slowly and patiently, like some enormous, cunning, and murderous beast, ready to devour, impossible to escape. I watched it come closer and I listened to the people around me, to their excitement and their pleasure. There was no doubt that it was real. I watched their shining faces and wondered if I were mad. For a moment I longed, with all my heart, to be able to feel whatever they were feeling, if only to know what such a feeling was like. As the boat moved slowly into the harbor, they were being moved into safety. It was only I who was being floated into danger. I turned my head, looking for Europe, but all that stretched behind me was the sky, thick with gulls. I moved away from the rail. A big, sandy-haired man held his daughter on his shoulders, showing her the Statue of Liberty. I would never know what this statue meant to others, she had always been an ugly joke for me. And the American flag was flying from the top of the ship, above my head. I had seen the French flag drive the French into the most unspeakable frenzies, I had seen the flag which was nominally mine used to dignify the vilest purposes: now I would never, as long as I lived, know what others saw when they saw a flag. "There's no place like home," said a voice close by, and I thought, *There damn sure isn't.* I decided to go back to my cabin and have a drink.

There was a cablegram from Harriet in my cabin. It said: Be good. Be quick. I'm waiting. I folded it carefully and put it in my breast pocket. Then I wondered if I would ever get back to her.

How long would it take me to earn the money to get out of this land? Sweat broke out on my forehead and I poured myself some whisky from my nearly empty bottle. I paced the tiny cabin. It was silent. There was no one down in the cabins now.

I was not sober when I faced the uniforms in the first-class lounge. There were two of them; they were not unfriendly. They looked at my passport, they looked at me. "You've been away a long time," said one of them.

"Yes," I said, "it's been a while."

"What did you do over there all that time?" — with a grin meant to hide more than it revealed, which hideously revealed more than it could hide.

I said, "I'm a singer," and the room seemed to rock around me. I held on to what I hoped was a calm, open smile. I had not had to deal with these faces in so long that I had forgotten how to do it. I had once known how to pitch my voice precisely between curtness and servility, and known what razor's edge of a pickaninny's smile would turn away wrath. But I had forgotten all the tricks on which my life had once depended. Once I had been an expert at baffling these people, at setting their teeth on edge, and dancing just outside the trap laid for me. But I was not an expert now. These faces were no longer merely the faces of two white men, who were my enemies. They were the faces of two white people whom I did not understand, and I could no longer plan my moves in accordance with what I knew of their cowardice and their needs and their strategy. That moment on the bridge had undone me forever.

"That's right," said one of them, "that's what it says, right here on the passport. Never heard of you, though." They looked up at me. "Did you do a lot of singing over there?"

"Some."

"What kind — concerts?"

"No." I wondered what I looked like, sounded like. I could tell nothing from their eyes. "I worked a few night clubs."

"Night clubs, eh? I guess they liked you over there."

"Yes," I said, "they seemed to like me all right."

"Well"— and my passport was stamped and handed back to me — "let's hope they like you over here."

"Thanks." They laughed — was it at me, or was it my imagination? — and I picked up the one bag I was carrying and threw my trench coat over one shoulder and walked out of the first-class lounge. I stood in the slow-moving, murmuring line which led to the gangplank. I looked straight ahead and watched heads, smiling faces, step up to the shadow of the gangplank awning and then swiftly descend out of sight. I put my passport back in my breast pocket — *Be quick. I'm waiting* — and I held my landing card in my hand. Then, suddenly, there I was, standing on the edge of the boat, staring down the long ramp to the ground. At the end of the plank, on the ground, stood a heavy man in a uniform. His cap was pushed back from his gray hair and his face was red and wet. He looked up at me. This was the face I remembered, the face of my nightmares; perhaps hatred had caused me to know this face better than I would ever know the face of any lover. "Come on, boy," he cried, "come on, come on!"

And I almost smiled. I was home. I touched my breast pocket. I thought of a song I sometimes sang, *When will I ever get to be a man?* I came down the gangplank, stumbling a little, and gave the man my landing card.

Much later in the day, a customs inspector checked my baggage and waved me away. I picked up my bags and started walking down the long stretch which led to the gate, to the city.

And I heard someone call my name.

I looked up and saw Louisa running toward me. I dropped my bags and grabbed her in my arms and tears came to my eyes and rolled down my face. I did not know whether the tears were for joy at seeing her, or from rage, or both.

"How are you? How are you? You look wonderful, but, oh, haven't you lost weight? It's wonderful to see you again."

I wiped my eyes. "It's wonderful to see you, too, I bet you thought I was never coming back."

Louisa laughed. "I wouldn't have blamed you if you hadn't. These people are just as corny as ever, I swear I don't believe there's any hope for them. How's your French? Lord, when I think that it was I who studied French and now I can't speak a word. And you never went near it and you probably speak it like a native."

I grinned. *"Pas mat. Je me défend pas mal."* We started down the wide steps into the street. "My God," I said. "New York." I was not aware of its towers now. We were in the shadow of the elevated highway but the thing which most struck me was neither light nor shade, but noise. It came from a million things at once, from trucks and tires and clutches and brakes and doors; from machines shuttling and stamping and rolling and cutting and pressing; from the building of tunnels, the checking of gas mains, the laying of wires, the digging of foundations; from the chattering of rivets, the scream of the pile driver, the clanging of great shovels; from the battering down and the raising up of walls; from millions of radios and television sets and jukeboxes. The human voices distinguished themselves from the roar only by their note of strain and hostility. Another fleshy man, uniformed and red-faced, hailed a cab for us and touched his cap politely but could only manage a peremptory growl: "Right this way, miss. Step up, sir." He slammed the cab door behind us. Louisa directed the driver to the New Yorker Hotel.

"Do they take us there?"

She looked at me. "They got laws in New York, honey, it'd be the easiest thing in the world to spend all your time in court. But over at the New Yorker, I believe they've already got the message." She took my arm. "You see? In spite of all this chopping and booming, this place hasn't really changed very much. You still can't hear yourself talk."

And I thought to myself, Maybe that's the point.

Early the next morning we checked out of the hotel and took the plane for Alabama.

I am just stepping out of the shower when I hear the bell ring. I dry myself hurriedly and put on a bathrobe. It is Vidal, of course, and very elegant he is, too, with his bushy gray hair quite lustrous, his swarthy, cynical, gypsylike face shaved and lotioned. Usually he looks just any old way. But tonight his brief bulk is contained in a dark-blue suit and he has an ironical pearl stickpin in his blue tie.

"Come in, make yourself a drink. I'll be with you in a second."

"I am, *hélas!,* on time. I trust you will forgive me for my thoughtlessness."

But I am already back in the bathroom. Vidal puts on a record: Mahalia Jackson, singing *I'm Going to Live the Life I Sing About in My Song.*

When I am dressed, I find him sitting in a chair before the open window. The daylight is gone, but it is not exactly dark. The trees are black now against the darkening sky. The lights in windows and the lights of motorcars are yellow and ringed. The street lights have not yet been turned on. It is as though, out of deference to the departed day, Paris waited a decent interval before assigning her role to a more theatrical but inferior performer.

Vidal is drinking a whisky and soda. I pour myself a drink. He watches me.

"Well. How are you, my friend? You are nearly gone. Are you happy to be leaving us?"

"No." I say this with more force than I had intended. Vidal raises his eyebrows, looking amused and distant. "I never really intended to go back there. I certainly never intended to raise my kid there —"

"Mais, man cher," Vidal says, calmly, "you are an intelligent man, you must have known that you would probably be returning one day." He pauses. "And, as for Pauli — did it never occur to you that he might wish one day to see the country in which his father and his father's fathers were born?"

"To do that, really, he'd have to go to Africa."

"America will always mean more to him than Africa, you know that."

"I don't know." I throw my drink down and pour myself another. "Why should he want to cross all that water just to be called a nigger? America never gave him anything."

"It gave him his father."

I look at him. "You mean, his father escaped."

Vidal throws back his head and laughs. If Vidal likes you, he is certain to laugh at you and his laughter can be very unnerving But the look, the silence which follow this laughter can be very unnerving, too. And, now, in the silence, he asks me, "Do you really think that you have escaped anything? Come. I know you for a better man than that." He walks to the table which holds the liquor. "In that movie of ours which has made you so famous, and, as I now see, so troubled, what are you playing, after all? What is the tragedy of this half-breed troubadour if not, precisely, that he has taken all the possible roads to escape and that all these roads have failed him?" He pauses, with the bottle in one hand, and looks at me. "Do you remember the trouble I had to get a performance out of you? How you hated me, you sometimes looked as though you wanted to shoot me! And do you remember when the role of Chico began to come alive?" He pours his drink. "Think back, remember. I am a very great director, *mais pardon!* I could not have got such a performance out of anyone but you. And what were you thinking of, what was in your mind, what nightmare were you living with when you began, at last, to play the role — truthfully?" He walks back to his seat.

Chico, in the film, is the son of a Martinique woman and a French *colon* who hates both his mother and his father. He flees from the island to the capital, carrying his hatred with him. This hatred has now grown, naturally, to include all dark women and all white men, in a word, everyone. He descends into the underworld of Paris, where he dies. *Les fauves* — the wild beasts — refers to the life he has fled and to the life which engulfs him. When I agreed to do the role, I felt that I could probably achieve it by bearing in mind the North Africans I had watched in Paris for so long. But this did not please Vidal. The blowup came while we were rehearsing a fairly simple, straightforward scene. Chico goes into a sleazy Pigalle dance hall to beg the French owner for a particularly humiliating job. And this Frenchman reminds him of his father.

"You are playing this boy as though you thought of him as the noble savage," Vidal said, icily. *"Ça verit d'où* — all these ghastly mannerisms you are using all the time?"

Everyone fell silent, for Vidal rarely spoke this way. This silence told me that everyone, the actor with whom I was playing the scene and all the people in the "dance hall," shared Vidal's opinion of my performance and was relieved that he was going to do something about it. I was humiliated and too angry to speak; but perhaps I also felt, at the very bottom of my heart, a certain relief, an unwilling respect.

"You are doing it all wrong," he said, more gently. Then, "Come, let us have a drink together."

We walked into his office. He took a bottle and two glasses out of his desk. "Forgive me, but you put me in mind of some of those English *lady* actresses who love to play *putain* as long as it is always absolutely clear to the audience that they are really ladies. So perhaps they read a book, not usually, *hélas!, Fanny Hill*, and they have their chauffeurs drive them through Soho once or twice — and they come to the stage with a performance so absolutely loaded with detail, every bit of it meaningless, that there can be no doubt that they are acting. It is what the British call a triumph." He poured two cognacs. "That is what you are doing. Why? Who do you think this boy is, what do you think he is feeling, when he asks for this job?" He watched me carefully and I bitterly resented his look. "You come from America. The situation is not so pretty there for boys like you. I know you may not have been as poor as — as some — but is it really impossible for you to understand what a boy like Chico feels? Have you never, yourself, been in a similar position?"

I hated him for asking the question because I knew he knew the answer to it. "I would have had to be a very lucky black man not to have been in such a position."

"You would have had to be a very lucky *man."*

"Oh, God," I said, "please don't give me any of this equality-in-anguish business."

"It is perfectly possible," he said, sharply, "that there is not another kind."

Then he was silent. He sat down behind his desk. He cut a cigar and lit it. puffing up clouds of smoke, as though to prevent us from seeing each other too clearly. "Consider this," he said. "I am a French director who has never seen your country. I have never done you any harm, except, perhaps, historically — I mean, because I am white — but I cannot be blamed for that —"

"But *I* can be," I said, "and I am! I've never understood why, if *I* have to pay for the history written in the color of my skin, *you* should get off scot-free!" But I was surprised at my vehemence, I had not known I was going to say these things, and by the fact that I was trembling and from the way he looked at me I knew that, from a professional point of view anyway, I was playing into his hands.

"What makes you think I *do?"* His face looked weary and stern. "I am a Frenchman. Look at France. You think that I — we — are not paying for our history?" He walked to the window, staring out at the rather grim little town in which the studio was located. "If it is revenge that you want, well, then, let me tell you, you will have it. You will probably have it, whether you want it or not, our stupidity will make it inevitable." He turned back into the room. "But I beg you not to confuse me with the happy people of your country, who scarcely know that there is such a thing as history and so, naturally, imagine that they can escape, as you put it, scot-free. That is what you are doing, that is what I was about to say. I was about to say that I am a French director and I have never been in your country and I have never done you any harm — but you are not talking to that man, in this room, now. You are not talking to Jean Luc Vidal, but to some other white man, whom you remember, who has nothing to do with me." He paused and went back to his desk. "Oh, most of the time you are not like this, I know. But it is there all the time, it must be, because when you are upset, this is what comes out. So you are not playing Chico truthfully, you are lying about him, and I will not let you do it. When you go back, now, and play this scene again, I want you to remember what has just happened in this room. You brought your past into this room. That is what Chico does when he walks into the dance hall. The Frenchman whom he begs for a job is not merely a Frenchman — he is the father who disowned and betrayed him and all the Frenchmen whom he hates." He smiled and poured me another cognac. "Ah! If it were not for *my* history, I would not have so much trouble to get the truth out of you." He looked into my face, half smiling. "And you, you are angry — are you not? — that I *ask* you for the truth. You think I have no right to ask." Then he said something which he knew would enrage me. "Who are you then, and what good has it done you to come to France, and how will you raise your son? Will you teach him never to tell the truth to anyone?" And he moved behind his desk and looked at me, as though from behind a barricade.

"You have no right to talk to me this way."

"Oh, yes, I do," he said. "I have a film to make and a reputation to maintain and I am going to get a performance out of you." He looked at his watch. "Let us go back to work."

I watch him now, sitting quietly in my living room, tough, cynical, crafty old Frenchman, and I wonder if he knows that the nightmare at the bottom of my mind, as I played the role of Chico, was all the possible fates of Paul. This is but another way of saying that I relived the disasters which had nearly undone me; but, because I was thinking of Paul. I discovered that I did not want my son ever to feel toward me as I had felt toward my own father. He had died when I was eleven, but I had watched the humiliations he had to bear, and I had pitied him. But was there not, in that pity, however painfully and unwillingly, also some contempt? For how could I *know* what he had borne? I knew only that I was his son. However he had loved me, whatever he had borne, I, his son, was despised. Even had he lived, he could have done nothing to prevent it, nothing to protect me. The best that he could hope to do was to prepare me for it; and even at that he had failed. How can one be prepared for the spittle in the face, all the tireless ingenuity which goes into the spite and fear of small, unutterably miserable people, whose greatest terror is the singular identity, whose joy, whose safety, is entirely dependent on the humiliation and anguish of others?

But for Paul, I swore it, such a day would never come. I would throw my life and my work between Paul and the nightmare of the world. I would make it impossible for the world to treat Paul as it had treated my father and me.

Mahalia's record ends. Vidal rises to turn it over. "Well?" He looks at me very affectionately. "Your nightmares, please!"

"Oh, I was thinking of that summer I spent in Alabama, when my mother died." I stop. "You know, but when we finally filmed that bar scene, I was thinking of New York. I was scared in Alabama, but I almost went crazy in New York. I was sure I'd never make it back here — back here to Harriet. And I knew if I didn't, it was going to be the end of me." Now Mahalia is singing *When the Saints Go Marching In.* "I got a job in the town as an elevator boy, in the town's big department store. It was a special favor, one of my father's white friends got it for me. For a long time, in the South, we all — depended — on the — *kindness* — of white friends." I take out a handkerchief and wipe my face. "But this man didn't like me. I guess I didn't seem grateful enough, wasn't enough like my father, what he thought my father was. And I couldn't get used to the town again, I'd been away too long, I hated it. It's a terrible town, anyway, the whole thing looks as though it's been built around a jailhouse. There's a room in the courthouse, a room where they beat you up. Maybe you're walking along the street one night, it's usually at night, but it happens in the daytime, too. And the police car comes up behind you and the cop says, Hey, boy. Come on over here. So you go on over. He says, Boy, I believe you drunk. And, you see, if you say, No, no sir, he'll beat you because you're calling him a liar. And if you say anything else, unless it's something to make him laugh, he'll take you in and beat you, just for fun. The trick is to think of some way for them to have their fun without beating you up."

The street lights of Paris click on and turn all the green leaves silver. "Or to go along with the ways *they* dream up. And they'll do anything, anything at all, to prove that you're no better than a dog and to make you feel like one. And they hated me because I'd been North and I'd been to Europe. People kept saying, I hope you didn't bring no foreign notions back here with you, boy. And I'd say, No sir, or No ma'am, but I never said it right. And there was a time, all of them remembered it, when I *had* said it right. But now they could tell that I despised them — I guess, no matter what, I wanted them to know that I despised them. But I didn't despise them any more than everyone else did, only the others never let it show. They knew how to keep the white folks happy, and it was easy — you just had to keep them feeling like they were God's favor to the universe. They'd walk around with great, big, foolish grins on their faces and the colored folks loved to see this, because they hated them so much. "Just look at So-and-So," somebody'd say. "His white is *on* him today." And when we didn't hate them, we pitied them. In America, that's usually what it means to have a white friend. You pity the poor bastard because he was born believing the world's a great place to be, and you know it's not, and you can see that he's going to have a terrible time getting used to this idea, if he *ever* gets used to it."

Then I think of Paul again, those eyes which still imagine that I can do anything, that skin, the color of honey and fire, his jet-black, curly hair. I look out at Paris again, and I listen to Mahalia, "Maybe it's better to have the terrible times first. I don't know. Maybe, then, you can have, *if* you live, a better life, a real life, because you had to fight so hard to get it away — you know? — from the mad dog who held it in his teeth. But then your file has all those tooth marks, too, all those tatters, and all that blood." I walk to the bottle and raise it. "One for the road?"

"Thank you," says Vidal.

I pour us a drink, and he watches me. I have never talked so much before, not about those things anyway. I know that Vidal has nightmares, because he knows so much about them, but he has never told me what his are. I think that he probably does not talk about his nightmares any more. I know that the war cost him his wife and his son, and that he was in prison in Germany. He very rarely refers to it. He has a married daughter who lives in England, and he rarely speaks of her. He is like a man who has learned to live on what is left of an enormous fortune.

We are silent for a moment.

"Please go on," he says, with a smile. "I am curious about the reality behind the reality of your performance."

"My sister, Louisa, never married," I say, abruptly, "because, once, years ago. she and the boy she was going with and two friends of theirs were out driving in a car and the police stopped them. The girl who was with them was very fair and the police pretended not to believe her when she said she was colored. They made her get out and stand in front of the headlights of the car and pull down her pants and raise her dress — they said that was the only way they could be sure. And you can imagine what they said, and what they did — and they were lucky, at that, that it didn't go any further. But none of the men could do anything about it. Louisa couldn't face that boy again, and I guess he couldn't face her." Now it is really growing dark in the room and I cross to the light switch. "You know, I know what that boy felt, I've felt it. They want you to feel that you're not a man, maybe that's the only way they can feel like men, I don't know. I walked around New York with Harriet's cablegram in my pocket as though it were some atomic secret, in *code,* and they'd kill me if they ever found out what it meant. You know, there's something wrong with people like that. And thank God Harriet was here, *she proved* that the world was bigger than the world they wanted me to five in, I *had* to get back here, get to a place where people were too busy with their own lives, *their private lives*, to make fantasies about mine, to set up walls around mine." I look at him. The light in the room has made the night outside blue-black and golden and the great searchlight of the Eiffel Tower is turning in the sky. "That's what it's like in America, for me, anyway. I always feel that I don't exist there, except in someone else's — usually dirty —mind. I don't know if you know what that means, but I do, and I don't want to put Harriet through that and I don't want to raise Paul there."

"Well," he says at last, "you are not required to remain in America forever, are you? You will sing in that elegant club which apparently feels that it cannot, much longer, so much as open its doors without you, and you will probably accept the movie offer, you would be very foolish not to. You will make a lot of money. Then, one day, you will remember that airlines and steamship companies are still in business and that France still exists. *That* will certainly be cause for astonishment."

Vidal was a Gaullist before De Gaulle came to power. But he regrets the manner of De Gaulle's rise and he is worried about De Gaulle's regime. "It is not the fault of *mon general*," he sometimes says, sadly. "Perhaps it is history's fault. I *suppose* it must be history which always arranges to bill a civilization at the very instant it is least prepared to pay."

Now he rises and walks out on the balcony, as though to reassure himself of the reality of Paris. Mahalia is singing *Didn't It Rain?* I walk out and stand beside him.

"You are a good boy — Chico," he says. I laugh. "You believe in love. You do not know all the things love cannot do, but" — he smiles — "love will teach you that."

We go, after dinner, to a Left Bank *discothèque* which can charge outrageous prices because Marlon Brando wandered in there one night. By accident, according to Vidal. "Do you know how many people in Paris are becoming rich — to say nothing of those, *hélas!,* who are going broke — on the off chance that Marlon Brando will lose his way again?"

He has not, presumably, lost his way tonight, but the *discothèque* is crowded with those strangely faceless people who are part of the night life of all great cities, and who always arrive, moments, hours, or decades late, on the spot made notorious by an event or a movement or a handful of personalities. So here are American boys, anything but beardless, scratching around for Hemingway; American girls, titillating themselves with Frenchmen and existentialism, while waiting for the American boys to shave off their beards; French painters, busily pursuing the revolution which ended thirty years ago; and the young, bored, perverted, American *arrivistes* who are buying their way into the art world via flattery and liquor, and the production of canvases as arid as their greedy little faces. Here are boys, of all nations, one step above the pimp, who are occasionally walked across a stage or trotted before a camera. And the girls, their enemies, whose faces are sometimes seen in ads, one of whom will surely have a tantrum before the evening is out.

In a corner, as usual, surrounded, as usual, by smiling young men, sits the drunken blonde woman who was once the mistress of a famous, dead painter. She is a figure of some importance in the art world, and so rarely has to pay for either her drinks or her lovers. An older Frenchman, who was once a famous director, is playing *quatre cent vingt-et-un* with the woman behind the cash register. He nods pleasantly to Vidal and me as we enter, but makes no move to join us, and I respect him for this. Vidal and I are obviously cast tonight in the role vacated by Brando; our entrance justifies the prices and sends a kind of shiver through the room. It is marvelous to watch the face of the waiter as he approaches, all smiles and deference and grace, not so much honored by our presence as achieving his reality from it; excellence, he seems to be saying, gravitates naturally toward excellence. We order two whisky and sodas. I know why Vidal sometimes comes here. He is lonely. I do not think that he expects ever to love one woman again, and so he distracts himself with many.

Since this is a *discothèque,* jazz is blaring from the walls and record sleeves are scattered about with a devastating carelessness. Two of them are mine and no doubt, presently, someone will play the recording of the songs I sang in the film.

"I thought," says Vidal, with a malicious little smile, "that your farewell to Paris would not be complete without a brief exposure to the perils of fame. Perhaps it will help prepare you for America, where, I am told, the populace is yet more carnivorous than it is here."

I can see that one of the vacant models is preparing herself to come to our table and ask for an autograph, hoping, since she is pretty — she has, that is, the usual female equipment, dramatized in the usual, modern way — to be invited for a drink. Should the maneuver succeed, one of her boy friends or girl friends will contrive to come by the table, asking for a light or a pencil or a lipstick, and it will be extremely difficult not to invite this person to join us, too. Before the evening ends, we will be surrounded. I don't, now, know what I expected of fame, but I suppose it never occurred to me that the light could be just as dangerous, just as killing, as the dark.

"Well, let's make it brief," I tell him. "Sometimes I wish that you weren't quite so fond of me."

He laughs. "There are some very interesting people here tonight. Look."

Across the room from us. and now staring at our table, are a group of American Negro students, who are probably visiting Paris for the first time. There are four of them, two boys and two girls, and I suppose that they must be in their late teens or early twenties. One of the boys, a gleaming, curly-haired, golden-brown type — the color of his mother's fried chicken — is carrying a guitar. When they realize we have noticed them, they smile and wave — wave as though I were one of their possessions, as, indeed, I am. Golden-brown is a mime. He raises his guitar, drops his shoulders, and his face falls into the lugubrious lines of Chico's face as he approaches death. He strums a little of the film's theme music, and I laugh and the table laughs. It is as though we were all back home and had met for a moment, on a Sunday morning, say, before a church or a poolroom or a barbershop.

And they have created a sensation in the *discothèque*, naturally, having managed, with no effort whatever, to outwit all the gleaming boys and girls. Their table, which had been of no interest only a moment before, has now become the focus of a rather pathetic attention; their smiles have made it possible for the others to smile, and to nod in our direction.

"Oh," says Vidal, "he does that far better than you ever did. Perhaps I will make him a star."

"Feel free, *m'sieu, le bon Dieu,* I got mine!" But I can see that his attention has really been caught by one of the girls, slim, tense, and dark, who seems, though it is hard to know how one senses such things, to be treated by the others with a special respect. And, in fact, the table now seems to be having a council of war, to be demanding her opinion or her cooperation. She listens, frowning, laughing; the quality, the force of her intelligence causes her face to keep changing all the time, as though a light played on it. And, presently, with a gesture she might once have used to scatter feed to chickens, she scoops up from the floor one of those dangling rag bags women love to carry. She holds it loosely by the drawstrings, so that it is banging somewhere around her ankle, and walks over to our table. She has an honest, forthright walk, entirely unlike the calculated, pelvic workout by means of which most women get about. She is small, but sturdily, economically, put together.

As she reaches our table, Vidal and I rise, and this throws her for a second. (It has been a long time since I have seen such an attractive girl.)

Also, everyone, of course, is watching us. It is really a quite curious moment. They have put on the record of Chico singing a sad, angry Martinique ballad: my own voice is coming at us from the walls as the girl looks from Vidal to me, and smiles.

"I guess you know," she says, "we weren't *about* to let you get out of here without bugging you just a little bit. We've only been in Paris just a couple of days and we thought for sure that we wouldn't have a chance of running into you anywhere, because it's in all the papers that you're coming home."

"Yes," I say, "yes. I'm leaving the day after tomorrow."

"Oh!" She grins. " Then we really *are* lucky." I find that I have almost forgotten the urchinlike grin of a colored girl, "I guess, before I keep babbling on, I'd better introduce myself. My name is Ada Holmes."

We shake hands. "This is Monsieur Vidal, the director of the film."

"I'm very honored to meet you, sir."

"Will you join us for a moment? Won't you sit down?" And Vidal pulls a chair out for her.

But she frowns contritely. "I really ought to get back to my friends." She looks at me. "I really just came over to say, for myself and all the kids, that we've got your records and we've seen your movie, and it means so much to us" — and she laughs, breathlessly, nervously, it is somehow more moving than tears — "more than I can say. Much more. And we wanted to know if you and your friend" — she looks at Vidal — "your *director,* Monsieur Vidal, would allow us to buy you a drink? We'd be very honored if you would."

"It is we who are honored," says Vidal, promptly, "*and* grateful. We were getting terribly bored with one another, thank God you came along."

The three of us laugh, and we cross the room.

The three at the table rise, and Ada makes the introductions. The other girl, taller and paler than Ada, is named Ruth. One of the boys is named Talley — "short for Talliafero" — and Golden-brown's name is Pete. "Man," he tells me, "I dig you the most. You tore me up, baby, tore me *up*."

"You tore up a lot of people," Talley says, cryptically, and he and Ruth laugh. Vidal does not know, but I do, that Talley is probably referring to white people.

They are from New Orleans and Tallahassee and North Carolina; are college students, and met on the boat. They have been in Europe all summer, in Italy and Spain, but are only just getting to Paris.

"We meant to come sooner," says Ada, "but we could never make up our minds to leave a place. I thought we'd never pry Ruth loose from Venice."

"I resigned myself," says Pete, "and just sat in the Piazza San Marco, drinking gin fizz and being photographed with the pigeons, while Ruth had herself driven *all* up and down the Grand Canal." He looks at Ruth. "Finally, thank heaven, it rained."

"She was working off her hostilities," says Ada, with a grin. "We thought we might as well let her do it in Venice, the opportunities in North Carolina are really terribly limited."

"There are some very upset people walking around down there," Ruth says, "and a couple of tours around the Grand Canal might do them a world of good."

Pete laughs. "Can't you just see Ruth escorting them to the edge of the water?"

"I haven't lifted my hand in anger yet," Ruth says, "but, oh, Lord," and she laughs, clenching and unclenching her fists.

"You haven't been back for a long time, have you?" Talley asks me.

"Eight years. I haven't really lived there for twelve years."

Pete whistles. "I fear you are in for some surprises, my friend. There have been some changes made." Then, "Are you afraid?"

"A little."

"We all are," says Ada, "that's why I was so glad to get away for a little while."

"Then you haven't been back since Black Monday," Talley says. He laughs. "That's how it's gone down in Confederate history." He turns to Vidal. "What do people think about it here?"

Vidal smiles, delighted. "It seems extraordinarily infantile behavior, even for Americans, from whom, I must say, I have never expected very much in the way of maturity." Everyone at the table laughs. Vidal goes on. "But I cannot really talk about it, I do not understand it. I have never really understood Americans; I am an old man now, and I suppose I never will. There is something very nice about them, something very winning, but they seem so ignorant — so ignorant of life. Perhaps it is strange, but the only people from your country with whom I have ever made contact are black people — like my good friend, my discovery, here," and he slaps me on the shoulder. "Perhaps it is because we, in Europe, whatever else we do not know, or have forgotten, know about suffering. We have suffered here. You have suffered, too. But most Americans do not yet know what anguish is. It is too bad, because the life of the West is in their hands." He turns to Ada. "I cannot help saying that I think it is a scandal —and we may all pay very dearly for it — that a civilized nation should elect to represent it a man who is so simple that he thinks the world is simple." And silence falls at the table and the four young faces stare at him.

"Well," says Pete, at last, turning to me, "you won't be bored, man, when you get back there."

"It's much too nice a night," I say, "to stay cooped up in this place, where all I can hear is my own records." We laugh. "Why don't we get out of here and find a sidewalk café?" I tap Pete's guitar. "Maybe we can find out if you've got any talent."

"Oh, talent I've got," says Pete, "but character, man, I'm lacking."

So, after some confusion about the bill, for which Vidal has already made himself responsible, we walk out into the Paris night. It is very strange to feel that, very soon now, these boulevards will not exist for me. People will be walking up and down, as they are tonight, and lovers will be murmuring in the black shadows of the plane trees, and there will be these same still figures on the benches or in the parks — but they will not exist for me, I will not be here. For a long while Paris will no longer exist for me, except in my mind; and only in the minds of some people will I exist any longer for Paris. After departure, only invisible things are left, perhaps the life of the world is held together by invisible chains of memory and loss and love. So many things, so many people, depart! and we can only repossess them in our minds. Perhaps this is what the old folks meant, what my mother and my father meant, when they counseled us to keep the faith.

We have taken a table at the Deux Magots and Pete strums on his guitar and begins to play this song:

Preach the word, preach the word, preach the word!
If I never, never see you any more.
Preach the word, preach the word.
And I'll meet you on Canaan's shore.

He has a strong, clear, boyish voice, like a young preacher's, and he is smiling as he sings his song. Ada and I look at each other and grin, and Vidal is smiling. The waiter looks a little worried, for we are already beginning to attract a crowd, but it is a summer night, the gendarmes on the corner do not seem to mind, and there will be time, anyway, to stop us.

Pete was not there, none of us were, the first time this song was needed; and no one now alive can imagine what that time was like. But the song has come down the bloodstained ages. I suppose this to mean that the song is still needed, still has its work to do. The others are all, visibly, very proud of Pete; and we all join him, and people stop to listen:

Testify! Testify!
If I never, never see you any more!
Testify! Testify!
I'll meet you on Canaan's shore!

In the crowd that has gathered to listen to us, I see a face I know, the face of a North African prize fighter, who is no longer in the ring. I used to know him well in the old days, but have not seen him for a long time. He looks quite well, his face is shining, he is quite decently dressed. And something about the way he holds himself, not quite looking at our table, tells me that he has seen me, but does not want to risk a rebuff. So I call him. "Boona!"

And he turns, smiling, and comes loping over to our table, his hands in his pockets. Pete is still singing and Ada and Vidal have taken off on a conversation of their own. Ruth and Talley look curiously, expectantly, at Boona. Now that I have called him over, I feel somewhat uneasy. I realize that I do not know what he is doing now, or how he will get along with any of these people, and I can see in his eyes that he is delighted to be in the presence of two young girls. There are virtually no North African women in Paris, and not even the dirty, rat-faced girls who live, apparently, in cafés are willing to go with an Arab. So Boona is always looking for a girl, and because he is so deprived and because he is not Western, his techniques can be very unsettling. I know he is relieved that the girls are not French and not white. He looks briefly at Vidal and Ada. Vidal, also, though for different reasons, is always looking for a girl.

But Boona has always been very nice to me. Perhaps I am sorry that I called him over, but I did not want to snub him.

He claps one hand to the side of my head, as is his habit. "*Comment vas-tu, mon frère?* I have not see you, oh, for long time." And he asks me, as in the old days, "You all right? Nobody bother you?" And he laughs. "Ah! *Tu as fait le chemin, toi!* Now you are *vedette*, big star — wonderful!" He looks around the table, made a little uncomfortable by the silence that has fallen, now that Pete has stopped singing. "I have seen you in the movies — you know? — and I tell everybody, I know *him!*" He points to me, and laughs, and Ruth and Talley laugh with him. "That's right, man, you make me real proud, you make me cry!"

"Boona, I want you to meet some friends of mine." And I go round the table: "Ruth, Talley, Ada, Pete" — and he bows and shakes hands, his dark eyes gleaming with pleasure — *"et Monsieur Vidal, le metteur en scène du film qui t'a arraché des larmes."*

"*Enchanté.*" But his attitude toward Vidal is colder, more distrustful. "Of course I have heard of Monsieur Vidal. He is the director of many films, many of them made me cry." This last statement is utterly, even insolently, insincere.

But Vidal, I think, is relieved that I will now be forced to speak to Boona and will leave him alone with Ada.

"Sit down," I say, "have a drink with us, let me have your news. What's been happening with you, what are you doing with yourself these days?"

"Ah," he sits down, "nothing very brilliant, my brother." He looks at me quickly, with a little smile. "You know, we have been having hard times here."

"Where are you from?" Ada asks him.

His brilliant eyes take her in entirely, but she does not flinch. "I am from Tunis." He says it proudly, with a little smile.

"From Tunis. I have never been to Africa, I would love to go one day."

He laughs. "Africa is a big place. Very big. There are many countries in Africa, many" — he looks briefly at Vidal — "different kinds of people, many colonies."

"But Tunis," she continues, in her innocence, "is free? Freedom is happening all over Africa. That's why I would like to go there."

"I have not been back for a long time," says Boona, "but all the news I get from Tunis, from my people, is not good."

"Wouldn't you like to go back?" Ruth asks.

Again he looks at Vidal. "That is not so easy."

Vidal smiles. "You know what I would like to do? There's a wonderful Spanish place not far from here, where we can listen to live music and dance a little." He turns to Ada. "Would you like that?"

He is leaving it up to me to get rid of Boona, and it is, of course, precisely for this reason that I cannot do it. Besides, it is no longer so simple.

"Oh, I'd love that," says Ada, and she turns to Boona. "Won't you come, too?"

"Thank you, mam'selle," he says, softly, and his tongue flicks briefly over his lower lip, and he smiles. He is very moved, people are not often nice to him.

In the Spanish place there are indeed a couple of Spanish guitars, drums, castanets, and a piano, but the uses to which these are being put carry one back, as Pete puts it, to the levee. "These are the wailingest Spanish cats I ever heard," says Ruth. "They didn't learn how to do this in Spain, no, they didn't, they been rambling. You ever hear anything like this going on in Spain?" Talley takes her out on the dance floor, which is already crowded. A very handsome Frenchwoman is dancing with an enormous, handsome black man, who seems to be her lover, who seems to have taught her how to dance. Apparently, they are known to the musicians, who egg them on with small cries of "*Olé!*" It is a very goodnatured crowd, mostly foreigners, Spaniards, Swedes, Greeks. Boona takes Ada out on the dance floor while Vidal is answering some questions put to him by Pete on the entertainment situation in France. Vidal looks a little put out, and I am amused.

We are there for perhaps an hour, dancing, talking, and I am, at last, a little drunk. In spite of Boona, who is a very good and tireless dancer, Vidal continues his pursuit of Ada, and I begin to wonder if he will make it and I begin to wonder if I want him to.

I am still puzzling out my reaction when Pete, who has disappeared, comes in through the front door, catches my eye, and signals to me. I leave the table and follow him into the streets.

He looks very upset. "I don't want to bug you, man," he says, "but I fear your boy has goofed."

I know he is not joking. I think he is probably angry at Vidal because of Ada, and I wonder what I can do about it and why he should be telling me.

I stare at him, gravely, and he says, "It looks like he stole some money."

"Stole *money?* Who, Vidal?"

And then, of course, I get it, in the split second before he says, impatiently, "No, are you kidding? Your friend, the Tunisian."

I do not know what to say or what to do, and so I temporize with questions. All the time I am wondering if this can be true and what I can do about it if it is. The trouble is, I know that Boona steals, he would probably not be alive if he didn't, but I cannot say so to these children, who probably still imagine that everyone who steals is a thief. But he has never, to my knowledge, stolen from a friend. It seems unlike him. I have always thought of him as being better than that, and smarter than that. And so I cannot believe it, but neither can I doubt it. I do not know anything about Boona's life, these days. This causes me to realize that I do not really know much about Boona.

"Who did he steal it from?"

"From Ada. Out of her bag."

"How much?"

"Ten dollars. It's not an awful lot of money, but" — he grimaces — "none of us *have* an awful lot of money."

"I know." The dark side street on which we stand is nearly empty. The only sound on the street is the muffled music of the Spanish club. "How do you know it was Boona?"

He anticipates my own unspoken rejoinder. "Who else could it be? Besides — somebody *saw* him do it."

"Somebody saw him?"

"Yes."

I do not ask him who this person is, for fear that he will say it is Vidal.

"Well," I say, "I'll try to get it back." I think that I will take Boona aside and then replace the money myself. "Was it in dollars or in francs?"

"In francs."

I have no dollars and this makes it easier. I do not know how I can possibly face Boona and accuse him of stealing money from my friends. I would rather give him the benefit of even the faintest doubt. But, "Who saw him?" I ask.

"Talley. But we didn't want to make a thing about it —"

"Does Ada know it's gone?"

"Yes." He looks at me helplessly. "I know this makes you feel pretty bad, but we thought we'd better tell you, rather than"— lamely — "anybody else."

Now, Ada comes out of the club, carrying her ridiculous handbag, and with her lace all knotted and sad. "Oh," she says, "I hate to cause all this trouble, it's not worth it, not for ten lousy dollars."

I am astonished to see that she has been weeping, and tears come to her eyes now.

I put my arm around her shoulder. "Come on, now. You're not causing anybody any trouble and, anyway, it's nothing to cry about."

"It isn't your fault, Ada," Pete says, miserably.

"Oh, I ought to get a sensible handbag," she says, "like you're always telling me to do," and she laughs a little, then looks at me. "Please don't try to do anything about it. Let's just forget it."

"What's happening inside?" I ask her.

"Nothing. They're just talking. I think Mr. Vidal is dancing with Ruth. He's a great dancer, that little Frenchman."

"He's a great talker, too," Pete says.

"Oh, he doesn't mean anything," says Ada, "he's just having fun. He probably doesn't get a chance to talk to many American girls."

"He certainly made, up for lost time tonight."

"Look," I say, "if Talley and Boona are alone, maybe you better go back in. We'll be in in a minute. Let's try to keep this as quiet as we can."

"Yeah," he says, "okay. We're going soon anyway, okay?"

"Yes," she tells him, "right away."

But as he turns away, Boona and Talley step out into the street, and it is clear that Talley feels that he has Boona under arrest. I almost laugh, the whole thing is beginning to resemble one of those mad French farces with people flying in and out of doors; but Boona comes straight to me.

"They say I stole money, my friend. You know me, you are the only one here who knows me, you know I would not do such a thing."

I look at him and I do not know what to say. Ada looks at him with her eyes full of tears and looks away. I take Boona's arm.

"We'll be back in a minute," I say. We walk a few paces up the dark, silent street.

"She say I take her money," he says. He, too, looks as though he is about to weep — but I do not know for which reason. "You know me, you know me almost twelve years, you think I do such a thing?" Talley saw you. I want to say, but I cannot say it. Perhaps Talley only thought he saw him. Perhaps it is easy to see a boy who looks like Boona with his hand in an American girl's purse.

"If you not believe me," he says, "search me. Search me!" And he opens his arms wide, theatrically, and now there are tears standing in his eyes.

I do not know what his tears mean, but I certainly cannot search him. I want to say, I know you steal, I know you have to steal. Perhaps you took the money out of this girl's purse in order to eat tomorrow, in order not to be thrown into the streets tonight, in order to stay out of jail. This girl means nothing to you, after all, she is only an American, an American like me. Perhaps, I suddenly think, no girl means anything to you, or ever will again, they have beaten you too hard and kept you in the gutter too long. And I also think, If you would steal from her, then of course you would lie to me, neither of us means anything to you; perhaps, in your eyes, we are simply luckier gangsters in a world which is run by gangsters. But I cannot say any of these things to Boona. I cannot say, Tell me the truth, nobody cares about the money any more.

So I say, "Of course I will not search you." And I realize that he knew that I would not.

"I think it is that Frenchman who say I am a thief. They think we all are thieves." His eyes are bright and bitter. He looks over my shoulder. "They have all come out of the club now."

I look around and they are all there, in a little dark knot on the sidewalk.

"Don't worry," I say. "It doesn't matter."

"You believe me? My brother?" And his eyes look into mine with a terrible intensity.

"Yes," I force myself to say, "yes, of course, I believe you. Someone made a mistake, that's all."

"You know, the way American girls run around, they have their sack open all the time, she could lose the money anywhere. Why she blame me? Because I come from Africa?" Tears are glittering on his face. "Here she come now."

And Ada comes up the street with her straight, determined walk. She walks straight to Boona and takes his hand. "I am sorry," she says, "for everything that happened. Please believe me. It isn't worth all this fuss. I'm sure you're a very nice person, and" — she falters — "I must have lost the money, I'm sure I lost it." She looks at him. "It isn't worth hurting your feelings, and I'm terribly sorry about it."

"I no take your money," he says. "Really, truly, I no take it. Ask him" — pointing to me, grabbing me by the arm, shaking me — "he know me for years, he will tell you that I never, never steal!"

"I'm sure," she says. "I'm sure."

I take Boona by the arm again. "Let's forget it. Let's forget it all. We're all going home now, and one of these days we'll have a drink again and we'll forget all about it, all right?"

"Yes," says Ada, "let us forget it." And she holds out her hand.

Boona takes it, wonderingly. His eyes take her in again. "You are a very nice girl. Really. A very nice girl."

"I'm sure you're a nice person, too." She pauses. "Good night."

"Good night," he says, after a long silence.

Then he kisses me on both cheeks. "*Au revoir, mon frère.*"

"*Au revoir, Boona.*"

After a moment we turn and walk away, leaving him standing there.

"Did he take it?" asks Vidal.

"I tell you, I *saw* him," says Talley.

"Well," I say, "it doesn't matter now." I look back and see Boona's stocky figure disappearing down the street.

"No," says Ada, "it doesn't matter." She looks up. "It's almost morning."

"I would gladly," says Vidal, stammering, "gladly —"

But she is herself again. "I wouldn't think of it. We had a wonderful time tonight, a wonderful time, and I wouldn't think of it." She turns to me with that urchinlike grin. "It was wonderful meeting you. I hope you won't have too much trouble getting used to the States again."

"Oh, I don't think I will," I say. And then, "I hope you won't."

"No," she says, "I don't think anything they can do will surprise me any more."

"Which way are we all going?" asks Vidal. "I hope someone will share my taxi with me."

But he lives in the sixteenth arrondissement, which is not in anyone's direction. We walk him to the line of cabs standing under the clock at Odéon.

And we look each other in the face, in the growing morning light. His face looks weary and lined and lonely. He puts both hands on my shoulders and then puts one hand on the nape of my neck. "Do not forget me, Chico," he says. "You must come back and see us, one of these days. Many of us depend on you for many things."

"I'll be back," I say. "I'll never forget you."

He raises his eyebrows and smiles. "*Alors, adieu.*"

"*Adieu, Vidal.*"

"I was happy to meet all of you," he says. He looks at Ada. "Perhaps we will meet again before you leave."

"Perhaps," she says. "Good-by, Monsieur Vidal."

"Good-by."

Vidal's cab drives away. "I also leave you now," I say. "I must go home and wake up my son and prepare for our journey."

I leave them standing on the corner, under the clock, which points to six. They look very strange and lost and determined, the four of them. Just before my cab turns off the boulevard, I wave to them and they wave back.

Mme. Dumont is in the hall, mopping the floor.

"Did all my family get home?" I ask. I feel very cheerful, I do not know why.

"Yes," she says, "they are all here. Paul is still sleeping."

"May I go in and get him?"

She looks at me in surprise. "Of course."

So I walk into her apartment and walk into the room where Paul lies sleeping. I stand over his bed for a long time.

Perhaps my thoughts travel — travel through to him. He opens his eyes and smiles up at me. He puts a fist to his eyes and raises his arms. "*Bonjour, Papa.*"

I lift him up. "*Bonjour*. How do you feel today?"

"Oh, I don't know yet," he says.

I laugh. I put him on my shoulder and walk out into the hall. Mme. Dumont looks up at him with her radiant, aging face.

"Ah," she says, "you are going on a journey! How does it feel?"

"He doesn't know yet," I tell her. I walk to the elevator door and open it, dropping Paul down to the crook of my arm.

She laughs again. "He will know later. What a journey! *Jusqu'au nouveau monde!*"

I open the cage and we step inside. "Yes," I say, "all the way to the new world." I press the button and the cage, holding my son and me, goes up.

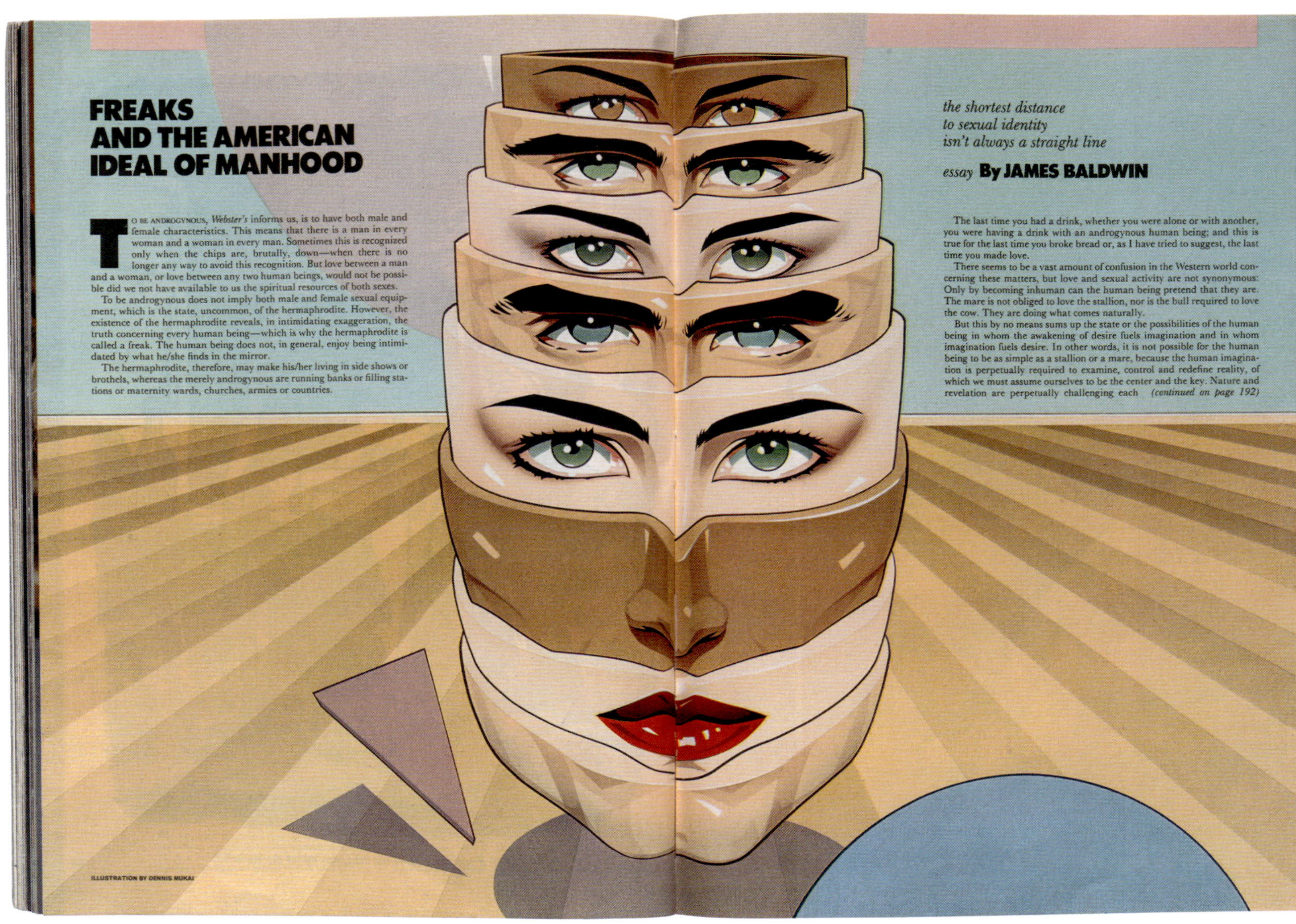

FREAKS AND THE AMERICAN IDEAL OF MANHOOD

the shortest distance to sexual identity isn't always a straight line

essay **By JAMES BALDWIN**

To be androgynous, *Webster's* informs us, is to have both male and female characteristics. This means that there is a man in every woman and a woman in every man. Sometimes this is recognized only when the chips are, brutally, down—when there is no longer any way to avoid this recognition. But love between a man and a woman, or love between any two human beings, would not be possible did we not have available to us the spiritual resources of both sexes.

To be androgynous does not imply both male and female sexual equipment, which is the state, uncommon, of the hermaphrodite. However, the existence of the hermaphrodite reveals, in intimidating exaggeration, the truth concerning every human being—which is why the hermaphrodite is called a freak. The human being does not, in general, enjoy being intimidated by what he/she finds in the mirror.

The hermaphrodite, therefore, may make his/her living in side shows or brothels, whereas the merely androgynous are running banks or filling stations or maternity wards, churches, armies or countries.

The last time you had a drink, whether you were alone or with another, you were having a drink with an androgynous human being; and this is true for the last time you broke bread or, as I have tried to suggest, the last time you made love.

There seems to be a vast amount of confusion in the Western world concerning these matters, but love and sexual activity are not synonymous: Only by becoming inhuman can the human being pretend that they are. The mare is not obliged to love the stallion, nor is the bull required to love the cow. They are doing what comes naturally.

But this by no means sums up the state or the possibilities of the human being in whom the awakening of desire fuels imagination and in whom imagination fuels desire. In other words, it is not possible for the human being to be as simple as a stallion or a mare, because the human imagination is perpetually required to examine, control and redefine reality, of which we must assume ourselves to be the center and the key. Nature and revelation are perpetually challenging each *(continued on page 192)*

ILLUSTRATION BY DENNIS MUKAI

Spread from **Playboy**, January 1985, featuring Baldwin's essay "Freaks and the American Ideal of Manhood"

Freaks and the American Ideal of Manhood

Playboy, January 1985

To be androgynous, Webster's informs us, is to have both male and female characteristics. This means that there is a man in every woman and a woman in every man. Sometimes this is recognized only when the chips are, brutally, down—when there is no longer any way to avoid this recognition. But love between a man and a woman, or love between any two human beings, would not be possible did we not have available to us the spiritual resources of both sexes.

To be androgynous does not imply both male and female sexual equipment, which is the state, uncommon, of the hermaphrodite. However, the existence of the hermaphrodite reveals, in intimidating exaggeration, the truth concerning every human being—which is why the hermaphrodite is called a freak. The human being does not, in general, enjoy being intimidated by what he/she finds in the mirror.

The hermaphrodite, therefore, may make his/her living in side shows or brothels, whereas the merely androgynous are running banks or filling stations or maternity wards, churches, armies or countries.

The last time you had a drink, whether you were alone or with another, you were having a drink with an androgynous human being; and this is true for the last time you broke bread or, as I have tried to suggest, the last time you made love.

There seems to be a vast amount of confusion in the Western world concerning these matters, but love and sexual activity are not synonymous: Only by becoming inhuman can the human being pretend that they are. The mare is not obliged to love the stallion, nor is the bull required to love the cow. They are doing what comes naturally.

But this by no means sums up the state or the possibilities of the human being in whom the awakening of desire fuels imagination and in whom imagination fuels desire. In other words, it is not possible for the human being to be as simple as a stallion or a mare, because the human imagination is perpetually required to examine, control and redefine reality, of which we must assume ourselves to be the center and the key. Nature and revelation are perpetually challenging each other; this relentless tension is one of the keys to human history and to what is known as the human condition.

Now, I can speak only of the Western world and must rely on my own experience, but the simple truth of this universal duality, this perpetual possibility of communion and completion, seems so alarming that I have watched it lead to addiction, despair, death, and madness. Nowhere have I seen this panic more vividly than in my country and in my generation.

The American idea of sexuality appears to be rooted in the American idea of masculinity. Idea may not be the precise word, for the idea of one's sexuality can only with great violence be divorced or distanced from the idea of the self. Yet something resembling this rupture has certainly occurred (and is occurring) in American life, and violence has been the American daily bread since we have heard of America. This violence, furthermore, is not merely literal and actual but appears to be admired and lusted after, and the key to the American imagination.

All countries or groups make of their trials a legend or, as in the case of Europe, a dubious romance called "history." But no other country has ever made so successful and glamorous a romance out of genocide and slavery; therefore, perhaps the word I am searching for is not idea but ideal.

The American *ideal*, then, of sexuality appears to be rooted in the American ideal of masculinity. This ideal has created cowboys and Indians, good guys and bad guys, punks and studs, tough guys and softies, butch and faggot, black and white. It is an ideal so paralytically infantile that it is virtually forbidden—as an unpatriotic act—that the American boy evolve into the complexity of manhood.

The exigencies created by the triumph of the Industrial Revolution—or, in other terms, the rise of Europe to global dominance—had, among many mighty effects, that of commercializing the roles of men and women. Men became the propagators, or perpetrators, of property, and women became the means by which that property was protected and handed down. One may say that this was nothing more than the ancient and universal division of labor—women nurtured the tribe, men battled for it—but the concept of property had undergone a change. This change was vast and deep and sinister. For the first time in human history, a man was reduced not merely to a thing but to a thing the value of which was determined, absolutely, by that thing's commercial value. That this pragmatic principle dictated the slaughter of the native American, the enslavement of the black and the monumental rape of Africa—to say nothing of creating the wealth of the Western world—no one, I suppose, will now attempt to deny.

But this principle also raped and starved Ireland, for example, as well as Latin America, and it controlled the pens of the men who signed the Declaration of Independence—a document more clearly commercial than moral. This is how, and why, the American Constitution was able to define the slave as three-fifths of a man, from which legal and commercial definition it legally followed that a black man "had no rights a white man was bound to respect." Ancient maps of the world—when the world was flat—inform us, concerning that void where America was waiting to be discovered, HERE BE DRAGONS. Dragons may not have been here then, but they are certainly here now, breathing fire, belching smoke; or, to be less literary and Biblical about it, attempting to intimidate the mores, morals, and morality of this particular and peculiar time and place. Nor, since this country is the issue of the entire globe and is also the most powerful nation currently to be found on it, are we speaking only of this time and place. And it can be said that the monumental struggles being waged in our time and not only in this place resemble, in awesome ways, the ancient struggle between those who insisted that the world was flat and those who apprehended that it was round.

Of course, I cannot possibly imagine what it can be like to have both male and female sexual equipment. That's a load of family jewels to be hauling about, and it seems to me that it must make choice incessant or impossible—or, in terms unavailable to me, unnecessary. Yet, not to be frivolous concerning what I know I cannot—or, more probably, dare not—imagine, I hazard that the physically androgynous state must create an all-but-intolerable loneliness, since we all exist, after all, and crucially, in the eye of the beholder. We all react to and, to whatever extent, become what that eye sees. This judgment begins in the eyes of one's parents (the crucial, the definitive, the all-but-everlasting judgment), and so we move, in the vast and claustrophobic gallery of Others, on up or down the line, to the eye of one's enemy or one's friend or one's lover.

It is virtually impossible to trust one's human value without the collaboration or corroboration of that eye—which is to say that no one can live without it. One can, of course, instruct that eye as to what to see, but this effort, which is nothing less than ruthless intimidation, is wounding and exhausting: While it can keep humiliation at bay, it confirms the fact that humiliation is the central danger of one's life. And since one cannot risk love without risking humiliation, love becomes impossible.

•

I hit the streets when I was about six or seven, like most black kids of my generation, running errands, doing odd jobs. This was in the black world—my turf—which means that I felt protected. I think that I really was, though poverty is poverty and we were, if I may say so, among the truly needy, in spite of the tins of corned beef we got from home relief every week, along with prunes. (Catsup had not yet become a vegetable; indeed, I don't think we had ever heard of it.) My mother fried corned beef, she boiled it, she baked it, she put potatoes in it, she put rice in it, she disguised it in corn bread, she boiled it in soup(!), she wrapped it in cloth, she beat it with a hammer, she banged it against the wall, she threw it onto the ceiling. Finally, she gave up, for nothing could make us eat it anymore, and the tins reproachfully piled up on the shelf above the bathtub—along with the prunes, which we also couldn't eat anymore. While I won't speak for my brothers and sisters, I can't bear corned-beef hash or prunes even today.

Poverty. I remember one afternoon when someone dropped a dime in front of the subway station at 125th Street and Lenox Avenue and I and a man of about 40 both scrambled for it. The man won, giving me a cheerful goodbye as he sauntered down the subway steps. I was bitterly disappointed, a dime being a dime, but I laughed, too.

The truly needy. Once, my father gave me a dime—the last dime in the house, though I didn't know that—to go to the store for kerosene for the stove, and I fell on the icy streets and dropped the dime and lost it. My father beat me with an iron cord from the kitchen to the back room and back again, until I lay, half-conscious, on my belly on the floor.

Yet—strange though it is to realize this, looking back—I never felt threatened in those years, when I was growing up in Harlem, my hometown. I think this may be because it was familiar; the white people who lived there then were as poor as we, and there was no TV setting our teeth on edge with exhortations to buy what we could never hope to afford.

On the other hand, I was certainly unbelievably unhappy and pathologically shy, but that, I felt, was nobody's fault but mine. My father kept me in short pants longer than he should have, and I had been told, and I believed, that I was ugly. This meant that the idea of myself as a sexual possibility, or target, as a creature capable of desire, had never entered my mind. And it entered my mind, finally, by means of the rent made in my short boy-scout pants by a man who had lured me into a hallway, saying that he wanted to send me to the store. That was the very last time I agreed to run an errand for any stranger.

Yet I was, in peculiar truth, a very lucky boy. Shortly after I turned 16, a Harlem racketeer, a man of about 38, fell in love with me, and I will be grateful to that man until the day I die. I showed him all my poetry, because I had no one else in Harlem to show it to, and even now, I sometimes wonder what on earth his friends could have been thinking, confronted with stingy-brimmed, mustachioed, razor-toting Poppa and skinny, popeyed Me when he walked me (rarely) into various shady joints, I drinking ginger ale, he drinking brandy. I think I was supposed to be his nephew, some nonsense like that, though he was Spanish and Irish, with curly black hair. But I knew that he was showing me off and wanted his friends to be happy for him— which, indeed, if the way they treated me can be taken as a barometer, they were. They seemed to feel that this was his business—that he would be in trouble if it became *their* business.

And though I loved him, too—in my way, a boy's way—I was mightily tormented, for I was still a child evangelist, which everybody knew, Lord. My soul looks back and wonders.

For what this really means is that all of the American categories of male and female, straight or not, black or white, were shattered, thank heaven, very early in my life. Not without anguish, certainly; but once you have discerned the meaning of a label, it may seem to define you for others, but it does not have the power to define you to yourself.

This prepared me for my life downtown, where I quickly discovered that my existence was the punch line of a dirty joke.

The condition that is now called gay was then called queer. The operative word was *faggot* and, later, pussy, but those epithets really had nothing to do with the question of sexual preference: You were being told simply that you had no balls.

I certainly had no desire to harm anyone, nor did I understand how anyone could look at me and suppose me physically capable of *causing* any harm. But boys and men chased me, saying I was a danger to their sisters. I was thrown out of cafeterias and rooming houses because I was "bad" for the neighborhood.

The cops watched all this with a smile, never making the faintest motion to protect me or to disperse my attackers; in fact, I was even more afraid of the cops than I was of the populace. By the time I was 19, I was working in the Garment Center. I was getting on very badly at home and delayed going home after work as long as possible. At the end of the workday, I would wander east, to the 42nd Street Library. Sometimes, I would sit in Bryant Park—but I discovered that I could not sit there long. I fled, to the movies, and so discovered 42nd Street. Today that street is exactly what it was when I was an adolescent: It has simply become more blatant.

There were no X-rated movies then, but there were, so to speak, X-rated audiences. For example, I went in complete innocence to the Apollo, on 42nd Street, because foreign films were shown there—The Lower Depths, Childhood of Maxim

Gorky, La Bête Humaine—and I walked out as untouched (by human hands) as I had been when I walked in. There were the stores, mainly on Sixth Avenue, that sold "girlie" magazines. These magazines were usually to be found at the back of the store, and I don't so much remember them as I remember the silent men who stood there. They stood, it seemed, for hours, with the magazines in their hands and a kind of miasma in their eyes. There were all kinds of men, mostly young and, in those days, almost exclusively white. Also, for what it's worth, they were heterosexual, since the images they studied, at crotch level, were those of women.

Actually, I guess I hit 42nd Street twice and have very nearly blotted the first time out. I was not at the mercy of the street the first time, for, though I may have dreaded *going* home, I hadn't *left* home yet. Then, I spent a lot of time in the library, and I stole odds and ends out of Woolworth's—with no compunction at all, due to the way they treated us in Harlem. When I went to the movies, I imagine that a combination of innocence and terror prevented me from too clearly apprehending the action taking place in the darkness of the Apollo—though I understood it well enough to remain standing a great deal of the time. This cunning stratagem failed when, one afternoon, the young boy I was standing behind put his hand behind him and grabbed my cock at the very same moment that a young boy came up behind me and put his cock against my hand: Ignobly enough, I fled, though I doubt that I was missed. The men in the men's room frightened me, so I moved in and out as quickly as possible, and I also dimly felt, I remember, that I didn't want to "fool around" and so risk hurting the feelings of my uptown friend.

But if I was paralyzed by guilt and terror, I cannot be judged or judge myself too harshly, for I remember the faces of the men. These men, so far from being or resembling faggots, looked and sounded like the vigilantes who banded together on weekends to beat faggots up. (And I was around long enough, suffered enough, and learned enough to be forced to realize that this was very often true. I might not have learned this if I had been a white boy; but sometimes a white man will tell a black boy anything, everything, weeping briny tears. He knows that the black boy can never betray him, for no one will believe his testimony.)

These men looked like cops, football players, soldiers, sailors, Marines or bank presidents, admen, boxers, construction workers; they had wives, mistresses, and children. I sometimes saw them in other settings—in, as it were, the daytime. Sometimes they spoke to me, sometimes not, for anguish has many days and styles. But I had first seen them in the men's room, sometimes on their knees, peering up into the stalls, or standing at the urinal stroking themselves, staring at another man, stroking, and with this miasma in their eyes. Sometimes, eventually, inevitably, I would find myself in bed with one of these men, a despairing and dreadful conjunction, since their need was as relentless as quicksand and as impersonal, and sexual rumor concerning blacks had preceded me. As for sexual roles, these were created by the imagination and limited only by one's stamina.

At bottom, what I had learned was that the male desire for a male roams everywhere, avid, desperate, unimaginably lonely, culminating often in drugs, piety, madness or death. It was also dreadfully like watching myself at the end of a long, slow-moving line: Soon I would be next. All of this was very frightening. It was lonely and impersonal and demeaning. I could not believe—after all, I was only 19—that I could have been driven to the lonesome place where these men and I met each other so soon, to stay.

•

The American idea of masculinity: There are few things under heaven more difficult to understand or, when I was younger, to forgive. During the Second World War (the first one having failed to make the world safe for democracy) and sometime after the Civil War (which had failed, unaccountably, to liberate the slave), life for niggers was fairly rough in Greenwich Village. There were only about three of us, if I remember correctly, when I first hit those streets, and I was the youngest, the most visible, and the most vulnerable. On every street corner, I was called a faggot. This meant that I was despised, and, however horrible this is, it is clear. What was *not* clear at that time of my life was what motivated the men and boys who mocked and chased me; for, if they found me when they were alone, they spoke to me very differently— frightening me, I must say, into a stunned and speechless paralysis. For when they were alone, they spoke very gently and wanted me to take them home and make love. (They could not take *me* home; they lived with their families.) The bafflement and the pain this caused in me remain beyond description. I was far too terrified to be able to accept their propositions, which could only result, it seemed to me, in making myself a candidate for gang rape. At the same time, I was moved by their loneliness, their halting, nearly speechless need. But I did not understand it.

One evening, for example, I was standing at the bottom of the steps to the Waverly Place subway station, saying goodbye to some friends who were about to take the subway. A gang of boys stood at the top of the steps and cried, in high, feminine voices, "Is this where the fags meet?"

Well. This meant that I certainly could not go back upstairs but would have to take the subway with my friends and get off at another station and maneuver my way home. But one of the gang saw me and, without missing a beat or saying a word to his friends, called my name and came down the steps, throwing one arm around me and asking where I'd been. He had let me know, some time before, that he wanted me to take him home—but I was surprised that he could be so open before his friends, who for their part seemed to find nothing astonishing in this encounter and disappeared, probably in search of other faggots.

The boys who are left of that time and place are all my age or older. But many of them are dead, and I remember how some of them died—some in the streets, some in the Army, some on the needle, some in jail. Many years later, we managed, without ever becoming friends—it was too late for that—to be friendly with one another. One of these men and I had a very brief, intense affair shortly before he died. He was on drugs and knew that he could not live long. "What a waste," he said, and he was right.

One of them said, "My God, Jimmy, you were moving so fast in those years, you never stopped to talk to me."

I said, "That's right, baby; I didn't stop because I didn't want you to think that I was trying to seduce you."

"Man," he said, indescribably, "why didn't you?"

But the queer—not yet gay—world was an even more intimidating area of this hall of mirrors. I knew that I was in the hall and present at this company—but the mirrors threw back only brief and distorted fragments of myself.

In the first place, as I have said, there were very few black people in the Village in those years, and of that handful, I was decidedly the most improbable. Perhaps, as they say in the theater, I was a hard type to cast; yet I was eager, vulnerable, and lonely. I was terribly shy, but *boys* are shy. I am saying that I don't think I felt absolutely, irredeemably grotesque—nothing that a friendly wave of the wand couldn't alter—but I was miserable. I moved through that world very quickly; I have described it as "my season in hell," for I was never able to make my peace with it.

It wasn't only that I didn't wish to seem or sound like a woman, for it was this detail that most harshly first struck my eye and ear. I am sure that I was afraid that I already seemed and sounded too much like a woman. In my childhood, at least until my adolescence, my playmates had called me a sissy. It seemed to me that many of the people I met were making fun of women, and I didn't see why. *I* certainly needed all the friends I could get, male *or* female, and women had nothing to do with whatever my trouble might prove to be.

At the same time, I had already been sexually involved with a couple of white women in the Village. There were virtually no black women there when I hit those streets, and none who needed or could have afforded to risk herself with an odd, raggedy-assed black boy who clearly had no future. (The first black girl I met who dug me I fell in love with, lived with and almost married. But I met her, though I was only 22, many light-years too late.)

The white girls I had known or been involved with—different categories—had paralyzed me, because I simply did not know what, apart from my sex, they wanted. Sometimes it was great, sometimes it was just moaning and groaning; but, ultimately, I found myself at the mercy of a double fear. The fear of the world was bearable until it entered the bedroom. But it sometimes entered the bedroom by means of the motives of the girl, who intended to civilize you into becoming an appendage or who had found a black boy to sleep with because she wanted to humiliate her parents. Not an easy scene to play, in any case, since it can bring out the worst in both parties, and more than one white girl had already made me know that her color was more powerful than my dick.

Which had nothing to do with how I found myself in the gay world. I would have found myself there anyway, but perhaps the very last thing this black boy needed were clouds of imitation white women and speculations concerning the size of his organ: speculations sometimes accompanied by an attempt at the laying on of hands. "*Ooo!* Look at him! He's cute—he doesn't like you to touch him there!"

In short, I was black in that world, and I was used that way, and by people who truly meant me no harm.

And they could *not* have meant me any harm, because they did not see me. There were exceptions, of course, for I also met some beautiful people. Yet even today, it seems to me (possibly because I am black) very dangerous to model one's opposition to the arbitrary definition, the imposed ordeal, merely on the example supplied by one's oppressor.

The object of one's hatred is never, alas, conveniently outside but is seated in one's lap, stirring in one's bowels and dictating the beat of one's heart. And if one does not know this, one risks becoming an imitation—and, therefore, a continuation—of principles one imagines oneself to despise.

I, in any case, had endured far too much debasement willingly to debase myself. I had absolutely no fantasies about making love to the last cop or hoodlum who had beaten the shit out of me. I did not find it amusing, in any way whatever, to act out the role of the darky.

So I moved on out of there.

In fact, I found a friend—more accurately, a friend found *me*—an Italian, about five years older than I, who helped my morale greatly in those years. I was told that he had threatened to kill anyone who touched me. I don't know about that, but people stopped beating me up. Our relationship never seemed to worry him or his friends or his women.

My situation in the Village stabilized itself to the extent that I began working as a waiter in a black West Indian restaurant, The Calypso, on MacDougal Street. This led, by no means incidentally, to the desegregation of the San Remo, an Italian bar and restaurant on the corner of MacDougal and Bleecker. Every time I entered the San Remo, they threw me out. I had to pass it all the time on my way to and from work, which is, no doubt, why the insult rankled.

I had won the Saxton Fellowship, which was administered by Harper & Brothers, and I knew Frank S. MacGregor, the president of Harper's. One night, when he asked me where we should have dinner, I suggested, spontaneously, the San Remo.

We entered, and they seated us and we were served. I went back to MacGregor's house for a drink and then went straight back to the San Remo, sitting on a bar stool in the window. The San Remo thus began to attract a varied clientele, indeed—so much so that Allen Ginsberg and company arrived there the year I left New York for Paris.

As for the people who ran and worked at the San Remo, they never bothered me again. Indeed, the Italian community never bothered me again—or rarely and, as it were, by accident. But the Village was full of white tourists, and one night, when a mob gathered before the San Remo, demanding that I come out, the owners closed the joint and turned the lights out and we sat in the back room, in the dark, for a couple of hours, until they judged it safe to drive me home.

This was a strange, great and bewildering time in my life.

Once I was in the San Remo, for example, I was *in*, and anybody who messed with me was *out*—that was all there was to it, and it happened more than once. And no one seemed to remember a time when I had not been there.

I could not quite get it together, but it seemed to me that I was no longer black for them and they had ceased to be white for me, for they sometimes introduced me to their families with every appearance of affection and pride and exhibited not the remotest interest in whatever my sexual proclivities chanced to be.

They had fought me very hard to prevent this moment, but perhaps we were all much relieved to have got beyond the obscenity of color.

Matters were equally bewildering, though in a different way, at The Calypso. All kinds of people came into our joint—I am now referring to white people—and one of their most vivid aspects, for me, was the cruelty of their alienation. They appeared to have no antecedents nor any real connections.

"Do you really *like* your mother?" someone asked me, seeming to be astounded, totally disbelieving the possibility.

I was astounded by the question. Certainly, my mother and I did not agree about everything, and I knew that she was very worried about the dangers of the life I lived, but that was normal, since I was a boy and she was a woman. Of course she was worried about me: She was my mother. But she knew I wasn't crazy and that I would certainly never do anything, deliberately, to hurt her. Or my tribe, my brothers and sisters, who were probably worried about me, too.

My family was a part of my life. I could not imagine life without them, might never have been able to reconcile myself to life without them. And certainly one of the reasons I was breaking my ass in the Village had to do with my need to try to move us out of our dangerous situation. I was perfectly aware of the odds—

my father had made that very clear—but he had also given me my assignment. "Do you really *like* your mother?" did not cause me to wonder about my mother or myself but about the person asking the question.

And perhaps because of such questions, I was not even remotely tempted by the possibilities of psychiatry or psychoanalysis. For one thing, there were too many schools—Freud, Horney, Jung, Reich (to suggest merely the tip of that iceberg)—and, for another, it seemed to me that anyone who thought seriously that I had any desire to be "adjusted" to this society had to be ill; too ill, certainly, as time was to prove, to be trusted.

I sensed, then—without being able to articulate it—that this dependence on a formula for safety, for that is what it was, signaled a desperate moral abdication. People went to the shrink in order to find justification for the empty lives they led and the meaningless work they did. Many turned, helplessly, hopefully, to Wilhelm Reich and perished in orgone boxes.

•

I seem to have strayed a long way from our subject, but our subject is social and historical—and continuous. The people who leaped into orgone boxes in search of the perfect orgasm were later to turn to acid. The people so dependent on psychiatric formulas were unable to give their children any sense of right or wrong—indeed, this sense was in themselves so fragile that during the McCarthy era, more than one shrink made a lot of money by convincing his patients, or clients, that their psychic health demanded that they inform on their friends. (Some of these people, after their surrender, attempted to absolve themselves in the civil rights movement.)

What happened to the children, therefore, is not even remotely astonishing. The flower children—who became the Weather Underground, the Symbionese Liberation Army, the Manson Family—are creatures from this howling inner space.

I am not certain, therefore, that the present sexual revolution is either sexual or a revolution. It strikes me as a reaction to the spiritual famine of American life. The present androgynous "craze"—to underestimate it—strikes me as an attempt to be honest concerning one's nature, and it is instructive, I think, to note that there is virtually no emphasis on overt sexual activity. There is nothing more boring, anyway, than sexual activity as an end in itself, and a great many people who came out of the closet should reconsider.

Such figures as Boy George do not disturb me nearly so much as do those relentlessly hetero (sexual?) keepers of the keys and seals, those who know what the world needs in the way of order and who are ready and willing to supply that order.

This rage for order can result in chaos, and in this country, chaos connects with color. During the height of my involvement in the civil rights movement, for example, I was subjected to hate mail of a terrifying precision. Volumes concerning what my sisters, to say nothing of my mother, were capable of doing; to say nothing of my brothers; to say nothing of the monumental size of my organ and what I did with it. Someone described, in utterly riveting detail, a scene he swore he had witnessed (I *think* it was a *he*—such mail is rarely signed) on the steps of houses in Baltimore of niggers fucking their dogs.

At the same time, I was also on the mailing list of one of the more elegant of the K.K.K. societies, and I still have some of that mail in my files. Someone, of course, eventually realized that the organization should not be sending that mail to this particular citizen, and it stopped coming—but not before I had had time to be struck by the similarity of tone between the hate mail and the mail of the society, and not before the society had informed me, by means of a parody of an Audubon Society postcard, what it felt and expected me to feel concerning a certain "Red-breasted" Martin Luther King, Jr.

The Michael Jackson cacophony is fascinating in that it is not about Jackson at all. I hope he has the good sense to know it and the good fortune to snatch his life out of the jaws of a carnivorous success. He will not swiftly be forgiven for having turned so many tables, for he damn sure grabbed the brass ring, and the man who broke the bank at Monte Carlo has nothing on Michael. All that noise is about America, as the dishonest custodian of black life and wealth; and blacks, especially males, in America; and the burning, buried American guilt; and sex and sexual roles and sexual panic; money, success and despair—to all of which may now be added the bitter need to find a head on which to place the crown of Miss America.

•

Freaks are called freaks and are treated as they are treated—in the main, abominably—because they are human beings who cause to echo, deep within us, our most profound terrors and desires.

Most of us, however, do not appear to be freaks—though we are rarely what we appear to be. We are, for the most part, visibly male or female, our social roles defined by our sexual equipment.

But we are all androgynous, not only because we are all born of a woman impregnated by the seed of a man but because each of us, helplessly and forever, contains the other—male in female, female in male, white in black and black in white. We are a part of each other. Many of my countrymen appear to find this fact exceedingly inconvenient and even unfair, and so, very often, do I. But none of us can do anything about it.

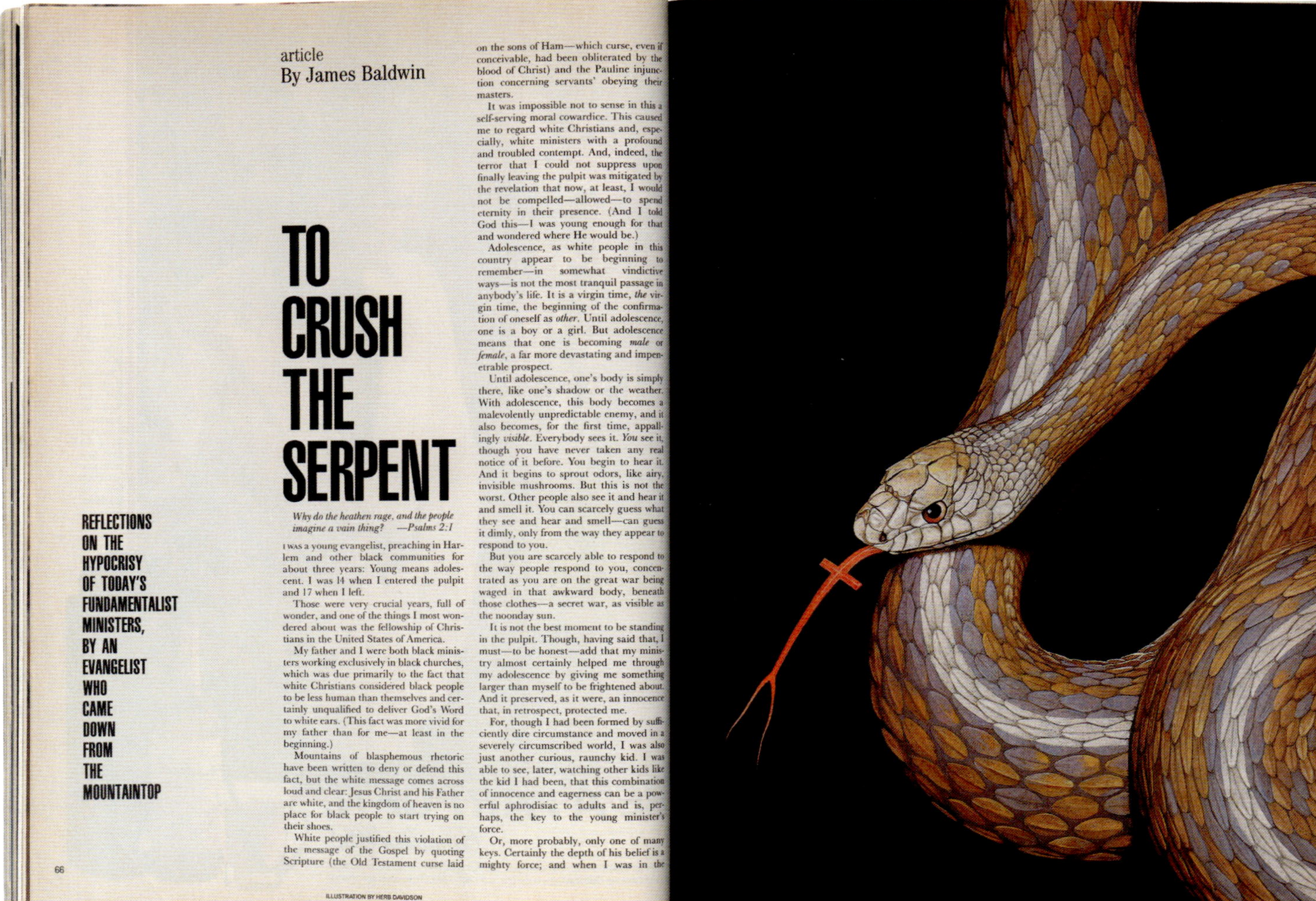

article

By James Baldwin

TO CRUSH THE SERPENT

REFLECTIONS ON THE HYPOCRISY OF TODAY'S FUNDAMENTALIST MINISTERS, BY AN EVANGELIST WHO CAME DOWN FROM THE MOUNTAINTOP

Why do the heathen rage, and the people imagine a vain thing? —*Psalms 2:1*

I WAS a young evangelist, preaching in Harlem and other black communities for about three years: Young means adolescent. I was 14 when I entered the pulpit and 17 when I left.

Those were very crucial years, full of wonder, and one of the things I most wondered about was the fellowship of Christians in the United States of America.

My father and I were both black ministers working exclusively in black churches, which was due primarily to the fact that white Christians considered black people to be less human than themselves and certainly unqualified to deliver God's Word to white ears. (This fact was more vivid for my father than for me—at least in the beginning.)

Mountains of blasphemous rhetoric have been written to deny or defend this fact, but the white message comes across loud and clear: Jesus Christ and his Father are white, and the kingdom of heaven is no place for black people to start trying on their shoes.

White people justified this violation of the message of the Gospel by quoting Scripture (the Old Testament curse laid on the sons of Ham—which curse, even if conceivable, had been obliterated by the blood of Christ) and the Pauline injunction concerning servants' obeying their masters.

It was impossible not to sense in this a self-serving moral cowardice. This caused me to regard white Christians and, especially, white ministers with a profound and troubled contempt. And, indeed, the terror that I could not suppress upon finally leaving the pulpit was mitigated by the revelation that now, at least, I would not be compelled—allowed—to spend eternity in their presence. (And I told God this—I was young enough for that and wondered where He would be.)

Adolescence, as white people in this country appear to be beginning to remember—in somewhat vindictive ways—is not the most tranquil passage in anybody's life. It is a virgin time, *the* virgin time, the beginning of the confirmation of oneself as *other*. Until adolescence, one is a boy or a girl. But adolescence means that one is becoming *male* or *female*, a far more devastating and impenetrable prospect.

Until adolescence, one's body is simply there, like one's shadow or the weather. With adolescence, this body becomes a malevolently unpredictable enemy, and it also becomes, for the first time, appallingly *visible*. Everybody sees it. *You* see it, though you have never taken any real notice of it before. You begin to hear it. And it begins to sprout odors, like airy, invisible mushrooms. But this is not the worst. Other people also see it and hear it and smell it. You can scarcely guess what they see and hear and smell—can guess it dimly, only from the way they appear to respond to you.

But you are scarcely able to respond to the way people respond to you, concentrated as you are on the great war being waged in that awkward body, beneath those clothes—a secret war, as visible as the noonday sun.

It is not the best moment to be standing in the pulpit. Though, having said that, I must—to be honest—add that my ministry almost certainly helped me through my adolescence by giving me something larger than myself to be frightened about. And it preserved, as it were, an innocence that, in retrospect, protected me.

For, though I had been formed by sufficiently dire circumstance and moved in a severely circumscribed world, I was also just another curious, raunchy kid. I was able to see, later, watching other kids like the kid I had been, that this combination of innocence and eagerness can be a powerful aphrodisiac to adults and is, perhaps, the key to the young minister's force.

Or, more probably, only one of many keys. Certainly the depth of his belief is a mighty force; and when I was in the

66

ILLUSTRATION BY HERB DAVIDSON

Spread from **Playboy**, January 1987, featuring Baldwin's essay "To Crush the Serpent"

To Crush the Serpent

Playboy, January 1987

What do the heathen rage, and the people imagine a vain thing?
—Psalms 2:1

Reflections on the hypocrisy of today's fundamentalist ministers, by an evangelist who came down from the mountain top

I was a young evangelist, preaching in Harlem and other black communities for about three years: Young means adolescent. I was 14 when I entered the pulpit and 17 when I left.

Those were very crucial years, full of wonder, and one of the things I most wondered about was the fellowship of Christians in the United States of America.

My father and I were both black ministers working exclusively for black churches, which was due primarily to the fact that white Christians considered black people to be less human than themselves and certainly less qualified to deliver God's Word to white ears. (This fact was more vivid for my father than for me—at least in the beginning.)

Mountains of blasphemous rhetoric have been written to deny or defend this fact, but the white message comes across loud and clear: Jesus Christ and his Father are white, and the kingdom of heaven is no place for black people to start trying on their shoes.

White people justified this violation of the message of the Gospel by quoting Scripture (the Old Testament curse laid on the sons of Ham—which curse, even if conceivable, had been obliterated by the blood of Christ) and the Pauline injunction concerning servants' obeying their masters.

It was impossible not to sense in this a self-serving moral cowardice. This caused me to regard white Christians and, especially, white ministers with a profound and troubled contempt. And, indeed, the terror that I could not suppress upon finally leaving the pulpit was mitigated by the revelation that now, at least, I would not be compelled—allowed—to spend eternity in their presence. (And I told God this—I was young enough for that and wondered where He would be.)

Adolescence, as white people in this country appear to be beginning to remember—in somewhat vindictive ways—is not the most tranquil passage in anybody's life. It is a virgin time, *the* virgin time, the beginning of the confirmation of oneself as *other*. Until adolescence, one is a boy or a girl. But adolescence means that one is becoming *male* or *female*, a far more devastating and impenetrable prospect.

Until adolescence, one's body is simply there, like one's shadow or the weather. With adolescence, this body becomes a malevolently unpredictable enemy, and it also becomes, for the first time, appallingly *visible*. Everybody sees it. *You* see it, though you have never taken any real notice of it before. You begin to hear it. And it begins to sprout odors, like airy, invisible mushrooms. But this is not the worst. Other people also see it and hear it and smell it. You can scarcely guess what they see and hear and smell—can guess it dimly, only from the way they appear to respond to you.

But you are scarcely able to respond to the way people respond to you, concentrated as you are on the great war being waged in that awkward body, beneath those clothes—a secret war, as visible as the noonday sun.

It is not the best moment to be standing in the pulpit. Though, having said that, I must—to be honest—add that my ministry almost certainly helped me through my adolescence by giving me something larger than myself to be frightened about. And it preserved, as it were, an innocence that, in retrospect, protected me.

For, though I had been formed by sufficiently dire circumstance and moved in a severely circumscribed world, I was also just another curious, raunchy kid. I was able to see, later, watching other kids like the kid I had been, that this combination of innocence and eagerness can be a powerful aphrodisiac to adults and is, perhaps, the key to the young minister's force.

Or, more probably, only one of many keys. Certainly the depth of his belief is a mighty force; and when I was in the pulpit, I believed. The personal anguish counts for something, too: It was the personal anguish that made me believe that I believed. People do not know on what this anguish feeds, but they sense the anguish and they respond to it. My sexuality was on hold, for both women and men had tried to "mess" with me in the summer of my 14th year and had frightened me so badly that I found the Lord. The salvation I was preaching to others was fueled by the hope of my own.

I left the pulpit upon the realization that *my* salvation could not be achieved that way.

But it is worth stating this proposition in somewhat harsher terms.

An unmanageable distress had driven me to the altar and, once there, I was—at least for a while—cleansed. But, at the same time, nothing had been obliterated: I was still a boy in trouble with himself and the streets around him. Salvation did not make time stand still or arrest the changes occurring in my body and my mind. Salvation did not change the fact that I was an eager sexual potential, in flight from the inevitable touch. And I knew that I was in flight, though I could not, then—*to save my soul!*—have told you from what I was fleeing.

And, at the same time, the shape of my terror became clearer and clearer: as hypnotic and relentless as the slow surfacing of characters written in invisible ink.

I threw all my anguish and terror into my sermons and I thus learned nearly all there was to know concerning my congregations. They trusted me because they sensed my anguish—and my anguish was the key to my love. I think I hoped to love them more than I would ever love any lover and, so, escape the terrors of this life.

It did not work out that way. The young male preacher is a sexual prize in quite another way than the female: and congregations are made up of men and women.

So, in time, a heavy weight fell on my heart. I did not want to become a liar. I did not want my love to become manipulation. I did not want my fear of my own desires to transform itself into power—into power, precisely, over those who feared and were therefore at the mercy of their own desires.

In my experience, the minister and his flock mirror each other. It demands a very rare, intrepid and genuinely free and loving shepherd to challenge the habits and fears and assumptions of his flock and help them enter into the freedom that enables us to move to higher ground.

I was not that shepherd. And rather than betray the ministry, I left it.

It can be supposed, then, that I cannot take seriously—not, at least, as Christian ministers—the present-day gang that calls itself the Moral Majority or its tongue-speaking relatives, such as follow the Right Reverend Robertson.

They have taken the man from Galilee as hostage. He does not know them and they do not know him.

Nowhere, in the brief and extraordinary passage of the man known as Jesus Christ, is it recorded that he ever upbraided his disciples concerning their carnality. These were roguh, hard-working fishermen on the Sea of Galilee. Their carnality can be taken as given, and they would never have trusted or followed or loved a man who did not know that they were men and who did not respect their manhood. Jesus made wine at the wedding, for example, by way of a miracle or otherwise—anyone who has been to a black fish fry knows how miraculously wine can appear. He appears not to have despised Mary Magdalene and to have got on just fine with other ladies, notably Mary and Martha, and with the woman at the well. Not one of the present-day white fundamentalist preachers would have had the humility, the courage, the sheer presence of mind to have said to the mob surrounding the woman taken in adultery, "He that is without sin among you, let him first cast a stone," or the depth of perception that informs "Neither do I condemn thee: Go and sin no more."

It is scarcely worth comparing the material well-being—or material aspirations—of these latter-day apostles with the poverty of Jesus. Whereas Jesus and his disciples were distrusted by the state largely because they respected the poor and shared everything, the fundamentalists of the present hour would appear not to know that the poor exist.

They are aided enormously in this blindness by the peculiar self-deception the American poor white applies to his own poverty. His poverty afflicts him with an eerie and paralyzing self-contempt, but he denies it: Poverty is meant for niggers. And, at the same time, he is aware that the ministers he sees on TV and to whom he sends his nickels and dimes were, once, no better off than he: He recognizes each as kin, so to speak.

These ministers, however, are of no interest in themselves—at least of no more intrinsic interest than any Deep South sheriff. And, indeed, the ministers remind me of the sheriffs and deputies I have encountered: the same lips, the same flat, slatelike eyes, the same self-righteous voices.

Now, I find it somewhat disturbing to mention the minister and the sheriff in the same breath, but I am black and they entered my life in the same breath. Both the white fundamentalist minister and the deputy are Christians—*hard-core* Christians, one might say. Both believe that they are responsible, the one for divine law and the other for natural order. Both believe that they are able to define and privileged to impose law and order; and both, historically and actually, know that law and order are meant to keep me in my place.

Or, I can put it another way, make another suggestion. Race and religion, it has been remarked, are fearfully entangled in the guts of this nation, so profoundly that to speak of the one is to conjure up the other. One cannot speak of sin without referring to blackness, and blackness stalks our history and our streets. Therefore, in many ways, perhaps in the deepest ways, the minister and the sheriff were hired by the republic to keep the republic white—to keep it free from sin. But sin is no respecter of skin: Sin stains the soul. Therefore, again and again, the republic is convulsed with the need for exorcism—sin has not only come to town but is in bed with us, churning out white niggers.

So something must be done. And what must be done, each time, is to attack the sexual possibility, to make the possibility of the private life as fugitive as that of a fleeing nigger.

The fundamentalist ministers remind me of my time in the pulpit, of ministers I have known and of my own choices. In some of my encounters with ministers, I found myself dealing with people from whose lives all possibility of earthly joy had fled. Joy was not even, to judge from the endless empty plain behind their eyes, a memory. And they could recognize, in others, joy or the possibility of joy only as a mighty threat—as something, as they put it, obscene.

The very first time I saw this—without knowing what I was seeing—was shortly after my conversion. I was not yet in the pulpit, so I was still 13.

The deacon of the church in which I had been converted was leaving to go to another church. This deacon's youngest son was my best friend, and this family had become my second family. They had been accused by the elders of the church of "walking disorderly." I had no idea what this meant, but I was told that if I did not stop seeing these people, I , too, would be walking disorderly. I concluded that walking disorderly meant that I had to choose between my friends and this particular church, and so I decided to walk disorderly and leave with my friends.

As I was leaving the church that night, the pastor's aide, a woman from Finland and the only white woman in our church, grabbed my arm as I started down the steps. She was standing just above me, leaning on the railing, dressed in white.

I was standing at the top of a steep flight of steps, and she had me off balance.

I knew she knew this.

Her face and her eyes seemed purple. I could not take my eyes from hers. Her lips seemed to be chewing and spitting out the air. She told me of the eternal torment that awaited boys like me. And, all the time, her grip on my arm tightened. She was hurting me, and I wanted to ask her to stop.

But, of course, she knew that she was hurting me. I wonder if she *knew* she knew it. She finally let me go, consigning me to perdition, and I grabbed the banister, just in time.

Quite a collision between a 13-year-old black boy and an aging, gaunt white woman—all in the name of Jesus and with my salvation as the motive.

But Jesus had nothing to do with it. Jesus would never have done that to me, nor attempted to make my salvation a matter for blackmail. The motive was buried deep within that woman, the decomposing corpse of her human possibilities fouling the air.

I was in love with my friend, as boys, indeed, can be at that age, but hadn't the faintest notion of what to do about it—not even in my imagination, which may suggest that the imagination is kicked off by memory. Or perhaps I simply refused to allow my imagination to wonder, as it were, below the belt.

Judging from my experience, I think that all of the kids in the church were like that, which is certainly why a couple of us went mad. Others simply backslid—went "back into the world." One relentless and realistic matron, a widow, determined to keep her 18-year-old athlete in the flock, in the pulpit and in his right mind, took him South and found him a bride and brought the son and the girl—who scarcely knew each other—back home. The entire operation could not have taken more than a week.

We went to see the groom one morning and, as we left, my friend yelled, "Don't do anything *we* wouldn't do!"

The groom responded, with a lewd grin, "You all better not be doing what *I*'m doing!"

Which suggests that we endured our repression with a certain good humor, at least for a time.

The Bible is full of prohibitions, tribal, domestic, practical, profound or seemingly useless; so the way of the transgressor is hard, is it? Thanks a lot.

We are not told that the way of the transgressor is *wrong*, nor are we told what a transgression is.

This means that I was challenged to discover for myself the meaning of the word transgressor: or the meaning of the Word. This challenge became the key to my journey through the Bible.

For example, it seemed to me that those people in Hitler's Germany who opposed the slaughter of, among others, the Jews, were transgressors. So was Mrs. Rosa Parks in Montgomery, Alabama, on the day she refused to surrender her seat on the bus to a white man. Where were the white Christian ministers then? (Christ was there. Mrs. Parks will tell you so.) A transgressor was the one white woman out of a white multitude who sat on the bus-stop bench in Charlotte to console the lone black girl whose life had been threatened by a mob of white Christians because she wanted to go to school. The South African horror was perceived and confronted by very few people: The Christian church cannot be numbered among those few. The Christian ministers who perceived the moral and actual horror of apartheid were transgressors. So are certain Catholic priests today, and so, for that matter, was the late Dr. Martin Luther King, Jr.

The Bible is not a simple or a simple-minded book, nad it is not to be reduced to a cowardly system of self-serving pieties.

The most crucial and celebrated Biblical prohibition, "Thou shalt not kill," is observed by virtually no one, either in or out of the Bible; and Christ recognizes—in ways having nothing to do with his desire or intention—that he brings not "peace but a sword."

In other words, you can glide through the Bible and settle for the prohibitions that suit you best.

The prohibitions that suit the fundamentalists best all involve the flesh.

And here I must, frankly, declare myself handicapped, even, or perhaps especially, as a former minister of the Gospel.

Salvation is not precipitated by the terror of being consumed in hell: This terror itself places one in hell. Salvation is preceded by the recognition of sin, by conviction, by repentance. Sin is not limited to carnal activity, nor are the sins of the flesh the most crucial or reverberating of our sins. Salvation is not flight from the wrath of God; it is accepting and reciprocating the love of God. Salvation is not separation. It is the beginning of union with all that is or has been or will ever be.

It is impossible to claim salvation and also believe that, in this life or in any life to come, one is better than another.

Or, let me try to put it another way: Salvation is as real, as mighty and as impersonal as the rain, and it is yet as private as the rain in one's face. It is never accomplished; it is to be reaffirmed every day and every hour. There is absolutely no salvation without love: This is the wheel in the middle of the wheel. Salvation does not divide. Salvation connects, so that one sees oneself in others and others in oneself. It is not the exclusive property of any dogma, creed or church. It keeps the channel open between oneself and however one wishes to name That which is greater than oneself. It has absolutely nothing to do with one's fortunes or one's circumstances in one's passage through this world. It is a mighty fortress, even in the teeth of ruin or at the gates of death. It protects one from nothing except one thing: One will never curse God or man.

Salvation repudiates condemnation, since we all have the right, for many reasons, to condemn one another. Condemnation is easier than wonder and obliterates the possibility of salvation, since condemnation is fueled by terror and self-hatred. I am speaking as the historical victim of the flames meant to exorcise the terrors of the mob, and I am also speaking as an actual potential victim.

Those ladders to fire—the burning of the witch, the heretic, the Jew, the nigger, the faggot—have always failed to redeem, or even to change in any way whatever, the mob. They merely epiphanize and force their connection on the only plain on which the mob can meet: The charred bones connect its members and give them a reason to speak to one another for the charred bones are the sum total of their individual self-hatred, externalized. The burning or lynching or torturing gives them something to talk about. They dare no other subject, certainly not the forbidden subject of the bloodstained self. They dare not trust one another.

One of them may be next.

And this accounts for the violence of our TV screen and cinema, a violence far more dangerous than pornography. What we are watching is a compulsive reliving of the American crimes: What we are watching with the Falwells and Robertsons is an attempt to exorcise ourselves.

This demands, indeed, a simplemindedness quite beyond the possibilities of the human being. Complexity is our only safety and love is the only key to our maturity.

And love is where you find it.

Acknowledgments

With great thanks to the friends who spent time with me during this project, chief among them being Jeff Posternak, and Mr. Baldwin himself. And, finally, this project would not be what it is without Rhea Combs, who not only builds bridges but is waiting for you on the other side.

Hilton Als

James Baldwin once noted, "History is not the past. It is the present. We carry our history with us. We are our history." *This Morning, This Evening, So Soon: James Baldwin and the Voices of Queer Resistance* embodies that ideal and is the result of the efforts and collaboration of many. When ruminating on this project and the legacy of Baldwin, I am indebted to those, both inside and outside of the National Portrait Gallery, who worked tirelessly to ensure that the exhibition and accompanying book reflect his ideas of connection, generosity, collective responsibility— and history.

The museum's staff contributed mightily to this project in myriad ways. I am grateful for the stalwart support, from the onset, of Kim Sajet, museum director, and wish to also thank the museum's executive team: Michael Hussey, director of history, for his efforts in assuring various historical facts were in order; Mahsa Javid, director of advancement, and her entire team, namely Raven Bradburn and Lindsay Gabryszak, for managing critical funding received for this project; Rebecca Kasemeyer, director of audience engagement, whose teams are instrumental in promoting this work to educators, spreading news about the exhibition and book, and developing critical connections with communities; Angie Kerns, director of finance and operations, for ensuring vital resources were available, and Tibor Waldner, director of collections and exhibitions, for his team's hard work.

Within the department of exhibitions, specific gratitude to Marlene Harrison, head of exhibitions, and Allison Keilman, exhibition program specialist, along with members of the design and production department. Special thanks to Peter Crellin, head of design and production, and Alex Cooper, exhibits specialist. And thanks to photographer Mark Gulezian for his above-and-beyond efforts and stellar photography.

Additional kudos to members of the registrar department, particularly Marissa Olivas and all the art handlers. This exhibition included many moving parts, and your attention to detail and professionalism ensured the safety of all the works as they arrived from afar. Erin Beasley, the Portrait Gallery's image rights specialist, offered crucial guidance for which I am tremendously appreciative.

Enormous thanks to Rhys Conlon, the museum's head of publicat who has been cheerleading this project from the onset and who stewa this publication through a remarkably short timeline. Not only has he editorial acumen assisted with ensuring the language is fine-tuned, bu is due to her heroic efforts that this text made it to the printers. We als thank Audio Transcription Center for their efficient work in transcrib the interview between Hilton Als and me. Tremendous gratitude to Mary DelMonico and Karen Farquhar of DelMonico Books for their enthusiastic support and dedication to this publication. We are gratef to have partnered with them and wish to also thank their colleague C Washburn. The book's design, by the talented Silas Munro and Brian Johnson of Polymode, not only honors Baldwin's legacy but is a beauti daring offering that epitomizes his spirit. I extend my deep, heartfelt t to them for their work and dedication.

Huge thanks to the curatorial and conservation departments as well. Special thanks to Ann Shumard, senior curator of photographs, her early enthusiasm and steadfast support, which resulted in finding wonderful photograph of Baldwin with civil rights activist James For The image became an important addition to the museum's collection this project.

I feel very lucky to have the wonderful curatorial and conservatic teams who also have been vital allies throughout this process: Robyn Asleson, curator of prints and drawings; Taína Caragol, curator of pair and sculpture and Latinx art; Charlotte Ickes, curator of time-based m art and special projects; along with collections managers Hallie Kroll McGrath and Casey Magrys, whose behind-the-scenes efforts have be critical. In addition, thank you to Im Chan, interim head of conservati and the entire conservation team. We received special support from A Ersenkal, Christina Finlayson, and Eric Knutzon, as well as Luke Mos time-based media conservator, who offered critical help with the pres tation of audio-visual materials. Their subject matter expertise provid guidance and oversight to better ensure the work remains presentable and for years to come.

Particular recognition for the yeoman's work of curatorial assista Amy Swartz. Amy's initiative, creative problem solving, and keen rese skills have been essential to ensuring this project stayed on course. He meticulous and unwavering support for every aspect of this project ha been the beacon I needed to remain on track.

I am also grateful to many throughout the Smithsonian Institution who have provided invaluable assistance, especially colleagues at the National Museum of African American History and Culture, namely Tulani Salahu-Din, museum specialist and Baldwin scholar. Her critic ctions to the Baldwin Estate proved to be priceless. Registrar Drew was extremely helpful in obtaining necessary loans, and huge s to Doug Remley, rights and reproduction specialist, as well as McDowell, time-based media archivist, whose timely assistance and :ise were essential. Tremendous gratitude, as well, to Tina Jones in ffice of Contracting, who always provides a bevy of vital knowledge aspects of the Smithsonian, as well as the Office of General Counsel lelissa Wright for her critical assistance in securing key licensing and essential loans.

:any individuals and institutions outside the Smithsonian also usly assisted with this project. Huge thanks to the teams at: ACA ies, Art Institute of Chicago, Atlantic Magazine, Richard Avedon lation, Beinecke Rare Book and Manuscript Library of Yale rsity, Blanton Museum of Art, Columbia University Libraries, n Family Collection, Gay Lesbian Bisexual Transgender (GLBT) ical Society, Lorraine Hansberry Literary Trust, Hauser & Wirth, y of Congress, Mead Art Museum, Museum of Contemporary Art go, National Museum of African American History and Culture, oy Magazine, Random House Records, Rennie Collection, 94, Schomburg Center for Research in Black Culture, Nina Simone :able Trust and Rich & Famous Records, Ltd., Whitney Museum erican Art, and David Zwirner Gallery. I am especially indebted to as Beard, Andrew Blackley, attorney Steven Ames Brown, Frederick right, Joi Gresham, Lyle Ashton Harris, Rebecca Hatcher, María ia Hidalgo, Emily Knapp, Julie McGarvie, Catherine Morris, Walker e, Kathy Pakay, Chris Rawson, Lynn Orilla Scott, Donald Spanel, as Teoh, Ken Winfield, and The Wylie Agency, particularly Jeffrey nak and Tucker Smith. Thanks, as well, to Darren Walker and The Foundation for believing in and supporting this project from its :ion.

xtra special hosannas to Savannah Downs at Marianne Boesky y and Donald Moffett for their patience, generous loan, and gness to think outside the box. Tremendous gratitude, as well, to ldwin Estate, who believed in this project as a gift to the nation ipported our efforts to honor Baldwin's centennial at the National it Gallery.

hroughout the development of this project, several friends and gues have offered important insights at pivotal moments. While are too many to name individually, a few must be recognized: Andrea vell Brownlee, LaToya Ruby Frazier, Thelma Golden for her critical luctions and steadfast support of artists and curators, and Valerie Oliver.

For their unconditional love and patience, I owe a huge debt of gratitude to my husband, Kojo Boateng, and our glorious daughter, Selah. Far too many late nights, weekends, and holidays have been devoted to "doing the work." Despite it all, you each take my passion and commitment with an open heart. The understanding, patience, and ability to keep me laughing—through it all—is heaven-sent.

And finally, this project is a result of thoughtful and generative conversations with Hilton Als, which began in late 2021 and were developed in earnest in 2022, after the success of his 2019 project at the David Zwirner Gallery in New York, *God Made My Face: A Collective Portrait of James Baldwin*. That exhibition revealed a complexity in thinking about portraiture and art history, and its impacts on representation and identity. As a result, our conversations blossomed into a project at the National Portrait Gallery that expands understandings about a great American artist, James Baldwin, and honors his circle of friends with whom his outsized platform often served as proxy for their internal values and personal struggles. I am deeply humbled and extremely grateful to Hilton Als for his support, encouragement, and critical engagement. Lastly, James Baldwin, thank you for your atistry, your daring, and your expectations of America. Your life and your words remain an inspriration.

Onward.

Rhea L. Combs, PhD

This book was published on the occasion of the exhibition *This Morning, This Evening, So Soon: James Baldwin and the Voices of Queer Resistance*, presented by the National Portrait Gallery, Smithsonian Institution, Washington, D.C., from June 28, 2024, to April 20, 2025.

Published in 2024 by the National Portrait Gallery, Smithsonian Institution, and DelMonico Books • D.A.P.

National Portrait Gallery
Eighth and G Streets NW
Washington, D.C. 20001
npg.si.edu

DelMonico Books
available through ARTBOOK | D.A.P.
75 Broad Street, Suite 630
New York, NY 10004
artbook.com
delmonicobooks.com

National Portrait Gallery

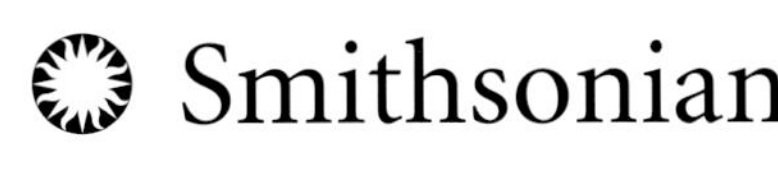

DelMonico Books

Design by Polymode: Brian Johnson and Silas Munro, Raleigh/Los Angeles
Typeset in: LaGrotesque by Naïma Ben Ayed and Dapifer by Joshua Darden Studio
Production: Karen Farquhar
Color separations: Altaimage, London and New York

Information about the exhibition is available at npg.si.edu

Printed and bound in China
ISBN: 978-1-63681-132-1
Library of Congress Control Number: 2024936884

Cover: Sedat Pakay, *James Baldwin, Istanbul,* c. 1965 (detail). See p. 40.
Back Cover: Sedat Pakay, *James Baldwin at Kilyos, Turkey,* 1965 (detail). See p. 38.
© Sedat Pakay | www.sedatpakay.com

Copyrights

Photography Credits

p. 13, p. 21, and p. 59: Courtesy of the National Museum of African American History and Culture.
p. 17: Photo by Stephen F. Somerstein/Archive Photos via Getty Ima
p. 18: Photo by Paul Slade/Paris Match via Getty Images.
p. 23: Photo by Sophie Bassouls/Sygma via Getty Images.
p. 24: Photo by Ulf Andersen/Hulton Archive via Getty Images.
p. 42 and p. 58: Courtesy of the Schomburg Center for Research in Bla Culture, the New York Public Library.
pp. 44–47, 49–55: Courtesy of the Beinecke Rare Book and Manuscrip Library, Yale University.
p. 48: Courtesy of Lynn Orilla Scott and Ken Winfield.
p. 60: Under license from the Nina Simone Charitable Trust and Rich Famous Records, Ltd., courtesy of Steven Ames Brown.
p. 63: Photo use granted by Joi Gresham and the Lorraine Hansberry Literary Trust.
p. 67: Photo by James Wang.
p. 68, pp. 70–72: Courtesy of the Library of Congress.
p. 75: Photo by Sarah Muehlbauer.
pp. 78–79: Photos by Liz Deschenes.
Special thanks to Mark Gulezian, photographer, National Portrait Ga Smithsonian Institution, who photographed works in the museum's collection and various ephemera.

All essays, letters, and other writing by Baldwin published courtesy of Permissions Company LLC, on behalf of the James Baldwin Estate.